P9-CRG-663

A CRITICAL APPROACH TO YOUTH CULTURE

Its Influence and Implications for Ministry

Pamela Erwin

youth specialties

ZONDERVAN.com/
AUTHORTRACKER
follow your favorite authors

ZONDERVAN

A Critical Approach to Youth Culture: Its Influence and Implications for Ministry
Copyright © 2010 by Pamela Erwin

YS Youth Specialties is a trademark of YOUTHWORKS!, INCORPORATED and is registered with the United States Patent and Trademark Office.

Requests for information should be addressed to:

Zondervan, *Grand Rapids, Michigan* 49530

ISBN 978-0-310-29294-4

Cover design: Mark Novelli, IMAGO
Interior design: SharpSeven Design

Printed in the United States of America

10 11 12 13 14 15 16 17 18 19 20 /DCI/ 23 22 21 20 19 18 17 16 15 14 13 12 11 10 9 8 7 6 5 4 3 2 1

CONTENTS

5   Acknowledgments

7   Introduction

13 PART ONE—THE NATURE OF CULTURE

15   Chapter 1   What Is Culture?

27   Chapter 2   What Makes Culture "Culture"?

35   Chapter 3   Expressing Culture: Signs, Symbols, Rituals, and Language

53   Chapter 4   Youth Culture: Is It Subculture?

61 PART TWO—ETHNOGRAPHY OF CULTURE

63   Chapter 5   The Need for Sharper Vision

67   Chapter 6   The Why and What of Ethnography

77   Chapter 7   Emic and Etic: The Eyes of an Ethnographer

91   Chapter 8   Being Ethical Youth Pastor-Ethnographers

103 PART THREE—ECOLOGIES OF CULTURE

105   Chapter 9   The Need for an Ecological Understanding of Adolescent Development

107   Chapter 10   An Ecological Model of Adolescent Development: The Influence on Culture and Experience

117   Chapter 11   The Cultures of Adolescent Relationships

147   Chapter 12   The Culture of Church and Religious Affiliation

159 PART FOUR—THEOLOGIES OF CULTURE

161 Chapter 13 Paul Tillich: Religion and Culture

169 Chapter 14 H. Richard Niebuhr: On Christ and Culture

181 Chapter 15 Karl Barth: Bearing Witness to Culture

193 Chapter 16 Kathryn Tanner: A Postmodern Response to a Theology of Culture

199 Chapter 17 Contextual Theology: Theology That Starts with Culture

211 Conclusion A Practical Approach to Understanding Youth Culture

219 Terms and Definitions

225 Bibliography

234 Index

ACKNOWLEDGMENTS

Writing is both a solitary and a communal pursuit. Without the neighborhoods of community surrounding me, the ability to withdraw and write would have been an arduous task, producing a text of much poorer quality. While I accept responsibility for the final product and any errors or weaknesses within, I am grateful for the many ways in which various people and groups helped make this book better.

The neighborhood of Bethel University provided me with both time and colleagues. Supporting me with a sabbatical, Bethel gave me the opportunity to focus on my writing and research, which allowed me to complete this manuscript in a timely manner. My colleagues encouraged me by sharing their insights, broadening my perspective and fine-tuning my research with ideas and authors to pursue, and, in general, improving this work. I would particularly like to thank Christian Collins-Winn, Karen McKinney, and Victor Ezigbo.

The classroom was another neighborhood that enriched the writing process and the final product. Students in all of my classes, but particularly in Understanding Adolescent Culture, posed questions, sometimes challenged my ideas, but always sharpened my thinking. I am humbled by their passion, their intellect, their pursuit of God's kingdom, and their desire to sacrificially serve Jesus Christ in youth ministry.

In the spring of 2009, students in Understanding Adolescent Culture allowed me to "test" this manuscript on them. These students—Rachel Allison, Alex Ducklow, Sandra Felten, Seth Goding, Megan Hansen, Alison Jungers, Adel Kahlow, Stephen Krueger, Kelsey Mickelsen, Laura Morgan, and Jenna Tieszen—brought tremendous insight to each class discussion and were eager and enthusiastic for each cultural observation and assignment. Their energy and excitement for this project motivated me in many ways to make this a better book.

Two other students also need to be mentioned here. Matthew Van Benschoten and Michael Roop were invaluable assistants. Matt sought out numerous books, manuscripts, and articles, and Michael read the final manuscript to offset my technology failings and get the manuscript in better form.

The neighborhood of youth ministry education colleagues gave me great support and encouragement. I am especially thankful for Calenthia Dowdy and Amy Jacober, who are not only great friends, but also amazing and stimulating research partners. They spent hours listening to me talk about my questions and concerns, sharing my excitement over new (to me) discoveries, reading and critiquing chapters, and celebrating the accomplishment of meeting each deadline.

This book would not have happened without all of the opportunities and great blessings I've received while working with many teenagers and youth groups over the years. In countless ways

I've been continually challenged to become a better student of culture and motivated to ask questions about the impact and influence of culture.

And, finally, thanks to all of my true neighbors in my community in St. Paul—Cindy Howard, Bridget and Will Berigan, and Todd and Mary Beth Carnicom. They witnessed my deadline anxieties and inability to put words on paper. They cooked, they listened, they prodded, and, when I needed it, they told me to "Go write."

I'd be remiss if I failed to thank the children on our block who've been a source of inspiration in a variety of ways. They've given me moments of re-creation and laughter and fun away from writing, while letting me watch them play and grow, and unknowingly egging me on in my pursuit of understanding the influences of culture on young lives. To Christine and Loice Howard; Frannie, Lucy, and Rosaleen Berigan; and especially my granddaughter, Cierra Erwin—thank you.

INTRODUCTION

In a report released in 2003, the United Nations reported that the number of young people between the ages of 10 and 19 was the largest in the world's history. With well over 1 billion young people, it is estimated that one in five people on the planet is an adolescent (Ranade). And as the stories related in the sidebar show, each and every adolescent is unique in personal characteristics and in cultural experience. Such a statement seems self-evident, as *no* two people are alike. Even identical twins aren't truly identical. They have many shared characteristics, for sure—but the differences in their taste, style, and even physicality will be far greater than their similarities.

So what accounts for our uniqueness? Is it strictly biological? If so, then identical twins would be wholly identical. Anthropologists and sociologists, confronted with similar questions about human differences, often use the example of raising a child in a different ethnic environment than her own. For example, consider a child of white European ancestry being adopted by a family from Beijing. She will have the *biological inheritance* of her white European ancestors, but in all other aspects of her self she'll reflect the *cultural inheritance* of her adopted Chinese family. As an adult any attempts to adopt the mannerisms and customs of white Europeans will be incomplete. The customs and lifestyle of her biological ancestors won't "fit" her as easily and smoothly as the customs and lifestyle of those of her cultural ancestors. She's been shaped by her

"Every day at 8 a.m., her straight black hair tied neatly in a braid, 16-year-old Neelam Aggarwal rides almost 5 kilometers [approximately 3 miles] to school in a horse-drawn buggy. She would like to be a doctor someday. But for girls like Neelam, who lives in [an extremely poor village in northern India], such a vocation seems remote. For starters, her school...doesn't even offer science classes for girls....Neelam, one of eight daughters of a sweets maker, has no intention of becoming a housewife. 'I want to make something of myself,' she says. So each day after school, Neelam operates what amounts to the village's only public telephone—a cellular phone owned by Indian cellular operator Koshika Telecom. By charging her fellow villagers to make calls, Neelam can make as much as $8.75 on a really good day. She's saving the money for computer classes, which she hopes will lead to a good job.... She is the very embodiment of India's youth—ambitious, technology-oriented, and confident." (Kripalani 1999)

Seven years ago, Jesse Jean was failing high school. The African-American teenager from Washington, D.C., had no family support. He missed two-thirds of the 10th grade and was surrounded by what he called a "thug mentality." [Growing up without a mother or father, Jean depended on support from mentors and other adults for support and encouragement. As he watched family members and neighborhood peers succumb to a life of violence and crime, Jean learned early on to be independent and] "go against the grain.…Jean says he spent many years as a loner—a protection mechanism." [After receiving a scholarship to attend a boarding school, Jean determined to rise above the environment he knew as a young child.] "This was Jean's survival plan: Stay in his room and play video games…[He reminded himself to] walk past the dealers with eyes cast down; just get up the block to the door of the local teen center. The teen center was his refuge." [Jesse completed college in June 2008 and is determined to make a difference. He wrote his college thesis on the need for more neighborhood teen centers] "because the centers can—and do—change lives." (Davis 2009)

"[18-year-old Ma Jingxuan lives in Beijing.] On weekends, Ma Jingxuan sheds her staid high school garb in favor of more offbeat, colorful clothes.…[She] spends her spare time reading Japanese comic books and creating outfits inspired by her favorite characters." *New York Times* style reporter Ann Mah writes that although the influence of American pop culture is widespread, many Chinese youth prefer the cultural trends of Japanese and Korean youth culture. "China's teenagers are more interested in the television shows and movies produced by their Pacific rim neighbors." Ma Jingxuan spends her time away from school dressed in the latest bright and vivid fashions from Japan, reading "manga comic books and creat[ing] outfits based on [her] favorite characters—from hair to makeup to shoes, [she] emulate[s] every minute detail." Ma Jingxuan depends on her parents to support her expensive entertainment habits and sometimes feels the outrage from adults. "People think we should avoid Japanese products…They think we're lazy." As Mah reports, "Others feel that teenagers' favorite activities—playing video games, shopping, hanging out at nightclubs, collecting robots and dolls based on comic book characters—are far too frivolous." (Mah 2005)

environment—her context. Her individuality—her uniqueness—isn't strictly a product of her biology, but in hugely significant ways, she's been shaped by her culture.

As infants and children, we learn our culture from those around us. Parents, siblings, other family members, and later on, teachers, peers, coaches, and mentors teach us what's appropriate, acceptable, and desirable. We learn culture in a variety of formal and informal ways, but primarily we learn it because others are *culture bearers*. That is, others transmit culture to us—they are carriers of cultural heritage and pass it on to children (and others) within a society.

In other words, we *inherit* culture from our elders. Culture is passed down to us not through biological means, but through our participation with others in our society. As human beings learn the ways of their culture, they become *culture bearers*—instruments of cultural transmission within their own context.

Culture, though, isn't solely a matter of inheritance and transmission. Human beings have the capability to be *culture makers*. That is, we don't simply receive and learn culture, but as we interact with others, we have the capacity and possibility of creating and shaping culture. As human beings in the context of a group (however small that number may be), we will influence and shape the customs and ways of life of that group. This bidirectional process of being both culture bearers and culture makers is an ongoing, never-ending process.

So at a very basic level, we can say that the uniqueness of each person can be attributed to both biological and cultural influences. As researchers seek to isolate and identify the influences that shape individuals, it's often difficult to tease out the significance of biology against culture.

In this text we'll focus on developing a greater understanding of how and why culture shapes the identity of adolescents. The premise of this book is twofold. First, trends and popular styles in youth culture change rapidly. When I was 16 years old, "Ain't No Mountain High Enough" by Diana Ross was the number one song on the *Billboard* charts, the greatest issue facing the world was the Vietnam War, and miniskirts reigned supreme. *Marcus Welby* was the top-rated television show and *Patton* won the Oscar for Best Picture. The top fiction novel of the year was *Love Story*, and *Everything You Always Wanted to Know About Sex but Were Afraid to Ask* beat out the *New English Bible* as the top-selling nonfiction book.

But as I write this, "I Kissed a Girl" by Katy Perry is the number one song on the *Billboard* charts, *The Dark Knight* is the top grossing film, and *America's Got Talent* is the top-rated television show (Billboard.com 2009, The People History 2009). By the time you read this paragraph, even these favorites will have been supplanted by new cultural trends and icons.

Knowing what teens are listening to and watching or even what they're wearing is helpful and might make you renowned for your knowledge of trivia. But youth culture is not some concrete, easily definable entity. It's constantly changing. Trends are merely surface reflections, giving us superficial glimpses into the lives of youth. This is not a book about current trends. Such a book would be out of date before the publisher could print it. So as we examine the influence of culture, we'll draw upon historical moments in youth culture to assist us in our understanding. But the goal isn't to make readers more hip and current on the latest fads in youth culture.

Second, because of the fluidity of youth culture, knowing what's popular today may be helpful, but it doesn't provide us much insight into the "tomorrows" of youth culture. As a young youth pastor, I thought I had to experience everything that young people did in order to understand them. So I spent a lot of time listening to music, watching television shows and movies, reading teen magazines, and playing video games. I soon realized there was no way I could ever experience every aspect of youth culture. And even if I could—the best I could achieve was to understand how youth culture *shaped me*, not how it shaped young people. Being a regular consumer of youth culture doesn't necessarily translate into a better understanding of youth.

This is a book for youth ministers who want to be discerners and critical thinkers of youth culture—*students* of youth culture, rather than simply *consumers*. Astute students of youth culture will develop a greater understanding. And with understanding comes a greater ability to speak to those who inhabit youth culture.

Culture is all around us. Some have described it like this: "Culture is to a human being as water is to a fish." It nourishes us, it defines us—we can't exist without it. And yet, culture is such an essential and inextricable part of our existence that we find it hard to see.

Part One of this book lays a foundation for our discussion of youth culture by exploring some of the basic questions about culture. What is culture? What are the different aspects and characteristics of culture? How does culture define us and our experiences? This section concludes with a discussion of youth culture as a subset of a larger social context.

One road-trip game that's been around for as long as families have been going on long trips together is "I Spy." You've probably played it dozens of times. A person who is "it" picks something in the surroundings and identifies it by color—for example, "I spy something orange." Everyone else takes turns trying to guess what the person has spied, looking for anything orange. Naturally, the goal for the person who's "it" is to spy something that no one else can identify. The meaning of the word *spy* in this context is to discover something by close observation. Likewise, youth workers need to "spy out" culture and its influences on youth.

Part Two explores the skills of a cultural ethnographer, one who spends time in close observation of culture and its effects. In particular, this section discusses the attitudes and skills of an ethnographer and presents ways for youth workers to consider the work of youth ministry as one of being a "pastor-ethnographer."

Eastman Kodak recently announced it would no longer produce Kodachrome film since demand for the product dramatically declined in the wake of digital camera technology. Photographers and filmmakers alike mourned the passing of Kodachrome because of its ability to bring images into sharp focus and the brightness and intensity of colors (Woodward 2009). The vividness of images captured on Kodachrome film was immortalized in "Kodachrome," written and sung by Paul Simon in 1973:

> They give us those nice bright colors.
> They give us the greens of summers.
> Makes you think all the world's a sunny day...
> So mama don't take my Kodachrome away.

The years in which an adolescent transitions through puberty often bring that sort of vivid intensity of experiences—experiences in which a young person awakens to greater clarity and awareness of his or her world. It's the same body the person had before; but suddenly it looks, feels, and responds in amazingly different ways. And the mind is now capable of thinking and expressing ideas and emotions that are totally novel and astonishing. A whole new world of relationship possibilities opens up as well, from knowing self to being able to know friends, parents, and others in completely fresh and exciting ways. All of these relationships intertwine to form vibrant and dynamic webs of relating.

Part Three examines these "cultures" of relationships, focusing on the immediate contexts of family, peers, and religious influences of the contemporary adolescent. This section explores how these contexts shape and form adolescents and vice versa.

Since the early days of the church, Christians have pondered the relationship between Christ and human culture. What are we to do with culture? Is culture good? Is it bad? Can we be faithful and still live in culture? Is it possible to live *without* culture? These deep questions are vital for Christians—and especially youth workers—to consider.

Part Four explores some contemporary theologians' responses to these questions. After reviewing the theologies of three twentieth-century theologians, this section will examine a postmodern theological perspective of culture and then conclude with a discussion of a method for doing theology that begins with culture.

This Introduction began with the analogy that culture is to human beings as water is to fish, meaning culture is essential to our survival, but it's difficult to see and even more difficult to grasp and hold on to. Throughout Parts One to Four, the intent is to describe ways to increase the capabilities of seeing culture and grasping its influence in the lives of young people. This text concludes by adapting the ideas presented into a framework for integrating such visual acuity into the everyday practices of youth workers.

REFLECTION ACTIVITY (5 TO 10 MINUTES)

Read back over the youth essays in the sidebar at the beginning of the Introduction. What cultural characteristics did these young people share (for example, dress, hairstyle, music, behavior)? What cultural characteristics were dissimilar? As you look at one particular story, can you identify the meaning behind an aspect of the person's culture? Can you determine different cultural values that have shaped how this young person thinks or acts?

DIGGING DEEPER (10 TO 15 MINUTES)

Read Acts 17:14-34. Compare and contrast ways in which Paul was a student or a consumer of culture in speaking with the Athenians. How did being a student of Greek culture give him greater access with the people in the marketplace?

- Every young person receives a biological inheritance from his or her family of origin.

- Every young person receives a cultural inheritance from the environment(s) in which he or she grows up.

WORKS CITED

Davis, Katie. 2008. Jesse's story: an urban teen beats the odds. *NPR*, August 22, 2008. http://www.npr.org/templates/story/story.php?storyId=93850513.

Kripalani, Manjeet. 1999. India's youth: they're capitalist-minded—and they're changing the nation forever. International—Asian Cover Story, *BusinessWeek Online*, October 11, 1999. http://www.businessweek.com/1999/99_41/b3650015.htm.

Mah, Ann. 2005. Japanese and Korean pop idols set trends for Chinese teens. *The New York Times*, March 4, 2005. http://www.nytimes.com/2005/03/04/style/04iht-rha.html?sq=chinese teens&st=cse&scp=1.

Nielsen Business Media, Inc. Billboard.com. http://www.billboard.com/bbcom/charts#/bbcom/charts.

Ranade, Supria. 2003. Global teen population is the highest ever, says U.N. report. *The Johns Hopkins News-Letter*, October 10, 2003. http://media.www.jhunewsletter.com/media/storage/paper932/news/2003/10/10/Science/Global.Teen.Population.Is.The.Highest.Ever.Says.U.n.Report-2246193.shtml.

Simon, Paul. 1973. "Kodachrome." *There Goes Rhymin' Simon*. http://www.allthelyrics.com/lyrics/paul_simon/kodachrome-lyrics-228765.html.

The People History: Where People Memories and History Join—1970s. http://www.thepeople-history.com/1970s.html.

Woodward, Richard B. 2009. Kodachrome fades to black. *The Wall Street Journal*. Arts & Entertainment. June 30, 2009. http://online.wsj.com/article/SB124631829284470853.html.

PART ONE

The Nature of Culture

CHAPTER 1
What Is Culture?

LEARNING OBJECTIVES

When you've finished this chapter, you should be able to:

1. Demonstrate an understanding of what culture is

2. Consider how culture shapes who we are

3. Apply the concept of culture to the social practices in which young people are engaged

4. Discuss some of the ways cultural experiences shape people

5. Articulate the seven different senses of culture

Culture. The word *culture* is common in our everyday vocabulary. We talk about *pop culture, youth culture*, and *American culture*. We use the word *culture* to explain our differences. For example, I'm from Minnesota. Minnesotans treat people with respect. We have a *culture* of niceness. We call it "Minnesota nice." We also use culture to explain what's important to us—what we believe in: "In America anyone can pursue the 'American dream.' Our culture makes it possible for anyone to succeed as long as they're willing to work hard." While these are ideological statements that may not be reality for every individual in the United States, these ideas exist as cultural beliefs that shape and form how Americans view themselves and how they view others.

But what is *culture*? As is often the case with a commonly used word, the definition is assumed. But when you dig deeper, you find that people may have given little thought to what the word really means or may have completely different understandings. What does it mean to say that youths have a culture? Does culture refer to what teenagers do? What they wear? What they buy? What they produce? What they think about—the ideas they have? Is youth culture some combination of all of these or none of these?

If there is such a thing as "youth culture," how do we define it? Obviously, youth culture has something to do with "youth" and with "culture." Though we could spend time discussing exactly what *youth* is, and we may do so later on in the book, I believe we should begin by clearly defining what *culture* is. Then we can talk more specifically about youth culture. So…culture. What is it? What does it look like? How does culture act? How do we know culture when we see it? A good place to start is by looking at the history and development of the word *culture*.

HISTORICAL UNDERSTANDINGS OF CULTURE

The word *culture* comes from the Latin *cultura* or *cultus,* meaning "cultivation or the state of being cultivated" (Freilich 1972). Even today, a lesser-known synonym of the word *culture* is *tillage,* meaning "to prepare the land or soil in preparation for growing" (Merriam-Webster). Inherent in the notion of culture is that it's being nurtured—that human activity helps it to grow and develop. Whatever culture is, it is not static, nor stagnant.

For early Germans, *kultur* meant the cultivation (nurture or development) of a "complex inner life" (Freilich 1972)—a life of knowledge in the arts and philosophy. This eventually came to be an understanding of culture in the larger society. So, for example, societies were considered cultured if they developed and participated in the development of the arts—literature, visual arts, and musical arts (what's sometimes referred to as "high culture").

Even today, a common understanding for the word *culture* is the collective consideration of a society's art, music, literature, and related intellectual activities. And to be a cultured person is to be someone who is intimately familiar with the artistic forms of a society. A closely related definition is one in which culture is considered a product of education and an accumulation of knowledge. Within this definition is an understanding of sophistication, in which a person or a society expresses a widespread knowledge and refinement.

Beginning in the late 1800s, as the field of anthropology (the science and study of human development) was in its infancy, anthropologists debated about how to define *culture*. Since that time, as they've worked to define the breadth and parameters of their own scientific discipline, they've endeavored to establish the parameters for understanding culture—both what it is and how one may adequately analyze it. This anthropological discussion will prove helpful for us as we begin our study of youth culture. In this first chapter, we'll begin to frame an explanation of culture by incorporating an analysis of Ward Goodenough's definitions of the seven senses of culture.

As we discussed earlier, culture isn't stagnant or static—it grows and develops. And growth and development mean change. Therefore, culture might be best imagined as a river. As you step into it, you are in the river; but even as you continue to stand at that same spot in the river, you're no longer standing in the same place that you first did. Everything around you has changed, from the silt under your feet to the microorganisms in the water around you—even the water coursing around your legs isn't the same.

Likewise, culture is a broad, constantly changing flow of social influences. The more complex a society becomes, the greater the complexity of these social influences and the greater the pace of change.

Simple Definition of *Culture*

Writing in 1870, E. B. Tylor set forth the first anthropological definition of *culture*. He said culture is "that complex whole which includes knowledge, belief, art, morals, law, custom, and any other capabilities and habits acquired by man as a member of society" (Goldstein 1957). Referring back to our discussion of the historical understandings of culture, Tylor suggested that only those peoples and societies that had developed sophistication in the arts and intellectual pursuits, as well as the social organization necessary to attain this development, had culture. Culture, in his estimation, was synonymous with civilization.

This assertion has been widely refuted over the years, but Tylor's general definition of *culture* is often touted as a solid beginning. For Tylor the total way of life of a people included the ways in which they thought and acted as a community. The response to this definition within the anthropological community has been a fruitful and intense discussion. Though by no means a thorough explication of this discussion, the following will provide a simple platform for our discussion of youth culture.

THE SEVEN SENSES OF CULTURE

Ward Goodenough, an anthropologist writing in the mid-twentieth century, identified seven "senses" or ways of visualizing culture (1989). Like a person's natural senses, our senses of culture operate independently yet simultaneously. One sense may take priority at certain moments, but there is the constant interplay of all the cultural senses.

For example, when a person enters a restaurant, the smells, sights, and sounds assault her senses. The sense of touch may be less engaged, but all of the senses help a person fully appreciate the experience. Ultimately, it's the sense of taste that carries the greater weight. However, as one begins to partake of the meal, the other senses contribute to the pleasure (or displeasure) of eating.

CULTURAL DISTINCTIONS

Human existence can be divided into two basic arenas: Natural and cultural. Natural refers to the aspects of human existence that aren't artificial, contrived, acquired, or learned. Basically, natural refers to what a human being *inherits* as a result of being born human, such as innate biological characteristics and behaviors. To be a living human being, one must breathe, eat, and sleep, among other things. These are natural behaviors. However, from that moment of birth on, our natural human behaviors are culturalized. That is, while all living human beings breathe, eat, and sleep, we don't all engage in those behaviors in the exact same ways. Instead, we develop customs and ways of life regarding these natural human behaviors.

Moreover, some senses may be more highly developed than others. But all are important to helping a person navigate her daily experiences, thereby shaping how she perceives them. Similarly, a person's sense of culture is a broad array of understandings, and it typically deepens as one develops greater abilities of cultural perception.

1. Systems of Standards

For Goodenough, the first sense of culture is a system of standards that frames a person's expectations for perceiving, believing, evaluating, and performing (1989). These expectations serve as guiding mechanisms and offer a basis for judging what are appropriate thoughts and actions. So, for example, a person in the United States would be expected to dress and act a particular way if he were attending a family barbecue. It's unlikely that he'd wear a suit and tie to the gathering. And he'd most likely interact informally with his family and friends in the backyard.

On the other hand, if this same person were attending his grandmother's funeral, there would be a different set of expectations for how he should dress and act. He might wear a suit and tie, but he'd certainly dress in a more formal manner than he would at the barbecue. His conversations and behavior would also be governed by the social practices for funerals. If he behaved outside of those social customs, his behavior would be viewed as inappropriate, perhaps even shameful.

In the same way that a child learns to integrate all of her physical senses to make judgments about life experiences, as she grows and matures, she'll develop a sense of the different systems of standards in the various arenas of her life. These senses will serve to help her make judgments about what she values and what behaviors she chooses.

CULTURAL SYSTEMS

A *system* is a group of sets of propositions about the world and the way the world operates, which serve as cultural boundaries that provide order and stability to a society. Broad sets of propositions exist in all social arenas—politics, economics, government, and the like. Smaller sets of propositions also exist within the contexts of families, neighborhoods, towns, schools, and even churches. These interlocking and overlapping *systems* teach people the customs and expectations of a particular culture.

These systems are an inevitable part and function of culture; however they're often oppressive and restrictive to some groups (for example, propositions that discriminate against people based on socioeconomic class, ethnicity, gender, religion, and so on).

Food for Thought

Can you identify cultural systems that are a part of your worship or youth group experiences?

2. Assigned Character Traits

In this second sense of culture, *culture* refers to specific attributes associated with or assigned to groups based on personal experiences with members of that group (Goodenough 1989). For example, I recently heard a travel writer, who's spent a lot of time in Southeast Asia, discuss tourism and tourists in Thailand. In talking about the numbers of tourists he'd observed, he made this comment: "You can always tell the American tourists. They are the ones in baggy shorts, ratty T-shirts, and flip-flops. Americans are slobs."[1] His experience with

---

1 This quote comes from a broadcast on National Public Radio in the spring of 2008. I wasn't able to aquire details regarding the particular interview.

American tourists had led him to conclude that all Americans dress like slobs. Furthermore, he'd assigned this character trait to American culture as a whole.

Two points should be noted here. First, these kinds of conclusions are just generalizations and certainly cannot be applied to all people within a group. However, in a general *sense*, this writer had learned something about American culture—that Americans tend to have a more casual style of dress. This leads us into the second point: This sense of cultural understanding is understood in *contrast* to one's own experience. This journalist perceived Americans as casual dressers because he experienced a more formal style of dress in his own culture or with people from other cultures.

It must be acknowledged that with this sense there is the danger of stereotyping people groups or individuals from a particular group, especially when we use our own cultural value to assign worth or when personal experience precludes our ability to see beyond generalizations. In this example the journalist placed a lower value on American tourists because they didn't dress as he thought was appropriate. His cultural standards led him to assign a negative stereotype to the cultural traits he observed in Americans and to act in an ethnocentric manner.

> ## Ethnocentrism
>
> *Paul Hiebert, and others, notes that "ethnocentrism occurs wherever cultural differences are found" both within and across societies (1985). People act ethnocentrically when they assume their personal cultural practices are superior to another's.*

> ## Food for Thought
> *How might American Christians be ethnocentric on mission trips?*

3. Operating Culture

Goodenough calls the third sense *operating culture* (1989). Like an operating system loaded on our computers, operating culture consists of those standards or systems that a society chooses to guide its own thoughts and actions or the standards a person chooses to judge another person's behavior. Without getting mired in a discussion about whether one's operating culture is consciously or subconsciously chosen, or whether it's merely imposed by others, it's important to note that a choice of operating culture is ongoing and influenced by one's own psychological and cognitive development, as well as an awareness of the breadth of possible choices.

So, for example, a person who's lived in one community for 50 years, rarely traveled beyond its borders, and had few social relationships outside of that context will have far less awareness of the great variety in potential worldviews. On the other hand, another person of a similar age who's spent a significant amount of time living in a variety of different cultures will have a greater reservoir of ways of perceiving, believing, evaluating, and performing.

Several years ago, I counseled with a young woman who'd been physically and emotionally abused by her mother. After a couple of years of living in a healthier family context, she made this comment to me:

> When I used to live with my mom and she would beat me, I thought that's what moms did. I thought all moms beat their kids. Then, I got out of it and realized that all moms didn't beat their kids. I realized that beating your kids wasn't normal. I thought it was.

This young woman had learned a new way of perceiving—a new possibility for what was appropriate. She'd developed a stronger sense of cultural standards. Though freedom to choose is not absolute, individuals and societies are in a fluid process of choosing a set of standards that will govern their lives.

4. Public Culture

The fourth sense of culture Goodenough calls *public culture* (1989). Public culture refers to those specific forms of thoughts and actions that are expected in the public social arenas of society. For those of us involved in youth ministry, there are two readily identifiable arenas of public youth culture—school and church or youth group. Youth workers often observe students acting one way at church and another way at school. At a very broad level, what we're observing is students adjusting their thoughts, actions, and behaviors to conform to the expectations of a specific public culture.

Goodenough speaks of how public culture limits the behavior of people within a specific group. For example, in some Arab cultures, public culture severely limits the

Therefore, I urge you, brothers and sisters, in view of God's mercy, to offer your bodies as a living sacrifice, holy and pleasing to God—this is true worship. Do not conform to the pattern of this world, but be transformed by the renewing of your mind. Then you will be able to test and approve what God's will is—his good, pleasing and perfect will. —Romans 12:1-2 (emphasis added)

CODE-SWITCHING

In *Code of the Street*, his book on life in the inner city, Elijah Anderson describes these sets of public cultures as "codes." As young people learn the codes of their schools, neighborhoods, churches, and homes, they become adept at "code-switching." In other words, they learn how to present themselves in a certain way in one context and another way in a different context. It's in these differing contexts—the "places where they are involved in the process of forging their own local identities"—that teenagers learn the codes (1999). And in their experiences within these multiple contexts, young people make decisions about who they will be and who they will become.

Anderson argues that context has a significant impact in shaping a young person's identity and that the ability to code-switch is often a matter of survival. That's why a young person can be known as a "good Christian young man" at home or at church, yet still be known on the streets as someone to be feared and respected. Such a young man has learned that to be feared and respected by his peers is important to his very survival on those streets (1999).

Codes aren't solely a part of the culture of inner-city life. Codes and code-switching are cultural phenomena for most young people, whether they're middle-class suburban youth, youth from rural Midwestern America, or youth living in the urban neighborhoods of L.A.

behavior and actions of women. Women in Saudi Arabia aren't allowed to go out in public unless a male family member accompanies them. They aren't allowed to vote or drive, are barred from certain professions, and cannot be treated in a hospital without the permission of an adult male family member (Eltahawy 2007). In this example, so different from the experiences of women living in Westernized cultures, it's easy to see how behaviors are limited. Less apparent is how these restrictive laws shape and limit the thoughts of men and women within Saudi Arabia. Cultural behavioral expectations for women shape how they view themselves and how others view them.

CULTURAL RELATIVISM: IS IT REALLY ALL RELATIVE?

As we've already discussed, culture shapes and influences human behavior. Further, different cultures make different decisions about what is appropriate, desirable, and acceptable. As students of culture and followers of Christ, how do we evaluate the values, beliefs, and behaviors of culture—say, for example, the culture of youth? Three principles can guide our critique and evaluation.

Culture Influences but Doesn't Determine

The influences of culture don't pressure all persons in a society in the same way, or to the same extent. Additionally, no one "can ever be truly free of cultural influence." Nevertheless, "we are not...determined by our culture" (Kraft and Kraft 2005). As youth workers, then, we don't reason away expectations for right and moral behavior because of the cultural influences on youth. We don't accept statements such as, "Everyone drinks at high school parties, so we can't expect our students not to." Nor do we adopt the contrary stance that youth can easily and readily resist the draw of culture to conform.

Cultural Relativism

As we seek to understand youth and their culture, this principle reminds us that teenagers' behavior should be understood in terms of their particular cultural context. As Charles Kraft, a Christian anthropologist, suggests, we must take "cultural practices and values seriously, though not necessarily approving of them" (2005). In this tension we can develop an appreciation for young people's choices and behaviors, setting aside our judgmental spirit and acknowledging that some questionable values and seemingly inappropriate behaviors might be totally appropriate in their particular context.

Ethical and Moral Imperatives

Adopting the principle of cultural relativism doesn't mean that everything in a culture is good or that we shouldn't critique cultural beliefs and values. Quite the opposite. It simply means that we don't judge another person's culture based on our own cultural experiences. Instead, we must evaluate a culture's values and beliefs from a broader ethical and moral imperative.

Public culture not only limits behavior, but also promotes certain behaviors. Behaviors that are acceptable—even encouraged—in some countries wouldn't be tolerated and might even be considered *illegal* in others. For example, in a number of countries, if a woman (but typically not a man) is suspected of engaging in premarital sex, "the males of her family may punish her, beat her, or even kill her" to protect the family's honor (Arnett 2007). Even the suspicion of a woman's wrongdoing can be considered grounds for violence toward her, including death (Eltahawy 2007).

These stark examples show how culture can be a negative influence in shaping thoughts, actions, and behaviors. But this dynamic isn't limited to countries outside the United States. One need spend only 20 to 30 minutes watching the latest sitcom or listening to music from the latest Top Ten lists to recognize the prevalent negative messages regarding sexuality, morality, and a host of other human behaviors.

A culture's influence in limiting and promoting behaviors, however, isn't always negative. Culture can also be a positive force in promoting good behaviors and restricting and limiting harmful ones. The work of Christian Smith and others shows that young people in the United States who are consistently involved in a church or youth group exhibit more positive behaviors and fewer negative behaviors. Therefore, we might conclude that the cultural influence of the church and youth group promotes positive behaviors and restricts less healthy thoughts and actions (Smith and Denton 2005).

5. A Set of Public Cultures

In most societies there are multiple public cultures. Goodenough describes this fifth sense of culture as "a set of public cultures that are functionally equivalent and mutually apprehensible. Each public culture in the set is a subculture" (1989). The idea here is that people within a society have access to a variety of public cultures (subcultures) that provide the same functions—limiting and promoting ideas, behaviors, and actions. Individuals within a particular society move in and out of these public cultures, evaluating and establishing a cultural hierarchy. "In this sense, culture is to subculture much as language is to dialect" (Freilich 1989).

I've lived in many regions of the United States during my life, and I've become familiar with a few of the American public cultures: Midwestern, Western, and Southern. As a southerner by birth, I'm most familiar with this public culture by far. It's my cultural inheritance. As a product of the South, much of the way that culture has limited and promoted certain ideas and behaviors has been, at least in the early years of my life, unconscious. My ideas of what was appropriate or "normal" were learned at an early age and without any awareness of other possibilities.

PROMOTING POSITIVE BEHAVIORS

Between 2002 and 2003, Christian Smith, along with a number of scholars and researchers, conducted the first in-depth, nationally represented study of the religious and spiritual lives of American teens. Collecting data from more than 3,300 teenagers (between the ages of 13 and 17) and their parents, Smith's study provides insight into the spiritual lives of adolescents and how their spirituality shapes a variety of outcomes, including "risk behaviors, quality of family and adult relationships, moral reasoning and behavior, community participation, media consumption, sexual activity, and emotional well-being" (Smith and Denton 2005).

This study found that religiously devoted adolescents were less likely to engage in risky behaviors. These teenagers regularly attended religious services (weekly or more), considered faith very important in their everyday lives, felt very close to God, were currently involved in a youth group, prayed at least a few times a week, and read Scripture at least once or twice a month.

Smith found that teens in this category were *far less* likely than other teenagers to:

- Smoke cigarettes regularly
- Drink alcohol weekly or more
- Get drunk every few weeks or more
- Cut classes in school
- Be expelled from school

And they were *more* likely to:

- Not drink at all
- Not smoke marijuana
- Get better grades (Smith and Denton 2005)

But as I began to mature, and especially as I moved to different regions of the country, I learned about new public cultures and different ways of being appropriate or normal. I learned there were different ways of thinking about the world and participating in society that were still American—but very different from America in the South. Each region has a different way of communicating about the same thing.

"WHAT ARE YOU DRINKING?"

If you've ever traveled in different regions of the United States and tried to order a soft drink, you may have experienced some confusion. 'For whatever reason, Americans cannot seem to come together on…the appropriate term for a soft or fizzy drink…In the southern [United States], stretching from New Mexico to Indiana, western North Carolina to most of Florida, all soft drinks are referred to as 'cokes,' which to everyone else is the name of a specific drink—a Coca-Cola. A Southerner may want a 'coke' and get a Pepsi-Cola—the archrival of Coca-Cola.…'Soda' is a term in use throughout California, Nevada, Arizona, and most of the Atlantic Seaboard.…In Boston and New England, one term for a soft drink is often a 'tonic,' which for everyone else is what you combine with gin.…The term 'tonic' is fading out with time, and more and more New Englanders have adopted the term 'soda.' Throughout most of the Midwest, from western Pennsylvania, through the Great Plains, to Oregon, the preferred usage is 'pop'" (Jordan 2008).

These regional public cultures, however, are still situated within the context of American culture. So many of the same beliefs and expectations are central to each public culture. In general, a person could travel to any region of the United States and expect that beliefs and values about freedom, democracy, and individual rights would be similar. Thus, while each regional subculture offers its own flavor in the ways these core values are lived out and experienced, they do so under the umbrella of American culture.

As a person develops a greater sense of public cultures, she'll be able to assess and rank them. As I've lived outside of the South, for example, I've made decisions between meeting the expectations of other regional cultures and my own understanding of southern culture. Do I continue to say, "I'm fixin' to go to the movies," as I might do in the South? Or do I adopt the preferred idiom in my local community? This decision-making strategy is an active process that involves engaging one public culture's norms and evaluating them against another's.

6. Society's Culture

In this sixth sense, Goodenough refers to the culture of a given society in its broadest sense (1989). In other words, *Culture* (capitalized) refers to the totality of all cultures within a society, both public and subcultures, and encompasses all activities within a given group of people. In Central and South America, there are a variety of cultures—a broad range of different ethnic and national experiences. However, all of these groups are often referred to as "Latin Americans" as a whole, noting an expectation that there are ideas, behaviors, and activities common to all peoples in this region of the world. Therefore, the Culture of Latin America refers to the broad range of common values, behaviors, and language (generally speaking) that subcultures within the geographical regions of Latin America share.

7. Culture Pool

Goodenough's seventh sense of culture refers to all of the possibilities of human culture—historical, present, and future—the total range of cultural possibilities from which to choose (1989).

Goodenough's argument about the different senses of culture and the ways human beings interact with them provides a good backdrop as we move forward to talk about the qualities of culture—that is, those aspects of culture that give culture its influence in our lives.

REFLECTION ACTIVITY (5 TO 10 MINUTES)

Consider the examples of Saudia Arabia and the media in our own culture. Reflect on the following questions: Who decides what gets promoted and encouraged in a culture? Who decides what gets restricted and discouraged in a culture? What role do youth play in promoting or discouraging their cultural norms?

DIGGING DEEPER (10 TO 15 MINUTES)

Read over the sidebar on the work of Christian Smith and his colleagues. Consider the significant patterns of behavior that promoted positive teenage choices and discouraged risky ones. How might your understanding of these cultural influences shape your ideas about how to practice youth ministry?

- Culture: All of the social dynamics of a society, including knowledge, beliefs, art, morals, laws, and customs.

- System of Standards: The sense of culture that frames expectations for perceiving, believing, evaluating, and performing.

- Assigned Character Traits: The sense of culture that refers to specific attributes associated with or assigned to groups based on personal experience with members of that group.

- Operating Culture: Those standards or systems that a society chooses to guide its own thoughts and actions or to judge others' behavior.

- Public Culture: Those specific forms of thoughts and actions expected in the public social arenas of society.

- Culture Pool: The total range of cultural possibilities from which human beings may choose.

CHAPTER 2

What Makes Culture "Culture"?

LEARNING OBJECTIVES

When you've finished this chapter, you should be able to:

1. Articulate the different characteristics of culture

2. Demonstrate an understanding of the bidirectional influence between human beings and culture

3. Discuss how culture shapes expectations for what is normal-abnormal, desirable-undesirable, and acceptable-unacceptable

A further debate in the anthropological discussion of culture has centered on ideas and behaviors. Experts in the study and practice of anthropology have debated whether culture was strictly a matter of (1) ideas and beliefs, (2) the actions of a group, or (3) both. Does culture constitute only those ideas or actions that could be considered communal? Or does it also incorporate the thoughts and actions of individuals?

Although the debate continues, the intensity of the discussion has mellowed within a number of camps in the anthropological community. Some scholars, such as Claude Lévi-Strauss and Clifford Geertz, considered culture to be mostly a matter of ideas—how a people make meaning. Others, such as Marvin Harris and Roy A. Rappaport, argued that culture is an adaptive mechanism. They saw culture from a systemic approach—that is, human beings create culture in response to a problem (Rappaport 1999).

The goal of this chapter is not to amplify the anthropological debate, but to use their discussion to help us frame our own discussion of youth culture.

A review of the literature offers us seven characteristics of culture.

1. CULTURE IS ABOUT THE HUMAN POTENTIAL FOR *IDEAS*

In *Culture: A Critical Review of Concepts and Definitions*, Alfred L. Kroeber and Clyde Kluckhohn (1952) state that culture is uniquely human. The development of culture isn't something animals can engage in because, at its essence, culture is about ideas. To construct a thought, an opinion, or a belief about something is strictly a human capacity. And this ability to construct ideas and assign value to them gives rise to culture. Not only that, but culture is something we humans will necessarily and automatically do. To be human is to have ideas—the very basis of culture.

What makes one society unique from another is the choices its people make when it comes to ideas. Hannerz claimed that culture was the "entire array of thought among a group or society" (1952). Margaret Mead called the range of human ideas the "great arc of human potentialities" (1934). So out of this wide range of potential ideas, societies select thoughts and beliefs, thereby giving them value and forming the nucleus out of which culture develops.

Namenwirth and Weber (1987) argued that culture was strictly about a system of ideas and had nothing to do with behaviors. It's an extreme view, not widely held by anthropologists. They do, however, focus on culture as a structured system of ideas.

2. CULTURE IS ABOUT PEOPLE ASSIGNING *MEANING*

If, as Mead contended, culture rests on a society choosing from the great arc of human potentialities of ideas, what causes a society to choose one particular idea, while another chooses an opposing idea? Geertz (1973) and others contend that culture is organized around those ideas that a society *values*. In other words, culture is about meaning. Groups choose from a range of possibilities based on what gives them meaning and purpose. In turn, meaning and purpose promote the development of social organization and social relationships and also help groups determine what ideas, acts, and practices are appropriate. Groups can then make determinations about how social relationships should be ordered and structured. This social organizing is a lengthy and ongoing process of establishing societal norms based on what is deemed to be valuable. Thereby, culture makes the meaning public (Hannerz 1952).

3. CULTURE IS ABOUT SOCIALLY CONSISTENT PATTERNS OF *BEHAVIOR*

As E. B. Tylor first articulated, culture is the customary way of life of a people. While some anthropologists differ on this point, contending that culture is solely about ideas (see the first cultural characteristic mentioned above), others argue that culture is about how those ideas shape and construct behavior. Namenwirth and Weber (1987) stated that culture is a system of ideas, not behavior nor any symbol or artifact of a society. Others, namely John W. Bennett, insisted that social norms lead to expected behaviors and that it's the intertwining of the two—norms and behaviors—that constitute the culture of a people (Freilich 1972).

Ruth Benedict (1934) noted that an anthropologist could begin to identify what ideas gave meaning and purpose to a people group by observing repeated patterns of behavior. Benedict also asserted that culture arises not solely based on ideas, but as the society develops a consistent pattern of thought and action. For Benedict the process of patterning behavior is essential in the development of a culture. The pattern of behavior arises, though, out of the development of a consistent pattern of thought and beliefs.

Benedict (1934) set forth three characteristics of culture addressing the issues of ideas and behavior:

1. Culture consists of a *consistent pattern of thoughts and actions*.

2. Each society promotes the development of characteristic purposes or meaning. That is, each society evaluates and selects a set of governing principles—*ideas*—that will guide its social interactions and practices.

3. As these ideas are solidified and normalized, *obedience* to these behaviors becomes more consistent and congruent. Cultural practices are established.

This interplay between ideas and behavior creates culture. This interplay also causes a kind of ebb and flow in the culture, making it difficult to realistically identify concrete cultural aspects—particularly from within a society. While behaviors can be observed, trends in patterned behaviors are fluid and constantly changing. This is particularly true in youth culture. This rapid change in cultural trends brings us back to the need to critically evaluate the behavior patterns we do see for any underlying meanings. That is where true understanding takes place.

> **Food for Thought**
>
> *How have you experienced the ordering of adolescent culture? What are some of the meanings assigned to specific adolescent behaviors?*

4. CULTURE IS *A HISTORICAL PHENOMENON (TRADITION)*

Paying attention to behavior trends helps us identify patterns of meaning, thereby allowing us to look for what is valued within a given culture. As Benedict, Freilich, Kroeber, and others contend, culture is deeply rooted in its historical context. As noted above, Benedict sets forth the framework for understanding culture as the process of socially transmitted and socially consistent patterns of behavior. This communal process of solidifying socially consistent patterns of thoughts and actions leads to long-established customs within a culture, otherwise known as "traditions."

As Benedict argues, tradition plays an enormous role in the development of culture (1934). Even in rapidly changing contemporary youth culture, the place of history and tradition cannot be denied. The trends in fashion, music, movies, language, and even technology build on the histories and traditions of the past. Culture is sustained by its historical context, and tradition provides the scaffolding upon which culture rests (Schusky and Culbert 1967).

CREATING CULTURAL PATTERNS

Culture is not biological, nor is it transmitted biologically. Culture happens as a result of normative social interactions within a specified group of people. In other words, culture happens as people normalize certain behaviors. For example, human beings within all societies mate and reproduce. While mating and reproduction are a part of the biological functions of human beings, not all societies and people groups share the same expectations. Each society has its own acceptable and unacceptable patterns of behavior regarding the process of selecting a mate, marriage, and reproduction. And those patterns develop and become formalized based on the valuing of certain ideas. They are *cultural patterns*.

In the country of Singapore, legislation discourages single women from becoming pregnant and raising children without a mate. The country's Ministry of Manpower Web site states that an eligible child qualifies Singaporean women for *government*-paid maternity leave of up to 12 weeks. However, an "eligible child" is defined as being a Singaporean citizen, legitimate, and the mother's first to fourth child. *Employers* are required to continue paying a female employee's salary during eight weeks of the maternity leave, provided that the woman has no more than two other children. Otherwise, the monetary benefit is reduced by 50 percent (Government of Singapore 2008).

On the other hand, the province of Ontario, Canada, provides parental leave of up to 37 weeks for either parent of a new baby. This provision includes biological as well as adoptive parents. In addition, mothers are entitled to take up to 17 weeks of pregnancy leave before the birth of their child (Ontario Ministry of Labour 2009).

The United States provides a third contrasting cultural perspective on parental leave. Family leave time for pregnant women and the parents of newborns is the responsibility of employers, not the federal government. And more than half of U.S. employers provide six weeks or less of maternity leave. Though a few states do provide better maternity and parental leave guidelines, federal guidelines cover only disability and discrimination of pregnant women or women on maternity leave. In 2007, the Institute for Women's Policy Research released a statement noting that there are only two provisions given to working women who are either pregnant or the parent of a newborn. The Pregnancy Discrimination Act of 1978 requires employers to treat pregnant women as they do other employees with short-term disabilities, forbidding employers from discriminating against pregnant employees or forcing them to take maternity leave. The Family and Medical Leave Act of 1993 provides job security for employees who are on leave because of a disability or illness, including pregnancy and childbirth. The United States doesn't have, however, any law mandating paid family leave—maternal or paternal, biological or adoptive—for parents of newborns. (Lovell, O'Neill, and Olsen 2007)

5. CULTURE IS *CREATIVITY*

Though culture is often rightly viewed as an external force that shapes and influences the communal dynamics of a group, people aren't passive participants in culture. On the contrary, people are the active, creative originators of culture. As Hannerz states: "People...manage meanings *from where they are* in the social structure" (1952). Only human beings are capable of developing culture because only human beings have the creative capabilities to adapt the ways they interact with their environment. This creative process of responding and adapting to the environment leads to culture building.

6. CULTURE IS ABOUT *PROBLEM SOLVING*

Culture isn't solely about the creative expression of people and groups. Likewise, culture happens when societies respond to problems, whether economic, political, or social. Culture allows for societies to exercise greater control over their environments. A relatively recent example of a society's response to a problem was the culture that grew up out of the events and crises of the Great Depression. Though it's a generalization,

THE BEATNIK GENERATION

In the post-war society of the United States (roughly 1946 to 1960), the Beat Generation came of age. Rooted in the experiences of World War II and the post-war growth of the middle class, suburbs, and the resulting prosperity and materialism, the Beat culture provided a way for young people to grapple with their feelings of alienation and disenchantment caused by the mainstream culture.

Middle-class youth who were disenchanted with the materialism and prosperity of their parents appropriated the cultural expressions of the disenfranchised poor and African-American youth. In stark contrast to their 1950's parents, these youth were easily identifiable by their fashions, language, and leisurely pursuits.

Fashion. In rejecting the well-groomed dresses and suits of the middle class, beatniks often dressed in black turtle-necks. Young men grew goatees, wore sunglasses, and grew their hair long. Young women wore their hair long and straight and favored black leotards, very much unlike their mothers' manicured style and weekly trips to the beauty parlor.

Language. As with other subcultures, language played a significant role in giving voice to the values and meaning of beatniks, further allowing them to identify themselves in contrast to mainstream American culture (Klinger-Vartabedian and Vartabedian 1992, Meisler 1959).

COMMON SLANG TERMS FROM THE BEATNIK GENERATION

Bad News	A person of bad character	"That cat is bad news."
Big Daddy	An older male	"Hey, big daddy!"
Bread	Money	"I need some bread."
Cat	A hip or younger person	"Look at that cat."
Cookin'	Doing well	"My man is cookin'."
Fast	Someone who's sexually active	"She's fast."
Heat	Police	"Look out; here comes the heat."
Pad	Home	"Jay has a new pad on 31st."
Rap	To tattle on someone	"Don't rap on that cat, man."

(Klinger-Vartabedian and Vartabedian 1992)

> ## Food for Thought
> *What are common words that youth use that are unique to the adolescent world?*

people who grew up during the 1930s have been characterized as being resourceful, creative when it comes to making do with little, consistent in saving, and able to stretch the value of a dollar. The most recent economic crisis of the first decade of the twenty-first century will certainly foster creative responses that will shape the culture of contemporary youth. Crises create a need

Leisure. As is the case with many subcultures, this culture formed out of a sense of alienation, emptiness, and abandonment by mainstream culture. (See the discussion of subcultures in chapter 4 of this book.) In the 1950s, the broader culture was experiencing an economic boom; the suburban middle-class phenomenon was in its infancy; and the pursuit of the middle-class lifestyle, including single-family homes in well-kept suburban neighborhoods and the increased emphasis on acquiring material goods as a statement of success, left many youth feeling disenchanted.

Reacting against the burgeoning materialism of the 1950s, beatniks rebelled and found comfort and meaning in societal expressions on the fringe of American culture. As a result, the world of the beatnik favored the cultural expressions of the downtrodden (for example, "beat down"), the jazz music of the African-American, and religious expressions of eastern religions (for example, Taoism).

During this time, coffeehouses sprung up in many cities throughout the United States (and eventually the rest of the Westernized world). These were gathering places for young people to find a place of belonging and engage with other beatniks in dialogue about contemporary issues and their search for spirituality and meaning.

Poetry readings and jazz sessions were commonplace here. As Klinger-Vartabedian and Vartabedian (1992) have argued, the culture of the beatniks was all about oral performance—whether poetry, prose, or jazz. So in addition to providing an environment for relationships and belonging, coffeehouses provided an arena for performers and participants to give voice to the longings of inner spirituality and to hear the voices of others.

The culture of the 1950s beatnik has influenced the lifestyle of succeeding generations of hippies, grunge rockers, and even hip-hop rappers.

Food for Thought

Many young people spend time in coffee shops today. How do modern-day coffee shop experiences relate to the 1950s coffeehouses?

---

for societal response, and as groups within a society respond to these needs, create solutions, and craft meaningful responses, values are shaped and formed.

7. CULTURE IS A GUIDANCE SYSTEM

Culture acts as a system of values, meanings, and beliefs to regulate social and, oftentimes, individual behaviors, including mating, reproduction, and control of emotions. They also establish ideals for what is "normal" within the context of society. Abnormality is defined by those persons who exhibit behaviors that are outside the normal range. For example, in the late 1960s, many young women wore granny dresses and clunky shoes, while young men wore polyester pants and wide ties. To dress in these fashions back in 1966 was considered normal. But our culture has changed in the last 40-plus years. Anyone dressing that way today would be considered weird or strange—he or she would be acting "abnormally."

A society's culture not only establishes expectations about what is normal, but also defines what is desirable. Again, what is undesirable is measured against what is valued in one's culture. In the North African countries of Tunisia, Morocco, and Algeria, obesity among women is highly valued. "Female fatness is viewed as a sign of social status and is a cultural symbol of beauty, fertility and prosperity" (Mokhtar, et al. 2001). Though the value of fatness in these cultures stands in contrast to the emphasis on extreme thinness in North American culture, there are similar processes at work. In each instance, cultural values determine what is desirable and undesirable.

As well, culture defines what and *who* is acceptable. An area of conflict within many churches centers on contrasting cultural views over what is acceptable and unacceptable behavior among youth. Particularly in those church communities in which a significant number of young people have little experience in a church setting, there are often clashes between youth workers and youth, or youth workers and other adults, over what teenage behaviors are acceptable. Though some of these expectations are rooted in biblical teaching, many flow out of cultural values and practice. For example, issues of dress, behavior during worship, language, and general behavioral protocol are frequently more about what church people feel is acceptable, rather than what is theologically appropriate.

Culture also offers a set of established, public, meaningful forms that can be used to evaluate and give worth to groups and individuals within a society. These cover all aspects, from language, law, art, morals, and beliefs, as well as science and technology. Holidays, for example, are part of a culture's meaningful forms. The specific holidays that are celebrated and the ways in which global holidays are celebrated convey what is particular and meaningful to a culture.

WHERE DOES IDEOLOGY FIT IN DEFINING CULTURE?

Merriam-Webster describes *ideology* as a "systematic body of concepts, especially about human life or culture" (Merriam-Webster 2009). These ideas provide a rationale for a society's political, social, economic, and, often, religious systems. Culture, then, is the vehicle through which a society communicates and transmits its values—including its ideological commitments.

Coined in the late eighteenth century, *ideology* mainly referred to the science of ideas. Writing in the mid-nineteenth century, Karl Marx and Friedrich Engels defined ideology in two ways. In a neutral sense, *ideology* is "any abstract or symbolic meaning system used to explain (or justify) social, economic, or political realities." Their second definition was more negative and was described as "a web of ideas that are distorted, contrary to reality, and subject to 'false consciousness'" (Jost 2006).

Even in these two definitions, however, we can see a broad understanding of ideology. Ideology refers to those aspects of a culture that involve the big ideas that provide a web—a system of meaning. In any society one can study social, economic, political, and religious arenas and begin to piece together the system of ideas that form the foundation for how people function in those arenas. So, for example, in the United States our system of government is built on a particular understanding of democracy. One *idea* is that democracy means "government is by the people and for the people." This *ideology*, and the way people interact with and act on it, permeates and helps to establish the parameters within which people function.

Building on Marx and Engels' negative understanding of ideology, some argue that ideology presupposes a class society—that the nature of any ideological system is that the system works to maintain structures and institutions, privileging some groups and disenfranchising others.

Food for Thought

Can you identify some norms (acceptable, normal, desirable behavioral expectations) in youth groups? How are these norms influenced by the broader youth culture?

This chapter has highlighted the qualities or characteristics of culture. As you engage in the arenas of youth culture, you can now begin to identify these qualities and how youth culture functions to provide a system that gives meaning, provides guidance, and serves to instruct adolescents about what society values as meaningful. From this broad foundation of cultural qualities, we can now begin to construct a framework for identifying the concrete elements of culture.

REFLECTION ACTIVITY (5 TO 10 MINUTES)

Consider the three countries' parental/maternity leave policies that were discussed earlier in this chapter (Singapore; Ontario, Canada; and the United States). Identify any cultural values that may be shaped and formed by these different policies. What are some possible cultural values about families, fathers, mothers, or children? What might be the governmental, political, or economic values of these countries?

DIGGING DEEPER (10 TO 15 MINUTES)

Review the key characteristics of culture. Apply your understanding of one or more characteristics to a particular issue in youth ministry and identify ways you might address this issue. For example, developing specific *practices* (or patterns of behavior) to *create* an atmosphere that fosters an acceptance of diverse groups of students. (This example draws on the third and fifth characteristics.)

- Every society develops cultural patterns that reinforce assumptions about what is normal or abnormal, desirable or undesirable, and acceptable or unacceptable.

- Culture is about the human potential for ideas and about how people assign meaning.

- Culture is about socially consistent patterns of behavior.

- Culture is a historical phenomenon.

- Culture is about finding solutions to problems and is a bounded system of expectations.

CHAPTER 3
Expressing Culture: Signs, Symbols, Rituals, and Language

LEARNING OBJECTIVES

When you've finished this chapter, you should be able to:

1. Demonstrate an understanding of how signs express cultural meaning

2. Articulate the nature and significance of rituals

3. Discuss how language functions as a cultural sign

Now we turn to the elements of culture—the pieces that work together to express culture in a society. Again, we look to other fields of study to help us understand the terms and concepts. Though there is some ambiguity regarding the terms, the discussions within the fields of anthropology and linguistics will serve as helpful guides.

Our goal is not to engage in the debates of other disciplines but to use their discussion to develop a framework to better understand how culture shapes and informs adolescents. To that end, this chapter highlights key points defining the basic elements of culture. The first section examines the broader category of signs. The subsequent sections discuss the dominant ways that signs are expressed in a culture, namely through symbols, rituals, and language.

SIGNS

At its most basic level, a *sign* is anything that represents something else. That is, a sign stands as a marker, pointing toward something else. It doesn't represent itself. In this capacity of representation, cultural signs serve a variety of functions.

First, signs are vehicles of meaning. It is through the use of signs that a society constructs meaning and communicates its values, beliefs, and convictions to its members. Signs provide a means for the "concrete embodiments of ideas, attitudes, judgments, longings, or beliefs" (Geertz 1973). As an example, the image on the next page reflects a sign that's used in our society as part of our system of traffic laws. The *denotation* of this sign is its physical characteristics. That is, this traffic sign can be described by its literal characteristics: The shape (octagonal), the color (red), and the word written on it in all-capital white letters (STOP).

A "stop" sign isn't significant on its own, however. A stop sign is useful only because it points to something else—the *idea* that you should stop at an intersection where a stop sign appears. Beyond the literal meaning denoted in its physical characteristics, there is the attributed meaning. When a driver approaches an intersection and sees a stop sign, he or she knows to stop because society has attributed that meaning to the physical sign. The *connotation* of the stop sign is the idea that you should stop when you see one (Berger 1995). Any sign—whether made up of words, physical objects, or sounds—expresses these two kinds of meanings.

A second function of signs is that they carry within them a multiplicity of meanings. They evoke emotions and sentiment. They compel people to take action. In other words, signs reflect the meaning(s) that society attaches to them. It is in the act of naming or pointing to by human actors (individual or group) that meaning, value, or worth is attributed. The same stop sign that represents the idea that one should stop at an intersection also carries with it meanings about being a responsible citizen, and the value of traffic laws and systems of government, among other things.

Another example of a sign is a cross. The cross evokes a variety of emotions and meanings. It represents much more than a physical cross. For some, it may point to the event of Christ's death; for others, it may point to the event of Christ's resurrection; and for still others, it may point to Christ's victory over sin. The point is that the image of the cross serves as a *sign* of something beyond the cross itself.

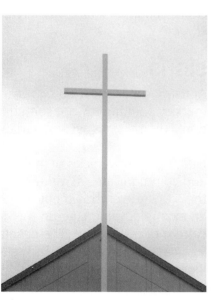

Ferdinand de Saussure, a linguist writing in the late nineteenth and early twentieth centuries, noted there were two aspects of signs. He labeled them *the signifier* and *the signified*. A signifier can be any material thing: A sound, an object, an image, an act, or some combination of all four. The signifier is the means by which a concept is represented. The represented concept is what is *signified* (Berger 1995). In the images of the cross (page 37), the cross is the signifier, and the meanings we highlighted are the concepts that are signified by the drawing.

As I write this, I hear the whistle of an approaching train. The sound signifies to me that a train is approaching the crossing

THE IMAGE OF THE CROSS

Christians all over the world use the symbol of the cross to point toward a deeper meaning of their faith. But not all Christian groups use the same symbol, nor do the symbols all point to the same meaning. The Catholic Church uses both the symbol of the cross and the crucifix. As for many Christians, the cross serves as a reminder of Christ's death and resurrection. The crucifix, a cross with Christ's body, is a symbol of Jesus' human death and suffering for humanity.

Historically, cross-like symbols have represented many meanings for different groups. A sample of the symbols and meanings follow:

Tau Cross. This version of a cross symbol was once an iconic representation for a druidic tree god. "Oak logs were stripped of their branches and fastened together to make a wooden idol that the druids called Thau" (Walker 1988). In Jewish tradition, this symbol represented the image the Israelites made on their doorposts at the first Passover in Egypt.

Coptic Cross. The original form of the coptic cross was a sun symbol representing the sun in the center of heaven surrounded and supported by four pillars that upheld the sky in each of the four directions. Coptic Christians added the four nails to symbolize the sacrifice of Christ and to "suggest that the blood drawn from his wounds by the nails had spread, symbolically, to the four corners of the world" (Walker 1988).

Cross Fourchée. Popular in medieval heraldry, this cross combined Christian meaning with pagan magic. The flaring points may have represented flames. "It was usually supposed that the torches at the tips of the cross would be extinguished with blood" (Walker 1988).

Greek Cross. Until the eighth or ninth century, this symbol was the usual Christian symbol. It is still commonly used in liturgical texts. Before being appropriated as a Christian symbol, the Greek cross "was an emblem of Hecate as the Goddess of Crossroads" (Walker 1988). It also represented the union of male and female.

Latin Cross. Authorized in the ninth century as the symbol representing Christ's sacrificial death.

down the street from my house. This example is also a reminder of the role of participants in the making of cultural signs. The sound of a whistle blowing indicates an approaching train because society has invested that sound with such meaning. The upcoming chart depicts the connections between signifier and signified.

Aspects of Cultural Signs

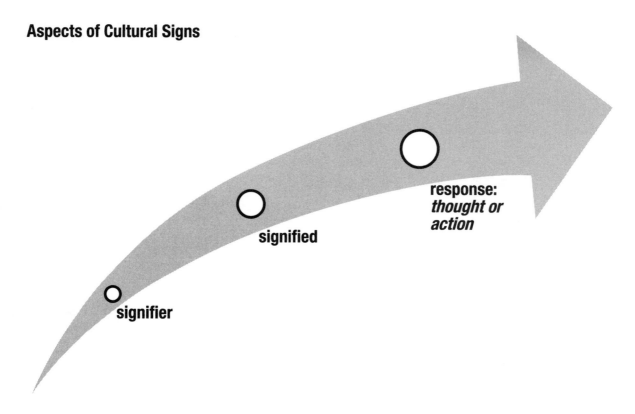

The signifier is a material object—a sound, an image, an object, or an act. The significance of the signifier is only in its pointing toward the signified.

The signified is an abstract concept; an expression of meaning that compels a receiver of a sign to some kind of thought or action.

Signs also function as part of the organic process of cultural meaning. As detailed earlier, culture isn't static. There is an ebb and flow to cultural processes. As Clifford Geertz contends, the general conceptions of value are formulated through cultural signs. There is, however, fluidity to the process (1973). As individuals and groups within a culture engage the cultural system of meanings by interpreting cultural signs and acting upon them, the general concepts are refined, renewed, and reconstructed (Spradley and McCurdy 2006).

C. S. Peirce, an anthropologist writing about the same time as Saussure, identified three modes of signs. In using modes, Peirce was attempting to explain the interlocking processes by which signs function in society to communicate meaning. He refrained from calling them "types" because he felt there were no pure types—that a sign was always a combination of at least two of these modes. It's helpful to examine each of the three modes to increase our understanding of signs and their influence in shaping one's cultural experience (Spradley and McCurdy 2006).

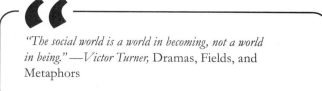

Imaging Signs

Peirce called this mode *icon* or *iconic* (Spradley and McCurdy 2006). In an effort to be more precise and avoid confusion with religious icons—which can actually be more symbolic than iconic—we will avoid his phrasing. The term *imaging* seems more appropriate because imaging represents how these kinds of signs function. Imaging signs resemble what they represent. They may be pictures, drawings, cartoons, scale models, or even replicated sounds.

Imaging Signs	Signifier	Signified
ID photo (passport, driver's license)	Photo	The real person
Architectural plans	Drawings	The building
Aerial maps	Map	Actual physical location
Mockingbird	Sounds	Specific people or things
Impersonators	Individual	Another person

Indicative Signs

Peirce labeled these signs *indexical signs* (Spradley and McCurdy 2006). Again, in an effort to clarify meaning, this category is referred to as *indicative.* With indicative signs, the signifier indicates the signified because there is a logical or causal connection between the signifier and the signified. The list on the next page offers a small sample of common indicative signs in our culture.

Indicative Signs	Signifier	Signified
Footprints on the beach	Impression in the sand	A human being
Animal footprints	Impression in snow or ground	An animal
Smoke from chimney	Smoke rising from chimney	Fire in fireplace
Food smells	Particular smells	Food to eat

SYMBOLS

The third mode of sign that Pierce identified is *symbolic*. Unlike imaging and indicative signs, there's no inherent or causal link between the signifier and the signified. Symbols can be understood as "anything that is disengaged from its mere actuality and used to impose meaning upon experience" (Spradley and McCurdy 2006). When a society adopts something material as a symbol, that something takes on new and different meanings.

In American culture, the bald eagle carries a connotation far removed from the literal reality of an eagle in its native environment. The bald eagle stands as a symbol for the American experience. Beliefs about freedom, power, and America's place in the world have been imposed on the image of an eagle. As Wuthnow states: "A symbol provides a bridge between raw experience and some sense of a larger reality" (1987). The raw experience in the symbol of the eagle is not the eagle in the wild, but the raw experience of groups and individuals in American society.

The symbol of the eagle and its imposed meanings connect groups and individuals to the larger ethos of American values and heritage. The symbols of a culture have power to influence and shape both the thinking and the identity of a people, partly because they connect individuals and smaller groups to the larger society.

As we continue to think about youth culture and its influence on adolescents, it is important to examine both the characteristics and influence of symbols. We will come back to this discussion as we begin to evaluate the symbols of youth culture. To that end, there are three key characteristics of cultural symbols.

Symbols	Signifier	Signified
Bald Eagle	Actual eagle or image of one	American freedom, power, etc.
Liberty Bell	The real bell in Philadelphia	Freedom, liberty, democracy
Traffic Light	Red, yellow, and green lamps	Traffic laws and responses
Road Map	Physical or Internet map	Lines represent streets, roads, and highways

Characteristics of Symbols

Symbols and their meanings must be learned. As already noted, with imaging and indicative signs, there is a natural connection. However, society constructs symbolic signs and imposes their meanings. In that regard, then, symbolic signs and their underlying meanings must be learned. In the introduction the text highlighted the importance of cultural inheritance—which includes language, values, and traditions—for shaping a person's identity. The symbols of a culture are a key way that one's cultural heritage is transmitted and received. People are born into a system laden with symbolic meaning. From the early stages of life, people learn from their social experiences the symbols of their culture, as well as the meanings attached to them. This process of learning helps people find their bearings and construct a reality (Geertz 1973).

Blueprints for behavior. Likewise, symbols provide a blueprint—a template for shaping public behavior. A blueprint guides and provides detailed instructions that, when followed, will lead to the completion of a specific structure, whether it's a bridge, a skyscraper, or a Quonset hut. Cultural symbols serve to give a people group an identity and to define what they value. Symbols delineate the boundaries of meaning for a culture.

I volunteer weekly in my granddaughter's fifth grade class. Typically, I arrive just in time to recite

THE SYMBOL OF THE BALD EAGLE

The largest bird of prey on the North American continent, the bald eagle is both a raptor (spends most of its time hunting) and a scavenger (often steals the prey killed by others). For early Americans, the eagle was believed to be an emblem of freedom, power, courage, and strength.

The bald eagle was adopted as the national symbol of the United States in 1782, when the country was still in its infancy. The design here is based on the preliminary sketch by artist Charles Thomson for the official seal of the United States. The olive branch in the right talon symbolizes peace and liberty; the 13 arrows held by the left talon signify the power of war. The ribbon held by the eagle's beak states *e pluribus unum,* which is translated, "out of many, one."

As a symbol of these ideas, the bald eagle appears on the reverse side of many coins and can be found on all sorts of cultural artifacts. The ideals expressed in the symbol of the American eagle serve to shape the notion of what it means to be an American and compels Americans to act in response to those ideals, whether positively or negatively (MacArthur 2008).

the Pledge of Allegiance. The Pledge acknowledges in its very first line that it's a sign—an oral reminder that the words being repeated are pointing to some dominant value or values of American life. It further acknowledges that the flag these fifth graders look to while saying the Pledge is a symbol—a reminder of American values. One may debate whether the values espoused in the Pledge of Allegiance ring true for all Americans, but it does define the values of liberty and justice as key components of American ideals.

Pledge of Allegiance

I pledge allegiance to the flag of the United States of America and to the republic for which it stands: One nation under God, indivisible, with liberty and justice for all.

"DO THIS IN REMEMBRANCE OF ME"

As with blueprints, symbols also invite response and produce action. Luke (in Luke 22:7-20) and Paul (in 1 Corinthians 11:23-34) give Christ's followers an account of Jesus' words to his disciples during their last Passover meal together. In both passages, the writers share Jesus' encouragement for his followers to reenact the Passover meal. And whenever they do it, Jesus says, "Do this in remembrance of me." (See Luke 22:19 and 1 Corinthians 11:24-25.)

The disciples would have been able to do what Jesus suggested as a literal remembrance because they physically shared that first memorial meal together. For all other followers, Jesus is establishing a symbolic blueprint—a guide for us to follow. To remember is to recollect, to recall something one has experienced. But you cannot remember something you never experienced. What Jesus is calling us to is a remembrance of meaning—the words Jesus spoke and the experience that's recorded for his disciples and future followers.

Jesus issues the invitation for us to respond by engaging in the physical act of sharing bread and wine together, but there is also an underlying call to respond to what the meal and Jesus' words represent. Jesus established the symbolic sign of communion to point toward who he was and the actions he was taking. The word translated here for "remembrance," *anamnesis*, is used only four times in the New Testament, once in Luke 22, twice in 1 Corinthians 11, and once in Hebrews 10:3 (NAS New Testament Greek Lexicon 2009). In all four instances, the word is connected to the concept of paying for sin and the one who is a sacrifice for sin. Though Jesus had not yet suffered his sacrificial death, the words he uses and the symbols he constructs point toward his ultimate death and sacrifice for our sin. Each time his followers recite these words and observe the Lord's Supper via communion, we remind each other of the depth of his sacrifice and his love for humanity.

System of meaning management. When taken together, the dominant values of a group of people function to create and sustain a system of values and norms. In a society there are myriad symbols from individuals and local communities, to larger towns, as well as national symbols. Dominant cultural symbols are those that establish and define the principles by which a society operates and serve to structure social organization, thereby conferring order and stability. These dominant symbols reflect the core values inherent in a society's systems—whether judicial, legislative, political, economic, or social. Creating an interlocking, overlapping system of meaning, dominant symbols function as a web to support social organization and delineate the boundaries within which a society functions.

RITUALS

Depending on your experience, one of two images probably comes to mind when you hear the word *ritual*. Strongly steeped in the traditions of liturgical faith, you may call to mind images of sacred religious practices. If you've read or studied the early histories of people groups (or read *National Geographic*), you may recall images of native rites of passage. Both are examples of rituals, but neither is all-encompassing to a full understanding of what ritual is.

Robert Wuthnow gives a clear, broad definition: "A symbolic-expressive aspect of behavior that communicates something about social relations, often in a relatively dramatic or formal manner" (1987). As we seek to understand Wuthnow's definition, we will explore the nature and characteristics of rituals.

Nature of Rituals

Inextricably intertwined with symbols. Wuthnow's definition immediately highlights a key aspect of the nature of rituals: They're intertwined

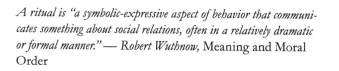

A ritual is *"a symbolic-expressive aspect of behavior that communicates something about social relations, often in a relatively dramatic or formal manner."* — Robert Wuthnow, Meaning and Moral Order

with symbols. The emphasis in Wuthnow's definition and what distinguishes ritual from symbol is behavior—the expressive aspect of ritual. Symbols invite a response and produce action. As Catherine Bell explains, "Ritual is to symbols as action is to thought" (1997). The diagram depicting the dynamic between signifier and signified (page 38) indicates that all cultural signs compel action on the part of a culture's participants. Behavior that is ritualistic, though, is not simply ordinary behavior. A ritual response to a symbol is an expressive behavior.

Rooted in behavior that is extraordinary. Rituals dramatize, enact, materialize, or perform a system of symbols. As Wuthnow (1987) notes, rituals aren't merely instrumental; they're expressive. They're not just functional; they, in some way, rise above the level of ordinary. Ritualistic experiences are those experiences and behaviors that people set apart as special. Consciously or unconsciously these experiences are given greater preference and status over the ordinary. And through these *consecrated* behaviors, people reinvigorate values and norms.

Furthermore, rituals are behaviors performed in a *ceremonial* fashion. That is, within the drama of rituals there is a given set of actions, a formality in the sense of an agreed-upon code of behaviors that may be socially constructed or, in some cases, individually defined. This code of behaviors may be a formal system (for example, communion) or a loosely held system (such as an athlete eating a specific meal before every game).

Rooted in public images and social identity. Rituals, as symbolic performances, are by nature about social interaction. Even as rituals may be individually performed, an aspect of their performance is that they serve to connect individuals to the larger social arena of meaning. Rituals provide a way for individuals to identify socially within a larger society.

Rooted in the history of a people. Though rituals may change over time, they are built and sustained out of the historical experiences of a people. So, for example, some rituals may be common to many cultures (religious holidays, for example), but they're enacted and experienced differently because of the history and traditions of each society.

AMERICAN THANKSGIVING: MYTHS AND REALITIES

Every year in scores of schools across the United States, students and teachers gather to reenact the first American Thanksgiving. School children dressed as Pilgrims and Indians sit down to enjoy a meal together. Additionally, most of us gather with friends and family to celebrate our own Thanksgiving meal as a ritual celebration of the values this holiday has come to hold for our culture.

As with any public ritual celebration, the truths communicated may be more ideals than facts. Further, as people participate in public ritual celebrations, the truths conveyed get reinterpreted, re-envisioned, and restructured, such that what is now experienced as "truth" may be far removed from the historical events from which the ritual performance first arose.

In exploring this aspect of ritual celebrations, this sidebar examines a few of the historical events of the "first" Thanksgiving and compares them with the myths that are often communicated in our present-day representations.

The first Thanksgiving was celebrated at Plymouth, Massachusetts, in 1621. Tradition holds that the first American settlers arrived on the shores of Plymouth Bay (modern-day Plymouth, Massachusetts) in 1620. The Native Americans welcomed the English settlers, teaching them how to hunt, fish, and survive in this new land. In return for their hospitality, the English settlers held a three-day feast in 1621, celebrating their first harvest and inviting the Indians to share in their first fruits.

Historians researching the history of eastern Native Americans and the arrival of Europeans to the Americas present a much different story. First, the lands of North America had significant populations of Indians; estimates range from a very low one million to tens of millions of people who already occupied these lands prior to the arrival of Europeans. Thus, the arrival of three ships to Plymouth Bay did not bring "settlers"—the land was already settled—but immigrants.

Second, this wasn't the first group of Europeans to arrive in North America. The Spanish arrived in St. Augustine, Florida, in the early 1500s. Others arrived from Great Britain before those Pilgrims landed at Plymouth Rock, too, settling in places such as Jamestown, Virginia. Additionally, the Spanish arrived in many parts of the West and Southwest years before those who came in 1620.

Third, celebrating a thanksgiving feast was not a new phenomenon. Eastern American Indians celebrated feasts of thanksgiving at various times throughout the year. As well, the British brought with them a tradition of celebrating feast days in recognition of God's pleasure. These feast days weren't held on specific dates but at any time throughout the year. As for this being the first Thanksgiving in America (setting aside the American Indian thanksgiving celebrations), some historians argue that earlier celebrations were probable. Historian Michael Gannon contends that the first American Thanksgiving happened on September 8, 1565, when Spanish explorer Pedro Menéndez de Avilés landed in St. Augustine, Florida, and celebrated a Catholic mass followed by a thanksgiving meal (Davis 2008). It would be more than 150 years after the gathering in Plymouth Bay before the first national thanksgiving celebration would be held to celebrate the American victory over the British in 1777.

Indigenous people helped the Pilgrims by providing food and teaching them how to fish and hunt. While there may be some truth to the idea that Indians helped the British survive in the new land by teaching them to hunt and cook the game native to New England, the myth presents a rosier picture than history indicates. Journals of those first Europeans to arrive at Plymouth share how these settlers robbed Indian graves and communities of food and other supplies and then justified their actions by assuming God had provided these provisions (Loewen 1996).

The Pilgrims prepared a thanksgiving meal and invited the Indians to join them. Most likely, the three-day feast in 1621 was not a thanksgiving meal but the negotiation of a political treaty between the Europeans and the Indians. Further, the food would have, again, most likely been provided by the Indians. As a side note of interest, the food would not have been like what we eat at our own Thanksgiving feasts. We know from journal accounts that the Indians provided venison. If they did share a meal that included fowl, it was most likely goose rather than turkey. And had they eaten turkey, it would have been wild turkey—far different from the giant domesticated birds we eat today. The meat would have been accompanied by dried corn porridge and stewed pumpkin. The heavy, sugar-laden fare we eat today would not have been part of their meal, since they didn't have sugar. So pumpkin pie, cranberry sauce, or any of the other desserts we typically eat were not a part of this meal.

The Pilgrims and Indians became friends. Within a generation, the Anglo-European population had increased significantly, while the native population, as a result of diseases brought over by the Europeans to the Americas, was almost completely wiped out. The remaining native populations were forced from their lands, massacred, sold into slavery, or driven to flee to Canada. For many Native Americans today, the Thanksgiving holiday is not a time of celebration but a reminder of the tragedies their people suffered at the hands of these early European settlers.

Thanksgiving wasn't declared an official American holiday until 1863, when Abraham Lincoln set aside the last Thursday in November as the official date of Thanksgiving. Then in 1941, President Franklin D. Roosevelt moved the date to the fourth Thursday of November.

As with all public ritual celebrations, Thanksgiving has evolved and now serves to uphold a set of values. Thanksgiving has become a celebration of American virtue and determination—the strength to endure during difficult times and to ultimately succeed. Further, Thanksgiving celebrations also carry with them a religious element, in that this public ritual avers God's blessings and provision (Linton and Linton 1949, Loewen 1996).

Food for Thought

How have you experienced ways that cultural values shape religious symbols?

Briefly, this next section describes the three key characteristics of rituals.

Story

Examined closely, rituals can be seen as the expressive performance of a story. Ritual is a reenactment of an event or events. The story may be told in part. It may not even be true, or fully true, but it's the retelling of events as an individual or group holds them to be.

Meaning—Messages—Intentions

In the telling of a story, rituals often articulate meaning through the incorporation of symbolic elements. The expressive behavior of rituals fosters a sense of meaning and purpose for participants as they also communicate messages of meaning to other participants. That is, there are both participants and an audience in ritual activity. (These two aspects of ritual activity are present even in an individual ritual. In such cases, the individual serves as both participant and audience.) The messages of rituals also serve as a means of declaring intentions about one's participation in the larger social identity espoused in the ritual story.

Set of Symbolic Acts

Already described in the above discussion about extraordinary behavior, this characteristic will only be briefly mentioned here. Social rituals can be identified by their formalized behavior, incorporating a set of symbolic behaviors.

LANGUAGE

Ferdinand de Saussure and others considered language to be a component of cultural signs. Building on the work of a number of theorists, this section will set forth ways in which language functions as a cultural sign. Before we delve into the topic, though, it's helpful to articulate a basic definition of what language is. Saussure separated language into two aspects. The first, *langue*, is the "system of rules and conventions which is independent of, and pre-exists, individual users" (Chandler 2003). *Parole* refers to the use of language—the system—in particular instances, oral or written (Chandler 2003).

Language as Signifier

First, language functions as a cultural sign because the vocal sounds of language, the physically written and spoken words, are signifiers pointing to concepts and meanings. The written and oral communication of language has meaning only if recipients have learned what particular sounds and words mean. Anyone who's tried to learn a second language knows that meaning must be learned along with the different sounds and words.

Language as Symbol

Second, the myriad meanings of any language system are symbolic because these meanings are socially constructed. Further, individuals and groups within a culture redefine, reformulate, and renew the meanings of words.

CHANGING SLANG OF YOUTH LANGUAGE

Today's teens aren't the first ones to have their own language. Every generation has a set of informal expressions, coined words and phrases, and standard vocabulary terms they use in new ways—in other words, *slang*. Other groups with common experiences and interests—for example, people who work in the same profession or share a hobby—often share a common language as well. But in every generation, some of the most vigorous slang terms seem to come from the language of teens.

As you read through the following lists of examples, you'll notice how quickly teenage slang changes when you see how many terms now seem out of date.

Teen Slang 1[2]

E-tact, n. Tact or appropriate expression used in electronic communications such as emails, IMs, texts, or blogging. *"He broke up with me by text. He has, like, no e-tact."*

Frontin', v. To be fake or put on a false exterior or façade, usually to impress someone or seem better than what you actually are. *"She is frontin'. Those heels are borrowed."*

Grill, n. Teeth or smile; n. Personal business or activities. *"Hey, why don't you stay out of my grill?"*

Hulk Out, v. To become really angry, perhaps violent (like The Hulk). *"When Dad finds out I failed my history test, he is so going to hulk out."*

Spim, n. An online ad solicitation sent on an instant-messaging program. *"Oh, sorry. I had to quit—too many spims at once slowed down my Internet."*

Trick Out, v. To adorn with accessories or make better. *"Mom, I really want to trick out my backpack. So can we go the store to buy some buttons?"*

2 Adapted from a list prepared by Vanessa Van Petten, "Teen Slang: Decoding What Your Kids Are Saying," http://www.radicalparenting.com/2008/01/09/teen-slang-decoding-what-your-kids-are-saying/.

Teen Slang 2[3]

Aight or *Ahigh* (one syllable), adv./adj. All right or okay. *"Aight, I'll go with you."*

Bam, int. Used when you have just dissed someone. *"Bam! Gotcha!"*

Bling, n. Anything shiny, specifically jewelry. *"How do you like my bling?"*

Booty, n. One's posterior. *"Watch her shake her booty."*

Booyah or *booya*, int. Used to express happiness or accomplishment. *"Booyah!"*

Buff, adj. To describe an attractive member of the opposite sex. *"Jess is so buff."*

Chill, v. To calm down, to be cool. *"Just chill, why dontcha?!"*

Cuz, n. Friend. *"That's Toby; he's my cuz."*

Diss, v. To treat somebody without respect. *"Hey, don't diss me like that."*

Holla, v. To talk. *"I'll holla at ya later."*

Hook up, v. To get something or to get with someone. *"Did ya hear that Kyle and Shelly hooked up?"*

Kev'd up, v. To enhance with extras. *"That motorcycle is kev'd up."*

Kickin', v. To hang out. *"No, we're not doing anything; we're just kickin'."*

My bad, n. A mistake. *"Oh, my bad. I didn't mean to do that."*

Peeps, n. Friends or people you hang out with. *"Staci is one of my peeps."*

Poppin', v. A happening. *"What's poppin'?"*

Smooth, adj. Cool. *"That guy is so smooth."*

Sup, int. To say hello. *"Sup?"*

Trippin', v. To imagine things; to do drugs, to jump to conclusions. *"That girl was trippin'."*

Wazzup, int. To say hello. *"Wazzup?"*

Whacked, adj. Crazy or weird. *"That dude is whacked."*

---

3 Adapted from a list prepared by Emma S., "How to Speak and Understand Teen Lingo." http://www.associatedcontent.com/article/11050/how_to_speak_and_understand_teen_lingo.html?page=3&cat=25.

Language Shapes Cultural Experience

Daniel Chandler (2003) contends that language is the most important of all the systems of signs and is the primary vehicle for shaping cultural experience. A given language system defines the boundaries within which a people may communicate and construct meaning. In the field of anthropology, the Sapir-Whorf hypothesis sets forth a basic definition of language. That is, "language...constitutes the means with which individuals think, and therefore...language conditions or determines cultural thought, perception and worldview" (Baugh and Sherzer 1984). Language is the most significant sign system in a culture because the "existence, maintenance and use" of all other elements of culture "are contingent upon language" (Rappaport 1999).

Language Is Shaped by Society

Discourse, the discussion and dialogue between individuals and groups, enables people to re-create, modify, and adapt language such that words change but, more importantly, meanings are modified and adapted.

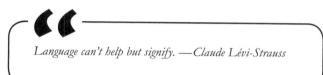

Language can't help but signify. —Claude Lévi-Strauss

USAGE'S INFLUENCE ON WORDS IN LANGUAGE

Anatoly Liberman, professor of language at the University of Minnesota, researches the origins and meanings of words. In a radio broadcast in 2007, Liberman noted that the meanings of words change over time. His discussion highlighted the interrelated process by which meanings are developed and maintained.

First, people must learn what words mean. As noted elsewhere in this text, the meanings of symbols—in this case, words—are socially constructed and must be learned. Words have the ability to shape and influence a culture's (or person's) thoughts and ideas only inasmuch as they're understood. So children learn from their social world—family and other social environments—what words mean.

Additionally, learners of a new language must also go through a process of connecting meanings to words. The meanings of words, though, are seldom static. Meanings may change slowly; but like culture in general, word meanings can be shaped and sometimes drastically altered.

As examples, Liberman cited the history of two words in the English language. A common adjective, *nice*, has changed significantly in the last 600 years. From the Latin *nescius*, meaning "ignorant," *nice* came into the English language from Old French during the fourteenth century. It initially meant "foolish or stupid." By the 1500s, the meaning of the word had shifted to mean "precise and careful," as in, "That is a *nice* distinction." Over the next 300 to 400 years, the meaning of the word migrated such that it began to take on a more positive meaning. Currently, the word typically means something that is pleasant or agreeable, but it's generally an adjective used where there is little depth of positive or negative meaning attributed. For example, "Oh, that's nice," or, "That's a nice dress you're wearing," meaning that it's fine, but it's not really good, not really bad.

Etymonline.com, quoting H. W. Fowler, states that, "By 1926, [*nice*] was too great a favorite with the ladies, who have charmed out of it all its individuality and converted it into a mere diffuser of vague and mild agreeableness" (Harper 2001).

The second word Liberman highlighted was the word *fond*. Of unknown origin, the word was first used in the fourteenth century and meant "foolish or silly." In Shakespeare's *King Lear* when the King speaks of being a "fond old man," he probably wasn't talking about being affectionate. Most likely he meant that he saw himself as a silly old man. Next, the word shifted to mean "being foolishly tender," and then it evolved once more to its more current meaning of "feeling love, affection, or preference for something or someone" (Liberman 2007).

I am a very foolish fond old man,
Fourscore and upward, not an hour more or less,
And to deal plainly,
I fear I am not in my perfect mind.

—*King Lear, Act 4, Scene 7 of* King Lear *by William Shakespeare*

In this section we've seen how symbols—including signs, rituals, and language—help to shape the ideas and beliefs of a society. Further, we've also identified ways that people, through their creative interaction, serve to refine, shape, and transform cultural beliefs and values.

REFLECTION ACTIVITY (5 TO 10 MINUTES)

Reflect on the *symbolic* in youth culture. What are two or three significant symbols and what are the accompanying concepts or meanings associated with each? One example is fashion. Young people often wear particular clothing styles or labels because they're associated with *coolness*, and coolness is an important value for many teens. Can you think of other symbols?

DIGGING DEEPER (10 TO 15 MINUTES)

Rituals instruct teens about what is meaningful and important. Take a few minutes to examine your youth ministry. Can you identify one or two rituals that are present? As you think about these rituals, answer these questions about each of them:

- What are the symbolic elements?

- How are the behaviors associated with this ritual *extraordinary*?

- How does this ritual help create a public and social identity for youth?

- How does this ritual derive from the history of your community and your particular youth group?

Take a few more minutes to consider an everyday, ordinary behavior in your youth ministry. Think about how it could be raised to the level of ritual behavior with a few simple changes.

- Signs, especially symbols, function within a culture to guide and communicate meaning.

- A ritual is a set of symbolic acts that helps a culture tell its story.

- Language shapes culture even as a people within a culture use and shape language to make and communicate meaning.

CHAPTER 4
Youth Culture: Is It Subculture?

LEARNING OBJECTIVES

When you've finished this chapter, you should be able to:

1. Demonstrate an understanding of subcultures and subcultural theory

2. Identify and discuss weaknesses in subcultural studies

3. Articulate principles for the study of youth cultures

To date, our focus has been on the broad concept of culture and cultural influences. In this chapter we'll shift our focus to youth culture. The broad concepts developed thus far certainly apply as we consider the specific aspects of the culture of young people. It's important, though, to consider how youth culture fits within the context of a larger society's culture. To accomplish this, chapter 4 will examine the history of the study of youth culture and conclude with the development of principles of youth culture. These principles will serve as the framework for the discussions in the next three chapters as we examine how youth workers may adequately and appropriately analyze youth as culture makers and culture consumers.

SUBCULTURAL THEORY

In the early to mid-twentieth century, social scientists formulated the concept of subculture, which gave rise to a wealth of research and study. Two primary schools of study developed—the American tradition greatly influenced by the University of Chicago and the British tradition out of Birmingham, England. There were common themes in both traditions, as well as a number of significant differences. In general, both schools of thought argued that subcultures formed within the context of a larger culture when individuals or groups encountered problems of status. That is, subcultures form when groups have difficulties achieving status within the normal, legitimate avenues of a dominant culture. Groups that are marginalized in a society (for example, working class, poor, minority populations, women, and so on) find solutions to the problems of their marginalization, resulting in cultural practices that "are distinct from the larger culture but borrow (and often distort, exaggerate, or invert) its symbols, values, and beliefs" (Scott and Marshall 2007). Interestingly, the study of subcultures was rooted in the work of social scientists on both sides of the Atlantic who studied the lives of adolescents on the fringe of cultures.

For this burgeoning school of thought, subcultures formed as a collective action as a response in resisting the authority of the dominant culture (Blackman 2005). So particularly in light of initial subcultural theory, these groups were considered deviant because they resisted conforming to the expected social and cultural standards of a society (in other words, they deviated from the norm).

> *Widely and broadly used, the core idea of subcultural theory is of the formation of subcultures as a collective solution to, or resolution of, problems arising from the blocked aspirations of members, or their ambiguous position in the wider society.*
>
> —*John Scott and Gordon Marshall,* A Dictionary of Sociology

In the years since, several critiques of subcultural theory have been put forth.

Dominant Culture as Homogenous

An initial failing of subcultural theory was that in its emphasis on the deviance of some groups, the diversity and plurality of dominant cultures was overlooked. This failing has grown only more pronounced in contemporary modern and postmodern cultures as the plurality and fragmentation within particular Western societies erodes the significance of deviance from a dominant culture as a defining element of a subculture.

Youth Cultural Practice Only in Response to Dominant Culture

The study of youth culture within the context of subculture confines all youth cultural practice to only those forms of cultural engagement that are a reaction against the dominant culture. In that regard, subcultural theory fails to adequately explain the cultural practices of youth in the wide arena within which youth function.

Much can be drawn from the field of subcultural studies. First, youth are a segment of society that develops its own aspects of culture. Second, there are issues of power and class that often serve to marginalize certain groups within a dominant culture. As we seek to understand youth and youth cultural influences, we need to keep in mind those powers of influence that contribute to the dynamics within which youth exist. In this text, however, we argue for a broader understanding of youth culture than the current field of subcultural studies affords.

Mary Bucholtz, in her study of the anthropology of youth, offers four principles that move us beyond the limited field of subcultural studies. First, Bucholtz contends that the lived experience of youth "involves its own distinctive identities and practices, which are neither rehearsals for the adult 'real thing' nor even necessarily oriented to adults at all" (2002). That is, the cultures of youth involve practices and identities that belong to the experience of young people and aren't solely about transitioning to adulthood.

Second, youth are agentive—meaning they're active agents in the process of culture-making through their various social and cultural practices. Youth are "cultural actors whose experiences are best understood from their own point of view" (Bucholtz 2002).

HIP-HOP: THE VOICE OF GLOBAL YOUTH CULTURE
Calenthia Dowdy[4]

Although rap music and hip-hop culture were birthed in the 1970s in Bronx, New York, its cultural style and form spread quickly from the East Coast of the United States, around the country, and then circled the globe. Though it's generally recognized as an African-American cultural art form, hip-hop's Bronx roots were diverse. Significant Latino influence was present from the beginning, and hip-hop's "founding fathers" were of Afro-Caribbean heritage. DJ Kool Herc was born in Jamaica but moved to the United States when he was 12. Afrika Bambaataa was born in New York to parents of Jamaican and Barbadian descent, and Grandmaster Flash was also born in New York to Barbadian immigrant parents. Afro-Caribbean flavor remixed with Latino and African-American styles within a particular social and historical context gave birth to what we now call "hip-hop."

These Bronx youth rediscovered and remixed graffiti, which can be traced back to Egypt. They recalled and reclaimed rap, which can be traced back to the African *griots* (storytellers). Some argue that the essential forms of break dancing can be traced to Angola's *capoeira* martial arts, still practiced in Brazil. DJ "breaks" come from Jamaica, while Grandmaster Flash gets a serious nod for adding a whole new dimension to the art of the DJ.

At its core, hip-hop's framework addresses identity, family and friendship, neighborhood, and credibility…or *Keepin' it real, me, my peeps, and my 'hood*. Who am I? Where am I from? Who are my friends? What do we care about? Universal in reach, rap offers voice, protest, and tools for reworking identity. The impact of youth agency is both local and global.

With the rise of satellites, international networking, cable television, and the Internet, rap music and hip-hop culture sped around the globe. Global capitalism and U.S. cultural flows made hip-hop accessible to young people everywhere. But when hip-hop landed in South America, Europe, Africa, and Asia, it began to look different "on the ground" in every location. Young people, as culture bearers and culture makers, weren't simply mimicking U.S. hip-hop; they were making it their own, based on their own social and historical contexts. Hip-hop thus becomes global and local, universal and particular, about the world and about my 'hood.

Hip-hop is a vehicle for global youth affiliations, similarities, differences, and mergers. It may look the same on the surface; but upon closer inspection, the local shape of hip-hop is always specific to time, place, and context.

4 Calenthia Dowdy is associate professor of youth ministry at Eastern University in St. Davids, Pennsylvania.

Third, cultural styles often flow out of social identity and meaning, rather than a direct form of resistance against dominant cultures.

And finally, the global dynamic of youth cultures has changed the ways youth function as cultural agents. As Bucholtz writes:

> The global spread of popular culture is often viewed as symptomatic of cultural leveling, yet many scholars have pointed out that how cultural forms are taken up and assigned meanings far from their places of origin is a process that involves creativity and agency...The same cultural resource can be put to use in radically different ways. Hence rap allows underemployed youth in Tanzania to participate politically in public discourse (Remes 1999), while in Zimbabwe, it enables privileged urban youth to display personal aspirations through cultural style (Neate 1994)...Thus cultural resources may be used locally in unpredictable ways. (2002)

Youth are active agents reacting, creating, and responding to global youth cultural forms, serving as both consumers and producers of culture.

REFLECTION ACTIVITY (5 TO 10 MINUTES)

Consider what you know about contemporary adolescent culture. What evidence do you see of the global dynamic of youth cultures?

DIGGING DEEPER (10 TO 15 MINUTES)

Reread the sidebar on the global influence of hip-hop culture. In what ways have you experienced the influence of hip-hop culture? In what ways have you experienced the influence of hip-hop in your youth community? In those instances, how have youth claimed it as their own experience? How have youth adopted and infused elements of hip-hop with their own messages and meanings? Write down your responses.

- Youth navigate the multiple worlds of youth cultures, negotiating cultural identities in a variety of contexts.

- Acting as both consumers of culture and agents of cultural formation, youth are creative actors in the world of youth culture.

WORKS CITED

Anderson, Elijah. 1999. *Code of the street: Decency, violence, and the moral life of the inner city.* New York: W. W. Norton & Company.

Arnett, Jeffrey Jensen. 2007. *Adolescence and emerging adulthood: A cultural approach.* 3rd ed. Upper Saddle River, NJ: Prentice Hall.

Baugh, John, and Joel Sherzer. 1984. *Language in use: Readings in sociolinguistics.* Englewood Cliffs, NJ: Prentice Hall Publishers.

Bell, Catherine. 1997. *Ritual: Perspectives and dimensions.* New York: Oxford University Press.

Benedict, Ruth. 1934. *Patterns of culture.* Boston: Houghton-Mifflin.

Berger, Arthur Asa. 1995. *Cultural criticism: A primer of key concepts.* Ed. Garth S. Jowett. Vol. 4 of *Foundations of popular culture.* Thousand Oaks, CA: Sage Publications.

Blackman, Shane J. 2005. Youth subcultural theory: A critical engagement with the concept, its origins and politics, from the Chicago school to postmodernism. *Journal of Youth Studies* 8 (1): 1–20.

Bucholtz, Mary. 2002. Youth and cultural practice. *Annual Review of Anthropology* 31: 525–552.

Chandler, Daniel. 2003. *Semiotics: The basics.* London: Routledge.

Davis, Kenneth C. 2008. A French connection. Opinion. *The New York Times*, November 25, 2008. http://www.nytimes.com/2008/11/26/opinion/26davis.html?_r=3.

Eltahawy, Mona. 2007. Punished for being raped. Opinion. *The New York Times*, November 29, 2007. http://www.nytimes.com/2007/11/29/opinion/29iht-edeltahawy.1.8528543.html.

Freilich, Morris. 1972. *The meaning of culture: A reader in cultural anthropology.* Lexington, MA: Xerox Publishing.

———. 1989. *The relevance of culture.* New York: Bergin & Garvey Publishers.

Geertz, Clifford. 1973. *The interpretation of cultures: Selected essays.* Boston: Basic Books.

Goldstein, Leon J. 1957. On Defining Culture. *American Anthropologist* 59 (6): 1075–1081.

Goodenough, Ward H. 1989. Culture, concept and phenomenon. In *The relevance of culture,* Morris Freilich, chapter 5. New York: Bergin & Garvey.

Government of Singapore. 2008. Ministry of Manpower. September 2, 2008. www.mom.gov.sg.

Hannerz, Ulf. 1952. *Cultural complexity: Studies in the social organization of meaning.* New York: Columbia Press.

Harper, Douglas. 2001. Online Entymology Dictionary. http://www.etymonline.com.

Hiebert, Paul G. 1985. *Anthropological insights for missionaries.* Repr., Grand Rapids, MI: Baker Book House Company, 1994.

Jordan. 2008. Regional dialects of the USA: An introduction. h2g2, a subsidiary of the BBC. March 14, 2008. bbc.co.uk/dna/h2g2/A30481706.

Jost, John T. 2006. The end of the end of ideology. *American Psychologist* 61 (7): 651–670.

Klinger-Vartabedian, Laurel, and Robert A. Vartabedian. 1992. Media and discourse in the twentieth-century coffeehouse movement. *Journal of Popular Culture* 26 (3): 211–219.

Kraft, Charles H. with Marguerite G. Kraft. 2005. *Christianity in culture: A study in dynamic biblical theologizing in cross-cultural perspective.* 25th Anniversary ed. Maryknoll, NY: Orbis Books.

Kroeber, Alfred L., and Clyde Kluckhohn. 1952. *Culture: A critical review of concepts and definitions.* Cambridge, MA: The Museum.

Liberman, Anatoly. 2007. An hour with the etymologist. Interview by Minnesota Public Radio. Minneapolis, MN (January 1, 2007). http://minnesota.publicradio.org/display/web/2007/01/01/midmorning2.

Linton, Ralph, and Adelin Linton. 1949. *We gather together: The story of Thanksgiving.* New York: Schuman.

Loewen, James W. 1996. *Lies my teacher told me: Everything your American history textbook got wrong.* New York: Simon & Schuster.

Lovell, Vicky, Elizabeth O'Neill, and Skylar Olsen. 2007. Maternity leave in the United States. Institute for Women's Policy Research Fact Sheet. Research assistance by Claudia Williams. http://www.iwpr.org/pdf/parentalleaveA131.pdf.

MacArthur, John D. 2009. Explanation of the great seal's symbolism. GreatSeal.com. http://greatseal.com/symbols/explanation.html.

Mead, Margaret. 1934. Preface. In *Patterns of Culture*, Ruth Benedict, viii. Boston: Houghton-Mifflin.

Meisler, Stanley. 1959. Letter from Washington. *The Nation* 189 (5): 99–101.

Merriam-Webster, Incorporated. 2009. Merriam-Webster Online Dictionary. http://www.merriam-webster.com/dictionary/ideology.

Mokhtar, Najat, et al. 2001. Diet culture and obesity in northern Africa. *Journal of Nutrition* 131 (3): 887S–892S.

Namenwirth, J. Zvi, and Robert Philip Weber. 1987. *Dynamics of culture.* Boston: Unwin Hyman.

NAS New Testament Greek Lexicon. 2009. Crosswalk.com. http://www.biblestudytools.com/Lexicons/Greek/grk.cgi?number=364&version=nas.

Ontario Ministry of Labour. 2009. Pregnancy and parental leave fact sheet. November 2009. http://www.labour.gov.on.ca/english/es/pubs/guide/pregnancy.php.

Rappaport, Roy A. 1999. *Ritual and religion in the making of humanity.* Cambridge: Cambridge University Press.

Schusky, Ernest L., and T. Patrick Culbert. 1967. *Introducing culture.* Englewood Cliffs, NJ: Prentice Hall.

Scott, John, and Gordon Marshall. 2007. *A dictionary of sociology.* New York: Oxford University Press.

Shakespeare, William. 1997. *King Lear.* Ed. R. A. Foakes. London: Thomas Nelson and Sons.

Smith, Christian, and Melinda Lundquist Denton. 2005. *Soul searching: The religious and spiritual lives of American teenagers.* New York: Oxford University Press.

Spradley, James, and David W. McCurdy. 2006. *Conformity and conflict: Readings in cultural anthropology.* 12th ed. Boston: Allyn & Bacon.

Turner, Victor. 1974. *Dramas, fields, and metaphors: Symbolic action in human society.* Ithaca, NY: Cornell University Press.

Walker, Barbara. 1988. *The woman's dictionary of symbols and sacred objects.* San Francisco: Harper Publishing.

Wuthnow, Robert. 1987. *Meaning and moral order: Explorations in cultural analysis.* Berkeley: University of California Press.

PART TWO

Ethnography of Culture

CHAPTER 5
The Need for Sharper Vision

LEARNING OBJECTIVES

When you've finished this section, you should be able to:

1. Articulate the need for a deeper ethnographic insight into youth cultures

2. Identify the characteristics for doing ministry as a youth pastor-ethnographer

Travis and Tyrone are eighth graders at a middle school in the upper Midwest. The boys live in the same neighborhood and attend the same local church youth group. Travis loves video games. The first thing he does when he arrives at youth group is head for the game console. He plays for as long as his leaders will allow, either with other teenagers or alone. When one of the adult volunteers asked him about his love of video games, Travis confided that he spends about two to three hours every day playing games at home. His mom makes sure he keeps up with his homework, but he always makes time for gaming.

Tyrone also likes playing video games, but he seems to have a number of other interests as well. At youth group you might find him playing video games with Travis, outside shooting hoops on the basketball court, or hanging with some of his friends.

What makes for the difference between Travis and Tyrone? Why does Travis seem obsessive about playing video games, while Tyrone can "take 'em or leave 'em"? It would take digging deeper into the lives of these two young men to gain a clearer picture of their motivations and the influence of this particular aspect of youth culture.

A red-tailed hawk is one of the largest members of the hawk family, although it isn't known for its size, but its incredibly sharp vision. From long distances the red-tailed hawk can see minute details far beyond what the human eye can see, catching the movement of a small mouse from a height of one mile. This hawk has "five times more visual sensory cells per millimeter of retina than do humans" (Pennsylvania State University 2003). Additionally, the red-tailed hawk has the physical capability to adjust its focus quickly as it detects and targets movement. Finally, the red-tailed hawk can sit in its perch for an hour or more as it patiently observes the landscape below it (Cornell Lab of Ornithology 2009, Day 1996).

These characteristics allow the red-tailed hawk to be aware of its surroundings—keeping track of danger as it also searches for food. The keen insight of this bird is why we sometimes say about teachers, parents, and others in authority: "She has the eyes of a hawk—she doesn't miss a thing." Youth workers need these same kinds of penetrating physical and mental visual skills when it comes to considering the influences of youth culture.

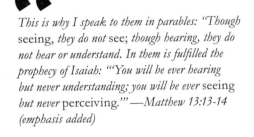

This is why I speak to them in parables: "Though seeing, they do not see; though hearing, they do not hear or understand. In them is fulfilled the prophecy of Isaiah: "'You will be ever hearing but never understanding; you will be ever seeing but never perceiving.'"—Matthew 13:13-14 (emphasis added)

The Gospels frequently characterize Jesus regarding his uncanny ability to see things, such as people's thoughts and true motivations, as well as the influence of the surrounding culture.[1] Like the red-tailed hawk, Jesus saw things that others missed. He saw behind people's surface actions and behaviors, identifying their underlying values and beliefs. Jesus called his followers to have this same kind of vision and to be wise in discerning the times. (See Luke 12:54-56.) Jesus cautions his followers not to get distracted by the world and its ways, but to pay attention—to develop a keener insight into the ways of the world.

This is the type of discernment youth workers must have as we anticipate culture's ability to shape and mold young people. We must increase our capabilities in critically analyzing the trends of youth culture with an eye toward understanding the motivations that lead young people to embrace these trends. Drawing on the practical skills of cultural ethnographers, youth workers can establish a framework for a deeper evaluation of youth culture.

This section explores the field of ethnography. As always, the goal is to be better equipped to see youth culture and to understand its influence on today's young people. Toward this goal, chapter 6 will examine ethnography, defining the broad parameters of ethnographic studies, as well as discussing the reasons why ethnographic skills are essential for youth workers. Chapter 6 concludes with a look at the attitudes necessary to be a youth pastor-ethnographer.[2]

Ethnographers rely on their abilities to perceive distinctions in cultures, both theirs and others'. The skills to discern a culture from the inside and outside give ethnographers the capability of assessing the deeply held beliefs and convictions of a group of people. Chapter 7 looks at these specific skills in ethnographic studies—an *emic* (or insider's) view and an *etic* (or outsider's) view. Integrated within this chapter will be a discussion of the contradictions of being an observer of culture.

As we move into the area of considering ways of observing young people in their culture and engaging in conversations with them, this naturally raises questions about privacy and ethical responsibilities of youth pastors to students as we immerse ourselves in their lives. In that regard,

---

1 For example, see Luke 5:17-26, Matthew 9:1-8, and 9:35-38.
2 Mary Clark Moschella uses the term *pastor-ethnographer* to describe the pastor who incorporates ethnographic skills into his or her work as pastor.

chapter 8 will explore these issues, particularly highlighting three aspects of youth workers' ethical responsibilities to students: Fiduciary responsibilities, confidentiality, and legal ethics.

MINISTRY AS ETHNOGRAPHY

Ethnography is a field of study in the broader scientific field of anthropology, the study of humankind. Specifically, ethnography explores groups of people in their natural setting through methods of inquiry and discovery. For ethnographers, the two key aspects are *behaviors* and *contexts*. By focusing their research on studying groups of people in their own communities, ethnographers are able to examine firsthand the behaviors and activities of those people. This kind of focused observation fosters a greater understanding of people's perspectives and motivations and sheds light on how the broader culture(s) shapes and influences them.

In the next chapter, we'll begin to explore an ethnographic approach to understanding youth culture, and it's the first of three pieces in developing our integrated approach to culture. (Developmental and theological considerations will follow in the next two chapters.) An ethnographic approach shifts the central focus from culture to people and groups.

REFLECTION ACTIVITY (5 TO 10 MINUTES)

This chapter suggests that youth workers need to develop a keener ability to see youth culture. What is your assessment of that argument? Is it valid? Why or why not?

DIGGING DEEPER (10 TO 15 MINUTES)

Reread the account of Travis and Tyrone at the beginning of this chapter. Develop a list of questions that might be helpful in discerning "below the surface" meanings for their choices and actions. What additional information might be helpful for you to find out about each of them?

- Ethnography is the study of people based on observing behaviors of groups of people in their particular environments.

- Developing the skills of ethnographers can equip youth workers to increase their understanding of youth and their influence with them.

CHAPTER 6
The Why and What of Ethnography

LEARNING OBJECTIVES

When you've finished this chapter, you should be able to:

1. Discuss the reasons why youth workers need to be pastor-ethnographers

2. Summarize the attitudes characterized by a pastor-ethnographer

THE WHY OF ETHNOGRAPHY

Ethnography is a broad field of study within cultural anthropology. The basis for ethnographic studies is the notion that people are best understood holistically—within their natural habitat or culture—so one may consider *all* aspects of a person's or group's existence in an attempt to understand a specific cultural dynamic. An ethnographer may use a variety of methods to gain a better understanding of a particular culture, but all of them will assist the ethnographer in developing a clearer picture of people in their given context and surroundings.

The goal of this chapter is not to fully explore the field of ethnography or turn youth workers into professional ethnographers. Our task is to consider some of the skills of the ethnographer and how they might deepen our abilities to be wise and discerning students of youth culture.

Ethnographic skills are a natural fit for the youth worker. First, the most prevalent method of ethnographic research is direct, firsthand observation of a group's cultural experiences. For example, an ethnographer might live in a community for six months in order to gain firsthand knowledge of the values, beliefs, and behaviors of the people. As youth workers, we are strategically situated to be ethnographers because we immerse ourselves in the worlds of youth every day. We are constantly surrounded by the personal experiences, actions, and beliefs of young people.

Another common method of ethnographic research is interviewing, which may include formal conversations with sets of preconceived questions or informal conversations in which the ethnographer lets the individual or group move the conversation in a particular direction. Again, youth workers are positioned to do ethnography because we intentionally seek to engage in conversations with young people in both informal and formal settings. Developing our ethnographic skills will enable us to take our natural skills of youth ministry and develop them so we can deepen our abilities to discern and act with wisdom.

STRENGTHS OF PASTORAL-ETHNOGRAPHY

Generally speaking, becoming skilled in ethnography will help youth workers not only analyze youth culture better, but also become more effective youth workers. Specifically, there are five strengths of doing pastoral-ethnography.[3]

Increased Understanding of Youth

While youth workers acknowledge that culture is constantly changing and the youth group is, too, we often get into a routine of believing that everything stays the same and thinking of the youth group as one large mass of students. Our programming tends to develop out of this latter perspective and is often a "one size fits all" approach that addresses broad biblical, theological, and cultural topics. The reality is that there is no OSFA approach that can fully take into account the cultural dynamics of a particular youth group.

In the typical youth ministry, around 10 to 20 percent of students age out or graduate and are replaced by a new group of younger students every year. And, of course, there are the regular changes of additions and withdrawals through a variety of other occurrences (for example, moves, friends joining friends, and so on). Each addition and exit alters the dynamics of the youth group, including its influence and relationship to youth culture.

The youth *group* is seldom, if ever, the same group for long. Youth leaders need the skills to assess and evaluate the dynamics of the youth group, and that's where ethnography comes in. Good ethnography explores the meanings, motivations, and actions of a group, thereby increasing our knowledge and understanding. By studying youth in their own context, youth workers become better equipped to understand how youth culture practices shape an adolescent's understanding of self.

An aspect of this increased understanding is increased knowledge concerning the cultural practices of the specific teenagers with whom we work. Usually, the average youth worker is proficient at talking about aspects of youth culture. We're often quite good at identifying the latest movies youth are watching, the top ten songs on their iPods, and even the latest fashions or hot topics. Our proficiency diminishes, however, when it comes to recognizing how the cultural practices of adolescents shape their understanding of self. Ethnography can help us become better at connecting the dots between the cultural experiences of young people and how those experiences help them construct their identities.

Adult Leader Training

A second reason for doing ethnography is that good ethnographic insights facilitate conversation and training with volunteer leaders and staff. Taking time to intentionally observe the cultural

---

3 This chapter draws and builds on the work of Mary Clark Moschella in her book *Ethnography as a Pastoral Practice: An Introduction* (Cleveland: The Pilgrim Press, 2008).

practices of youth establishes a framework for identifying pertinent topics for instruction and discussion with youth leaders. Working together with the adult leadership, youth workers can develop schedules for youth group Bible studies, leader training and discipleship, as well as parent and family discussions that focus on issues prevalent in the contemporary experiences of a particular group.

Recently, one of the young people I work with had a close friend who was injured in an alcohol-related car accident, sustaining multiple injuries that will require months of hospitalization and even more months of rehabilitation. As I sat with this young woman and her friends and family, all kinds of issues came up, such as death, alcohol use, and the value of prayer. Late one evening, when my brain seemed to be on autopilot, I almost missed a significant comment; but somehow what this young woman was saying clicked in my brain. As she agonized over the pain and suffering that her young friend was facing—and would face for a long time—she said, "I just wish she'd been able to say no to letting Kelly drive her home; that she'd called her mom or another friend to pick her up. It's happened to me a couple of times, where so-and-so had a few drinks but thought she was sober enough to drive and wouldn't listen to any of us. But even if she had, I don't know if we really would have been any better, ya know? You don't want to make a scene, and you don't want to embarrass yourself by calling your mom to pick you up."

Later, I was able to reflect on that conversation, and I realized the need to start a conversation with volunteers and staff about how we could talk with the youth about making wise decisions concerning alcohol and driving.

There is never enough time to teach on all of the critical cultural, biblical, and theological issues in the short span of time that students are in our programs. Ethnographic skills sharpen our abilities to critically evaluate the essential topics that need to be addressed with adult leaders, youth, and parents.

Community Matters

Building on the second strength, the third strength is a greater ability to see what matters in a community. Though there is certainly a global youth culture and similar cultural themes from one youth context to the next, there are also things of interest that are unique to each youth community. Honing ethnographic skills will help shine a light on these things. It takes concerted effort at being involved in the local youth context to learn and discern what's really important.

Ethnography helps youth workers identify not only patterns of history and tradition in the context of a community, but also insights into how those patterns shape the particular cultural experiences of the youth group. Many a youth pastor has learned—too late—the importance of the annual winter retreat after replacing it with a different event or the meaning of the quarterly youth Sunday service once the traditional order of service was changed. Developing a more penetrating insight into the practices and traditions of a community helps identify how those practices and traditions influence contemporary cultural practices and values.

Facilitate Theological Thinking

A fourth reason for youth workers to engage in the practices of ethnography is that developing ethnographic skills promotes critical theological reflection. As youth workers discover more about the lives of young people, this knowledge will give rise to greater theological questioning. Mary Clark Moschella uses the metaphor of excavating. As youth workers dig deeper into the culture of youth, studying issues that are important to the lives of young people, we'll confront theological questions.

For example, a youth minister I know observed a group of seventh and eighth grade students who were listening to this "really cool song." The youth pastor filed that away until later, when she had an opportunity to ask one of the students about that "really cool song" they were listening to. He told her the name of the song was "Low" and the artist was Flo Rida. She talked to him for a few minutes about what he liked about the song, showing a genuine interest in the student's love of music. Later that evening, she had an opportunity to review the lyrics online and to gather data on the artist. The major themes in the song—sexuality and male-female relationships—motivated her to reflect on an appropriate theology regarding those issues.

These kinds of experiences can facilitate theological thinking among adults—both parents and leaders—as well as with young people. "Rather than imposing abstract doctrines upon people" the youth pastor-ethnographer "becomes an interpreter of the theology that the people are already expressing through their lives" (Moschella 2008). Good theology is theology that addresses the issues of a particular context. Focused ethnography helps youth workers identify the particular themes and issues in a youth group and can encourage both the youth and the leaders to engage in critically reflective thinking about the theological considerations they raise.

Facilitate New Practices

A fifth reason is that good ethnography facilitates a new youth ministry practice that more accurately fits the context of a particular youth group. It naturally follows that just as doing pastoral-ethnography facilitates theological thinking, it also facilitates new practices in youth ministry. In the example above, the youth worker was compelled by her reflection on some song lyrics to have discussions with youth leaders and to consider particular teaching topics with students. This critical theological reflection leads youth workers to identify new responses and new ways of encountering the culture of youth.

Additionally, youth pastor-ethnographers become adept at recognizing the gaps in ministry practices and considering new practices to address those gaps. Again, in the example above, the youth leadership team developed a practice of encouraging students to submit song lyrics for discussion groups. The lyrics were submitted beforehand, allowing youth leaders time to critically reflect on the cultural themes and to develop questions that would help facilitate critical thinking on the part of the students. This new practice came out of the adults' understanding that one of the gaps that needed to be filled was helping students develop their own skills in critically evaluating music lyrics.

THE WHAT OF ETHNOGRAPHY

> The first service that one owes to others in the fellowship consists in listening to them. Just as love to God begins with listening to His Word, so the beginning of love for the brethren is learning to listen to them...Christians, especially ministers, so often think they must always contribute something when they are in the company of others, that this is the one service they have to render. They forget that listening can be a greater service than speaking. (Bonhoeffer 1978)

As noted above, since those in the vocation of youth ministry consciously immerse themselves in the lives and cultures of a specific group of young people, we youth workers are ethnographers in some fashion, whether or not we acknowledge it. As we engage in the practices of ministry, we are continuously seeking to discover what is meaningful and purposeful to those we serve as we encourage them on their spiritual journeys. And these practices of seeking and discovery are the practices of an ethnographer.

Therefore, I urge you, brothers and sisters, in view of God's mercy, to offer your bodies as a living sacrifice, holy and pleasing to God—this is true worship. Do not conform to the pattern of this world, but be transformed by the renewing of your mind. Then you will be able to test and approve what God's will is—his good, pleasing and perfect will. —Romans 12:1-2

Good ethnographic practices rely on inculcating appropriate attitudes as we engage in youth work as pastor-ethnographers. This section explores the attitudes that are necessary for a pastor-ethnographer to cultivate.

Cultivating Watchfulness

When I think of what it means to be watchful, I think of someone who is somewhat at a distance, but not really. Being watchful demands that a person cultivate all of her senses to be vigilant and alert to what is going on around her. It's developing an attitude of readiness, being attentive to what people are saying and doing. At an even deeper level, watchfulness is paying attention to meanings and motivations behind words and actions. This is an attitude that comes only through discipline and practice (Tierney 2002, Moschella 2008).

An aspect of watchfulness is the practice of being a part of a group without losing a sense of both subjectivity and objectivity. Subjectivity is the personal interpretation—that eye to seeing what is happening around you and working to define the actions and behaviors. Objectivity is the ability to view situations and people impartially, without bias. So, as pastor-ethnographers, we need to be able to suspend judgment in our watchfulness in order to gain a fuller understanding of youth and their culture (Moschella 2008).

Watching isn't solely about the careful, thoughtful observation of others. It's also about self-examination. As a pastor-ethnographer, a person needs to be cognizant of his own reactions to youth and their cultural activities. Gerry Tierney (2002) cautions us to be watchful for our own feelings of superiority, unease, suspicion, and hostility. And I would add the need to be attentive to our own *positive* feelings regarding youth culture as well.

The apostle Paul encourages us to be people who don't conform to the world and its culture but are transformed through the renewing of our minds (Romans 12:2). The practices that Paul exhorts us to engage in are practices of watchfulness. We must pay attention to what is going on around us and how we're being shaped and molded by culture. Our minds are renewed as we judge our own motivations and attitudes and allow the Spirit to teach us about inappropriate feelings—whether negative or positive—toward culture.

Cultivate an Attitude of Listening

As Bonhoeffer notes in the quote above, Christian leaders often feel as though they have a responsibility to offer something to others through a constructive or instructive word. However, cultivating an attitude of listening creates an atmosphere that allows youth workers to learn more about students and their culture. A disciplined practice of listening requires youth workers to give up some things, while at the same time incorporating other active practices.

> **Food for Thought**
>
> *Listening seems to be an especially difficult trait for some youth workers to develop. Why do you think that is?*

What We Give Up

In order to cultivate an attitude of listening, youth workers must give up being in control. When we encourage young people to talk, to tell their stories about what is important to them, we enter territory where we don't control the direction of the conversation. That can be a risky place for a youth worker to be. A student may tell you something you don't want to know, take you places you don't want to be, force you to confront issues you don't want to deal with. To engage in active listening, youth workers need to acknowledge the riskiness of doing so and be willing to let go of control, trusting the students and, ultimately, God. This means we also have to give up our fear—of the unknown, of what we might discover, and of what such knowledge might mean for us both personally and professionally. Trusting students and God is a risky thing and can make for messy ministry.

My dear brothers and sisters, take note of this: Everyone should be quick to listen, slow to speak and slow to become angry. —James 1:19

Furthermore, when we take the step of giving up control, we will also have to set aside a desire to judge. If we truly want to learn about the lives and culture of teenagers, we need to develop the disciplined practice of listening without judging. We don't have to set aside our convictions and theological beliefs, but an attitude of judgment will quickly thwart any willingness or trust on the part of adolescents to share their lives with us.

Finally, as Moschella notes, "Listening is difficult because it requires us to give up the role of expert and become a learner again" (2008). An attitude of listening takes us into the role of discovery and learning, increasing our knowledge of those around us. It is in this place of deeply listening that youth workers have the opportunity to get clearer glimpses into youth culture and its influence in the lives of young people.

Incorporating New Practices

In addition to giving up practices, youth workers must incorporate *new* practices in order to cultivate an attitude of listening. Like many youth workers, I meet young people for coffee at local coffee shops around the city where I live. As we engage in conversation, I often find my eyes darting anywhere but on the young person in front of me—watching people come through the door, observing what the baristas are doing behind the counter, or listening to snippets of conversations from the tables around me. Sometimes I'm quickly brought back around when the student says something that grabs my attention. And then I wonder what else he's been saying and what I've missed.

There are also times when I'm on the receiving end of such disrespect, when the person across from me is reading a text message, answering a cell phone, or writing notes in her PDA. Cultivating an attitude of listening demands that we practice honoring and respecting youth and the stories they're willing to share with us. As Moschella states, "Listening can be a means of grace, bringing forth stories through which people make sense of their lives" (2008). Listening is a way of honoring and acknowledging the one who is speaking.

Ultimately, cultivating an attitude of listening is an act of love. Ethnography in pastoral ministry is not just about seeing and understanding culture, it's about knowing young people in a deeply personal way. It's about treating students respectfully and with compassion.

> Therefore if you have any encouragement from being united with Christ, if any comfort from his love, if any common sharing in the Spirit, if any tenderness and compassion, then make my joy complete by being like-minded, having the same love, being one in spirit and of one mind. Do nothing out of selfish ambition or vain conceit. Rather, in humility value others above yourselves, not looking to your own interests but each of you to the interests of the others. In your relationships with one another, have the same attitude of mind Christ Jesus had. —Philippians 2:1-5

Cultivate All of Your Senses

Moschella also suggests that pastors are like novice connoisseurs of art. The first time you stand in front of a painting of one of the great masters, you're overwhelmed with the beauty and immensity of the work of art. But as you stand and watch, patiently, unaware of the time passing, you become more aware of the intricate details of different aspects of the painting.

And as you continue looking, bit by bit you begin to see more of the painting. It was there all the time, but you hadn't focused enough to be able to see it.

Henri Nouwen speaks of this phenomenon in his book *The Return of the Prodigal Son* (1994). As Nouwen sat for hours in front of Rembrandt's painting by the same name, he began to notice intricate details he'd missed in a cursory first look: The differences between the father's left and right hands; the torn sandals, worn feet, and shaven head of the prodigal son; the austere countenance of the elder son. (See Luke 15:11-32.)

Moschella contends that the work of a pastor-ethnographer is like that kind of revelation that comes from a deeply penetrating eye. There is a need to move from the forest mentality—focusing on the big picture—to directing our focus to small, revealing details around us. Spend time watching the individual student. Concentrate on her actions, her interactions. Consider the context of those actions and interactions. Pay attention to material aspects of these encounters. Think about the influence and meaning of dress, attitudes, words, and facial expressions and notice how the whole package comes together.

Cultivate an Attitude of Humility

Most Christians who grew up in a church community learned early on about Moses' hesitation at accepting the position of leadership to which God called him. (See Exodus 3 and 4.) Though God had prepared Moses to confront the Pharaoh and rescue the Israelites from their enslavement in Egypt, Moses didn't seem to relish being in such a significant place of leadership. However, he eventually grew into his role as leader of the Israelites. And by the end of his life, we see a man who speaks with authority:

> Listen, you heavens, and I will speak; hear, you earth, the words of my mouth. Let my teaching fall like rain and my words descend like dew, like showers on new grass, like abundant rain on tender plants. I will proclaim the name of the Lord. Oh, praise the greatness of our God! —Deuteronomy 32:1-3

The one who initially resisted God's calling to leadership was now confident and comfortable in his authority and his ability to speak and proclaim in the name of the Lord.

For all the wisdom and maturity Moses developed, however, he never lost an attitude of humility. Numbers 12:3 describes him as "more humble than anyone else on the face of the earth." Being unassuming and respectful of the people one serves doesn't diminish one's authority and responsibility. The example of Moses shows us quite the opposite. Because Moses embraced his responsibilities as God's servant leader and approached his work with humility, he was able to lead with greater authority and respect. Cultivating a sense of humility will also foster a greater awareness and ability to learn from others.

Cultivate an Attitude of Curiosity

Curiosity may have killed the cat, but a *lack* of curiosity will kill the ability to observe and see beyond the surface of youth culture. Develop a thoughtful and questioning attitude that wants to know *why* a particular young person thinks the way he does or *why* this particular fad has become so important to the youth group or *why* a particular young woman consistently makes wise choices when it comes to academics—even when her friends make fun of her for doing so. The desire to find out the reasons behind actions, thoughts, and behaviors makes us better pastor-ethnographers.

Cultivate a Sense of Humor

Youth ministry is often characterized as a place for fun and games, and it can be. Yet, the work and responsibility can also overwhelm us and weigh us down. Sometimes it seems that fun and games are a means of dealing with the serious nature of our work. As pastor-ethnographers, we need to cultivate a sense of humor. This is not the wild wackiness that often characterizes youth ministry, but a sense of noting the strange and amusing aspects of life and culture.

Cultivate a Sense of Ethics

Professional researchers who engage in formal ethnographic study have developed very stringent guidelines for the practices of researching human subjects. As youth pastors and pastor-ethnographers, we also need to be cautious and ethical in our dealings with students. I'm not advocating that we adopt the stringent guidelines of the professional ethnographer, but we need to be aware of and respectful of students. This means we have the privilege of knowing personal, intimate aspects of their lives. As such, we should approach that privilege with an attitude of respect, acknowledging the gift—but also the responsibility—we've been given. All youth ministries need to develop a consistent, coherent policy of confidentiality. (Chapter 8 will explore in greater detail the ethical responsibilities of a pastor-ethnographer.)

The "what" of ethnography involves developing the attitudes that allow youth workers to see into the motivations, meanings, and actions of young people. That's the first step. The next step for a pastor-ethnographer is to develop and hone the practical skills of ethnography that increase our ability to see youth culture.

REFLECTION ACTIVITY (5 TO 10 MINUTES)

This chapter suggests that youth workers should cultivate a particular set of attitudes. Reflect on which of these attitudes is your strongest and why. Which one would you like to strengthen and why?

DIGGING DEEPER (10 TO 15 MINUTES)

As noted in this chapter, Mary Clark Moschella says: "Rather than imposing abstract doctrines upon people," the youth pastor-ethnographer "becomes an interpreter of the theology that the people are already expressing through their lives" (2008). Write a one-page response to this statement, then answer these questions: What does it mean for youth workers to be "interpreters"? In what ways does doing ethnography help youth workers become better interpreters?

- Youth workers serve cross-culturally in the world of youth and are natural ethnographers.

- Ethnographic skills equip youth workers to more effectively understand the culture of youth, as well as to discern what matters to a youth community.

- Ethnographic skills facilitate theological thinking and youth ministry practices.

- A youth pastor-ethnographer needs to cultivate attitudes of watchfulness, listening, humor, and humility, as well as a sense of curiosity and ethics.

CHAPTER 7
Emic and Etic: The Eyes of an Ethnographer

LEARNING OBJECTIVES

When you've finished this chapter, you should be able to:

1. Articulate the similarities and differences in emic and etic descriptions of culture

2. Explain the four steps in the S. E. E. Spiral

3. Discuss the contradictions of experiences in a study of culture

Mission trips are an omnipresent part of youth ministry programs because youth workers recognize them as opportunities to teach students what it means to be God's kingdom servants by serving others. Youth workers also know that regardless of the work their students do and where they do it, the potential for the greatest transformation is not with the people and places visited but in the lives of the students who go.

On one such trip, a group of poor, inner-city youth traveled to Guatemala to help construct a dormitory at an orphanage for girls who'd been rescued from living on the streets and working as prostitutes to survive and support their families. After a week of long days spent working in extremely hot, humid conditions, the youth group had finished the new dormitory and gotten to know some of the girls who'd be living in it.

As the group processed what they'd learned during the trip, one young man shared, "I learned a lot about poverty. I thought I knew what it was like to be poor. But I'm not poor. I've learned what real poverty is." Because of his experience at the orphanage, he'd gained greater insight into the experiences and lives of those young girls. As he stood on the periphery and looked at their lives, he increased his knowledge about them and his understanding of his own life.

These two ways of seeing are at the core of ethnographic study. Both are essential skills for the ethnographer to analyze and understand culture. Ethnographers need to develop the ability to see inside a culture from the *outside*—an *etic* perspective—as well as the ability to see from *within* a culture—an *emic* perspective. This chapter explores each of these perspectives and identifies ways that youth workers can hone their skills at understanding youth culture. We'll dig deeper into both perspectives, highlighting some of the specific observational skills that will assist youth workers in becoming better etic and emic observers of youth culture.

In the example of mission trips, much of what's described may seem like everyday youth ministry. Youth workers are masters at hanging out where students are, doing the kinds of things youth do, and crafting programs and activities to meet the needs of young people. So how is this approach any different from what youth workers are already doing? This chapter argues for a subtle shift in how we view the work that youth leaders do.

Alice Reich, professor of anthropology at Regis University in Colorado, contends that the primary goal for studying a people and their culture is to overcome misunderstandings (1998). Metaphorically speaking, a student of culture needs a set of bifocals—one set of lenses to correct the visual impairment caused by the misunderstandings of another culture and a second set to correct the visual impairment caused by the misunderstandings of one's *own* culture. Closeness to one's own culture without reflection will blind a person from clearly seeing the cultural experiences of young people. The distance (experientially, developmentally, emotionally, and so on) from contemporary youth culture without deep, critical reflection will also blind adult leaders from clearly seeing how young people are being shaped and formed by their culture. Thus, the skills of an ethnographer equip youth workers to do what they're already doing—but do it better.

GETTING OUR CLOSE-UP VISION IN FOCUS

A number of years ago, I required a class of college students to attend a training workshop for youth pastors. These students would be graduating in a few weeks, and I wanted to encourage them to get into the routine of continuing their education and help them network with youth pastors who'd been in the profession for a number of years.

Following the weekend workshop, students came to class prepared to discuss the sessions they'd attended. When class began, I asked the students to share about their experiences. Todd was quick to respond, noting that he was quite surprised by what he'd experienced. His exact words were:

> I was scared. In my first session, there were about 20 youth pastors, all men, and almost all of them were in their late 30s, 40s, and 50s—except for me. The first thing we did was play a game that I play with my youth group all the time. But what scared me was how these guys were so into playing the game. It might've just been me, but I looked around and thought, *This is gonna be me in 20 years*, and it frightened me. I don't want to be some middle-aged man still trying to hold on to his youth. Youth ministry has to be more than that.

The point of this illustration isn't that playing games or having fun with your students makes you juvenile. The point is that sometimes in youth ministry there is too little reflection on how we participate and consume the elements of youth culture. We need to gain greater clarity of vision by developing a better inside view of our own perspectives.

An Emic Perspective: A View from the Inside

Drawing from studies of language and meaning, ethnographers have labeled two approaches to studying culture: *Emic* (the inside view) and *etic* (the outside view). The inside view starts with the youth worker's personal emic. The goal is for the youth worker to develop greater self-understanding, and this begins with acknowledging that our beliefs and convictions about youth and youth culture are culturally and historically bound. Whenever you hear someone say, "Things weren't like that when I was a kid," or "The world today is not like it was when I was young," you can be certain their perceptions are being shaped by their own personal history. This is not a critique of the people who make those comments (we make them, too). It's an acknowledgment that contemporary experience is often measured by one's past.

Another aspect of this dilemma is that it's *true* that youth culture is very different now than it was 10 years ago. In fact, it's different than it was just *one* year ago. Therefore, it's that very reality that affirms the cross-cultural nature of youth work because youth workers engage in cross-cultural ministry every day when they show up in the world of youth. In other words, the nature of our profession is that we bring the lens of our own culture to work, which means we are—to some degree—*out of focus* with the world of adolescents.

The first step in adjusting our focus is becoming aware of our own perceptions. As Alice Reich (1998) iterates, misunderstandings are a common part of interacting cross-culturally and often result because we don't recognize how our own perspectives shape the reality we see in the other culture.

An Etic Perspective: A View from the Outside

The goal of an etic perspective is for a person who's outside of a particular culture to describe the actions, beliefs, or behaviors of that culture. Though a completely unbiased account is impossible, the goal is to be as neutral and objective as we can. Most often, etic accounts are derived from firsthand observation, but they can also be built on historical and documented sources (for example, magazines, newspapers, online data, and so on).

When I lead a discussion in my classes or youth group about the pros and cons of dating, I often start by asking, "Is dating an appropriate activity for today's youth?" Students are always eager to share their opinions. Interestingly, adult leaders have their own perspectives, too. College-aged adults are often engaged in their own practices of dating, bringing fresh ideas and opinions from their own experiences. Older adults, whether married or single, will have a longer history and different cultural experiences than their younger counterparts. And the students frequently laugh in disbelief over the teenage dating practices of adult leaders who are now in their 50s, 60s, or even older. Likewise, adults may be dismayed by what seems casual and informal in the contemporary practices of dating.

After lively conversation and the sharing of a variety of perspectives, I typically ask a follow-up question: "Where do your beliefs about dating come from?" Often, students and leaders will endeavor to offer up support for or against different dating practices based on biblical guidelines. I then give them a brief history about the cultural practices of dating in the ancient Middle East (it wasn't practiced) and the Scripture passages that address the practice of dating (there aren't any). The stage is then set for everyone to critically evaluate the cultural and historical foundations of their own beliefs about dating.

Many times, students begin to see how their personal experiences and the values of their culture have contributed to their convictions. Students then have a much clearer perspective of their own values, which enables them to look at contemporary dating practices of adolescents in a much more focused way.

In this example we see evidence of both emic and etic perspectives among students and leaders. As these two groups reflect on their own experiences, they're bringing into focus an emic perspective. As they reflect on each other's experiences, they're bringing into focus an etic perspective.

These kinds of critical evaluative exercises in no way diminish the belief that Scripture can provide instruction into today's youth culture. Nor do they mean that youth workers must set aside their personal convictions or moral imperatives. However, it does motivate us not to hold so tightly to our personal convictions that we're hindered in being able to see the culture, motivations, and convictions of the youth in our care. This kind of thoughtful, personal reflection actually affords youth workers greater insight and sensitivity, thereby giving us a voice with which to speak more clearly regarding our concerns about the issues of youth culture, whether they be dating practices, sexuality, or a consumer mentality.

THE S. E. E. SPIRAL OF EMIC-ETIC PERSPECTIVES

Building on the work of Kenneth Pike and Marvin Harris,[4] a colleague of mine, Linde Getahun, developed a framework for observing the cultural world around us. In her work as a professor of developmental psychology, Dr. Getahun uses this framework to instruct students how to complete service-learning projects in her courses.[5] The diagram to the right describes her four-part strategy for gaining an emic-etic perspective, entitled the "S. E. E. Spiral."

---

4 See *Emics and Etics: The Insider/Outsider Debate* (Newbury Park, CA: Sage Publications, 1990).
5 Service-learning is a teaching method that strives to connect classroom learning with real-life situations, giving students the opportunity to apply what they're learning to specific community and group needs. An aspect of this kind of learning is the opportunity to reflect meaningfully about the issues and responsibilities in a particular cultural setting.

THE S.E.E. SPIRAL

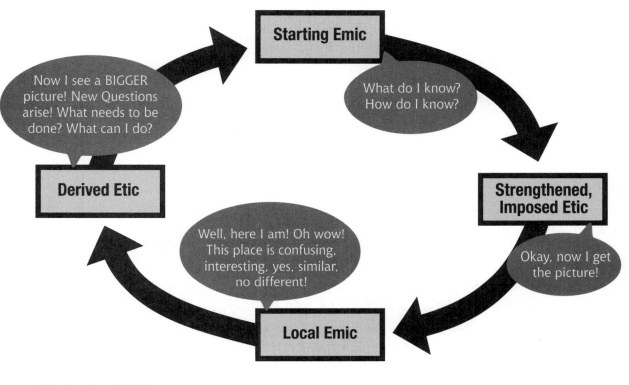

© L. Getahun (2006)
Bethel University, St. Paul, MN

Starting Emic: What Do I Know and How Do I Know It?

This approach begins with an intentional critical reflection on an element of culture—looking inside one's own culture to explore how you initially understand that phenomenon. Two questions guide the work of this reflection: What do I know? How do I know it?

So, for example, if a youth leadership team wanted to explore the practice of tattooing, they'd begin by reflecting on their own experience and knowledge of tattooing. Each member of the team would answer questions about tattoos:

- What is their personal reaction to the idea of body tattoos?

- Do they have any tattoos?

  - If they do, what kind do they have and why that particular design?

  - Why did they get a tattoo?

- What was the process in making a decision to get or not to get a tattoo?

- What are the beliefs and values they hold regarding tattoos? What are these beliefs based on?

From there the leadership team would move to what they know about the practice of tattooing within the youth group and the broader youth culture and how they know it. This, again, is a starting approach and allows youth workers to set out their assumptions and preconceived ideas about tattoos.

"IF YOU WANT TO KNOW WHO I AM, LOOK AT MY TATTOO"

Recently I was at my local Home Depot buying materials for a fence. As the young man helped load my construction materials, I noticed he had many intricate tattoos on his legs and arms. Fortunately, for me, I'd bought a lot of lumber, and it took Ted 10 to 15 minutes to load it all into my Jeep. In that amount of time, I was able to learn a lot about Ted's love of tattoos, as well as his love of art and Minnesota.

He explained how he spends months researching each new tattoo. Many of the tattoos reflect his love of Minnesota and the outdoors (for example, a tattoo of the map of Minnesota, a loon, and so on). Once he makes a decision about a new tattoo, he sets up a consultation with one of the three tattoo artists he uses to discuss and plan what the tattoo will look like and where it will be placed on his body. Once he is satisfied, he then sets up the necessary appointment(s) to complete the tattoo.

As I listened to him speak with pride and enthusiasm about the artwork on his body, I got a glimpse into how Ted used tattoos to express his personality. It reminded me of times when I've asked my students to draw a rough outline of their bodies and then fill in those outlines with symbols representing their experiences, values, or beliefs. Tattooing was a way for Ted to say, "This is who I am and this is what's important to me."

Most young people don't go through the elaborate process that Ted does, but tattooing is a way they can engage in self-expression. Tattoos have been a part of many cultures for thousands of years. Archaeologists have found Egyptian mummies with tattoos and tattooing implements dating back to around 2000 BC. In all of the evidence discovered thus far, it appears that women received the tattoos, which served as "amulets, status symbols, declarations of love, signs of religious beliefs, adornments, and even forms of punishment" (Lineberry 2007).

The contemporary art form among North American youth and young adults has its own particular expression. The data on tattoos presents some interesting findings. Statistics show that one to eight percent of youth have at least one tattoo. Between the ages of 18 and 29, however, there is a significant increase, with roughly one in three young people having at least one tattoo (Brown, Perlmutter, and McDermott 2000; Youth Culture 2001). Surveys have also found that young women are more likely than young men to get tattoos, with three out of five tattoos going to women (Youth Culture 2001).

A Youth Culture report (2001) on youth piercings and tattoos found that there is a strong correlation between teens with tattoos and their use of alcohol, cigarettes, and marijuana. There is also a strong correlation between tattooing and other risk-taking activities, preference for particular music styles (heavy metal, for example), and an increased tendency to hang out with friends.

The matter of Christians getting tattoos is hotly debated. Some believe tattooing dishonors God and the body as God's temple. Others believe tattooing is a personal decision and doesn't automatically dishonor God or a person's witness. The most frequent Scripture cited against tattooing is Leviticus 19:28. This verse discusses the surrounding pagan countries' practice of marking the dead, which was common in ancient Palestine. But the passage as a whole talks about the many practices that God cautions the Israelites to avoid so they can maintain their covenant relationship with God, proclaim the one true God to the nations around them, and be holy and set apart. The emphasis here is on honoring God.

Christians today aren't bound by many of the Old Testament laws set forth in Leviticus. For example, we eat pork and shellfish, which is forbidden in Levitical law. This is not to say that tattoos are appropriate for youth and youth workers, but that each youth group must wrestle in their own context and community to consider what appropriately honors God and self (Gerwig 2007).

> *"'Do not cut your bodies for the dead or put tattoo marks on yourselves. I am the Lord.'" —Leviticus 19:28*

As youth groups reflect and consider the contemporary practice of tattooing, two questions should be a part of the consideration. First, what is an appropriate practice regarding youth leaders and tattoos? Suppose a devout church member in his 40s with a tattoo on his arm—a leftover from his days in the military 15 years ago—volunteers to work with the youth. Should he be allowed to volunteer? What about the young female volunteer and recent college graduate who has a cross tattoo on her ankle—should she be allowed to volunteer?

Second, what is an appropriate teaching practice regarding tattoos for teens? Using the ethnographic process outlined in this chapter, youth leaders should establish a plan that is based on their particular context and community. Chuck Gerwig, a pastor of students and families in Southern California, has developed a list of questions for students to review as they consider getting a tattoo. These questions can be helpful to you as you work through the process of developing an appropriate theological perspective:

• Am I legally old enough to get a tattoo?

• If I live with my parents, would my parents support my decision?

• Would I be defying my parents' God-given authority over me?

• Would I still want this particular image when I get older?

• What if my future mate wouldn't like seeing this image for a lifetime?

• Would this tattoo be in an area of my body that would be plainly visible? Many people **do** unfairly judge people with tattoos as being "second-class."

• Would this image bring God glory?

• Do I feel **fully** convinced that tattoos are allowable for Christians? (Gerwig 2007)

Food for Thought

How important is it for you to develop a "theology" of tattoos? How do you evaluate the impact of having a tattoo?

Strengthened, Imposed Etic: What Can I Expect to See?

This next step in the S. E. E. Spiral moves from initial perspectives to data gathering. At this point, the intent is to gather supporting background information that will help youth leaders gain greater perspective on a particular phenomenon of culture. Possible sources for gathering information might include:

• Youth culture online resources

• Youth ministry and youth culture books, magazines, and other print resources, such as newspapers

• Expert opinions regarding the particular cultural product (for example, talking to tattoo artists regarding the practice of tattooing)

• Opinions of others who might have insight into a cultural practice (for example, youth pastors, parents, teachers, school administrators, and so on)

This can be a formal or informal process, as warranted by the particular aspect of culture. The goal is to strengthen knowledge and understanding from an outsider's perspective.

Local Emic: What Do I See and Hear Around Me?

The third step in the S. E. E. Spiral involves getting a firsthand look at the particular cultural dynamic. It is at this stage that outside knowledge is integrated with personal—inside—experience. The data gathering at this stage comes from actual personal interactions with young people and might include:

- Collecting data on the practices of youth, both informally and formally

- Holding group discussions and asking questions similar to those found in the "Starting Emic" section above, inviting students to tell what they know and how they know it

- Surveying students:

  - Informal surveys or questions that come out of individual conversations

  - Formal survey and data gathering

Derived Etic: What Do I Now Know?

The fourth step in the S. E. E. Spiral brings the youth pastor-ethnographer to a place of deeper understanding. Of course, this doesn't mean the pastor-ethnographer has a particular cultural experience all figured out. At this point the pastor-ethnographer will, most likely, have more questions than at the start. This step includes many of the processes noted at the beginning of the previous chapter in "Strengths of Pastoral-Ethnography." (See page 68.) Working through the Spiral to this point increases understanding of youth culture, raises questions about theological matters and appropriate youth ministry practices, and helps a youth worker understand what matters to a community and what areas of training and education need to be addressed.

Two final points need to be made in concluding an explanation of the S. E. E. Spiral. First, as Dr. Getahun has noted, this strategy is a spiral. The process of cultural learning is ongoing. New questions and new points to ponder send the pastor-ethnographer back to the starting point on the journey of observing and learning about culture.

Second, these four steps overlap, particularly for youth workers who are constantly immersed cross-culturally in youth culture. Thus, the youth pastor-ethnographer often ends up doing them simultaneously. The point of the Spiral is to give structure and guidance to the process of analyzing culture.

A discussion of the particular ethnographic skills that youth workers may employ at this stage of the S. E. E. Spiral follows this section.

SKILLS FOR DOING A LOCAL EMIC: IDENTIFYING THE CONTRADICTIONS

Alice Reich (1998) has argued that the work of an ethnographer is oxymoronic. The word *oxymoron* comes from two Greek words: *Oxy*, meaning "sharp," and *moros*, meaning "foolish." In Reich's estimation, ethnography is oxymoronic because the work of being a cultural observer requires a person to engage in foolish endeavors in order to become sharp—to gain greater understanding.

Perhaps that's what my former student, Todd, observed when he watched the older youth pastors play games—they were being foolish in order to gain clarity. Part of our job as youth workers is to participate in youth culture in ways that, to outside observers, might appear foolish. But we don't do it for the sake of folly; we do it for increased understanding.

To that end, Reich has identified five contradictions or tensions that exist for the person who's interested in becoming an ethnographer of youth culture. This section is particularly salient for the third step in the S. E. E. Spiral as we immerse ourselves in gaining an emic perspective of youth culture.

The Subject-Object Phenomenon

In an ethnographic observation, the researcher is not the *expert*; the individual (or group) living in context is the *expert*. This creates a tension between the subject and the object of research. In traditional research experiences, the individuals being studied are treated as subjects—the "somebody treated or acted upon" (Merriam-Webster 2009). Researchers *subject* individuals to questionnaires, tests, surveys, and so on.

In an ethnographic observation, there is the tension between people as subjects and people as objects. That is, the group being studied is the intended purpose of the study—they aren't just the things being studied, but also the recipients of the study. As objects of study, individuals teach us about their world—their culture. Researchers are the recipients (the learners), and the individuals being observed are the teachers. This is to gain greater understanding and to allow them to speak, in a sense. They are, therefore, both teacher and subject. Thus the role of "expert" is shared by the researcher (youth worker) and the subjects (youth).

A youth pastor I know regularly hangs out at a local bagel shop in our community, and he does so at times when he knows the youth will be there. He uses that time to write and reflect on the day-to-day experiences in his church and community. But as he does that, he has one ear—and perhaps one eye—on the activities and conversations of the young people nearby. Occasionally, students will join him. He's been going there for years now, and most of the youth know who he is and the work he does. In that setting, he doesn't see himself as the expert or professional. The students are the experts. He's merely allowing them to teach him about their world. In addition, they aren't solely the subjects—the "what" that he's studying. They're also the objects. He knows that with greater clarity he'll be able to speak to them with greater effectiveness and integrity. The tension between the two dynamics of subject-object is a necessary tension, and youth workers must be able to manage it.

The Familiar Strange

For five years, I've taken virtually the same route to my office twice a day at least four to five times a week. A little over a year ago, I was driving down a street that I'd driven thousands of times before, when I noticed a house that looked like a Gothic mansion in a horror movie. For years I'd driven past this house and never noticed it. But on this random morning, the strangeness of the house stood out to me, and I noticed it for the first time. In my comfortableness with my daily routine, the oddness of this house had been overlooked.

Ethnographers are often called to study contexts that are familiar—or at least *seem* familiar—to their own experience. Since we spend a great deal of time with youth in their own context, we youth workers are certainly familiar with our surroundings. We become comfortable in believing we have a thorough knowledge and understanding of this context. Reich (1998) insists there are ways to strengthen our ability to see beyond the familiar, to identify the strange in the familiar.

For example, we can focus on taking apart our "taken-for-granted" knowledge. Practice looking again and again at an ordinary scene in your youth work experience, and try to build new ways of seeing, hearing, and understanding their world. As researchers enter an environment that they're somewhat familiar with (either through personal experience or study), there is the contradiction that as we become more familiar with a context, we are conditioned by that context and less able to *see* the unfamiliar or the strange.

Researchers need to develop new ways of seeing, hearing, and understanding the context. Practice becoming familiar with *looking* again and again at an ordinary scene and seeing it with new eyes.

The Strange Familiar

I recently took my granddaughter, Cierra, to London. We spent an incredible two weeks exploring the city's museums, art galleries, and restaurants. As an 11-year-old and a budding scientist, Cierra was very inquisitive. Frequently, she remarked at how British people were really weird; they didn't do things in a "normal" way. She enjoyed keeping track of the strange phrases Brits used in "their English."

I encouraged her not to think of them as abnormal, merely different. I suggested she begin looking for things that were similar to what she knew at home. She quickly compiled a list and realized how similar British and American people are.

When someone goes into a new setting, that person is typically struck by (and sometimes overwhelmed by) the strangeness of the situation. It's often easier in this kind of context to identify what is different, what feels weird, what makes us uncomfortable. In this kind of experience, the student of culture must work to develop a sense for seeing beyond the strange in order to identify things that might be predictable or familiar.

FUNDAMENTALS OF BEING HUMAN

As we noted in chapter 2, meaning making is at the center of social and cultural activities. All human beings—all cultures—seek meaning and purpose for their existence (Who am I and why am I here?). Underneath cultural practices one can find answers to these kinds of questions.

In all cultures and with all groups of people, there are universal aspects of culture that are specific to being human. Further, the more one endeavors to understand self and others, the more one recognizes the unknowable nature of what it means to be human. The tension for students of culture is not only to work to identify these universal aspects of humanity, but also to recognize that in every human being and in every human context there are universal aspects that are unknowable. The researcher must acknowledge that human nature is mysterious. And part of that mystery is that an individual's culture limits our ability to know and be known.

Creators and Created

The student of culture must also acknowledge the bidirectional relationship between human beings and culture: We are both creators *of* culture and created *by* culture. The youth pastor-ethnographer seeks to understand the creator-createdness of specific contexts, giving voice to human experiences. "To be human is to have a voice that names the world in relation to one's own experience. To be human is to seize the right to one's own voice and to work for the rights of everyone to have a voice" (Reich 1998).

Developing emic and etic perspectives of youth culture allows the youth pastor-ethnographer to take what youth workers do well—building relationships with young people—and dig deeper into the lives of youth to critically evaluate the impact and influence of youth culture.

REFLECTION ACTIVITY (5 TO 10 MINUTES)

Take an everyday experience—one that you engage in regularly—and consider "the strange" in the familiar of the activity. How does the consideration of the strange increase your ability to see more critically into that activity?

DIGGING DEEPER (10 TO 15 MINUTES)

Identify a cultural practice of youth with which you're familiar (for example, tattooing). Write a brief response that answers the two starting emic questions: What do you know? and How do you know it?

- An emic perspective is the description of a cultural belief or behavior from an insider's perspective.

- An etic perspective is the description of a cultural belief or behavior from an outsider's perspective.

- "Familiar-Strange" means looking for the strange in the familiar.

- "Strange-Familiar" means looking for the familiar in the strange.

CHAPTER 8
Being Ethical Youth Pastor-Ethnographers

LEARNING OBJECTIVES

When you've finished this chapter, you should be able to:

1. Discuss the fiduciary relationship between youth workers and students

2. Articulate reasons a youth ministry needs a policy of confidentiality

3. Explain clergy privilege and mandated reporting

Evan's youth pastor had observed significant changes in Evan's behavior in the last six months. Typically an active part of the youth group, Evan had gone from being one of the leaders with lots of friends to sitting by himself, not talking to anybody (if he showed up to youth group at all). When adult leaders tried to engage him in conversation, the once-talkative tenth grader would give only one- or two-word responses. Kate, Evan's youth pastor, had an opportunity to talk with Evan one Wednesday night. He seemed more vulnerable than usual. When Kate compassionately shared her concern about the changes she'd seen, Evan broke down and said he was in trouble and needed help.

"But if I tell you," he said, "you have to promise not to tell anyone, especially my parents."

Sensing an opportunity to help and not wanting Evan to shut down, Kate said, "Yes, I promise I won't tell anyone. Now, let me help you."

Evan began to share about his journey of experimenting with drugs, which now controlled his life. He couldn't stop, and he knew he needed help. Drugs were destroying his life. He was failing in school, and many of his friends had deserted him. He also knew that if his parents found out, it would kill them. After much prayer and discussion about how to get him the help he needed, Evan left Kate's office with a referral to a drug counseling program and the promise to follow up with Kate in a day or two. Kate's closing words to Evan were an encouragement to tell his parents about the situation. Kate told Evan she knew his parents loved him and would be there to help him if he let them.

He dejectedly shook his head and said, "No, I can't do that to them. I can't tell them."

After Evan left, Kate sat in her office and prayed for Evan. She knew his parents needed to know what was happening—that they'd be angry with her if they found out she knew and hadn't told them. But she rationalized to herself, "I don't even know them. I've met his mom only once. My responsibility is to Evan—to be there for him. Besides, I promised him I wouldn't tell anyone."

Situations like this one happen all too frequently in youth ministry. Whether it's as serious as drug use or as relatively minor as teens sharing their everyday experiences with adult youth leaders, youth work brings us into close proximity to the intimate details of adolescent lives. Further, if youth workers seek to understand youth culture, they will necessarily focus on increasing their knowledge of the activities, values, and beliefs of the young people with whom they work.

All of this means that youth workers must act with great care and compassion as young people open up their lives to them. There are both ethical and legal considerations involved when youth workers build relationships with young people, especially when those young people either willingly or at our suggestion volunteer details about their personal lives.

It is this aspect of care that motivates this chapter on the ethical and legal considerations of the youth pastor-ethnographer. Specifically, there are three aspects that need to be considered: A youth worker's fiduciary duty, the nature and responsibility of confidentiality, and the legal mandate to report what is shared.

Sometimes it's difficult to ascertain the legal and ethical responsibilities of youth workers. From a legal standpoint, most states—and in some cases, the federal government—have established guidelines that cover the relationships between adults in a professional relationship with children and youth. Sometimes those guidelines are specific, as in the case of adults who are teachers, health care professionals, or counselors. There are also laws that specify responsibilities of clergy who work with children and youth. The difficulty comes in trying to clarify the role of youth workers.

The first step for someone who works with youth, whether volunteer or paid staff, is to clarify with the church or ministry the exact role and responsibility of each person who works with youth and children. This process should involve ministry insurance company representatives and the specific leadership board of the ministry, as well as appropriate legal counsel. A written guideline of responsibilities regarding responsible care should be established and given to every person who has direct contact with youth. Even if a volunteer only sets up and takes down the room every week, he or she should still know the policies regarding conversations with young people.

The seriousness of this situation isn't meant to stifle conversation and relationship building with teenagers, but to equip adults to offer the best care possible. Toward that end, this section offers general guidelines for understanding the fiduciary duties, confidentiality, and mandated reporting. But in no way should the information offered here be used as a substitute for the formal work suggested above.

FIDUCIARY DUTY

The legal understanding of fiduciary duty dates back hundreds of years in the United States and the United Kingdom and covers many professions, such as financial management and banking, health care, and clergy. Specific to the context of youth ministry, fiduciary duty covers an adult's relationship with a young person. This section highlights three aspects of the fiduciary relationship: Acting for another's benefit, trust and reliance, and power.

Acting for Another's Benefit

An adult is in a fiduciary relationship with another person when that adult, at his or her own initiative, takes on the responsibility to "act primarily for the benefit of another" (Easterbrook 1993). In the case of youth ministry, all youth leaders would be in a fiduciary relationship with their students because we participate in youth ministry for the benefit of the young people we serve.

As fiduciaries, youth leaders have certain responsibilities. Our primary one is to "act at all times for the sole benefit and interests of another [youth], with loyalty to those interests" (Frankel 1998). That means youth leaders must attempt to provide the highest standards of care from a legal, ethical, and moral standpoint. In part, this means we mustn't put our personal interests ahead of the students' interests.

Further, from a legal standpoint fiduciaries are expected to "meet a stricter standard of behavior" than the average person. This includes not placing ourselves in a relationship with youth if there might be a conflict of interest, and making decisions relative to youth that exhibit appropriate advice and counsel (Frankel 1998). Legally, this stricter standard of behavior usually isn't defined until there's a case of malfeasance. That means it's incumbent on the adult leader to always act in the best interest of the students.

Trust and Reliance

A second aspect of a fiduciary relationship is one of trust and reliance. Inherent in the youth worker-youth relationship is a dynamic of confidence that the adult leader will act for the good of the youth. Young people expect that they can trust and depend on adult leaders. And parents and the broader ministry communities have a similar expectation. Because of the trust and confidence placed on youth workers, we're held to a higher standard of care.

Unequal Power Dynamic

Third, in a fiduciary relationship there is an aspect of unequal power because one party (the youth worker) possesses greater knowledge and skill, and the other party (the student) relies on or has an expectation that the youth worker has such knowledge and skill. Furthermore, partly because of the expectation of trust and reliance, but also because of the adult-adolescent dynamic, young people "do not deal on equal terms" with youth leaders. In a legal sense, youth leaders are in a position "to exert unique influence over" youth (Lack and Traina 2009). Youth may share details with youth workers that they wouldn't share with other adults. They may also feel compelled to act in certain ways because of their relationship with youth workers.

Youth workers may dispute this notion of power, believing they function more as "older friends" to youth. The reality is that youth workers have significant influence in shaping the actions and behaviors of their students. Youth workers are in a unique position of power, and, therefore, we must act ethically and responsibly with the influence we do have. This takes us back to the first point—youth workers must always act for the benefit of the student.

Some argue that pastors are not in a fiduciary relationship with the people in their ministries because it's not typically a legal counseling relationship and, therefore, the expectation of trust, reliance, and power isn't inherent in the relationship. Court decisions have been mixed—affirming the pastor-congregant relationship as fiduciary in some cases and sometimes not. Whether or not there is a legal basis, simply from an ethical and moral standpoint, we know that youth place their trust and confidence in youth workers. And youth workers have the ability to influence the thoughts and choices of their students because of the unique relationship they have with them. That means youth workers should act with greater care and responsibility toward youth.

> **Food for Thought**
>
> *How do you rate yourself when it comes to maintaining confidentiality?*

KEEPING THINGS CONFIDENTIAL

The Council of the American Anthropological Association (a governing body for professional ethnographers) states in their research guidelines:

> Anthropological researchers must do everything in their power to ensure that their research does not harm the safety, dignity, or *privacy* of the people with whom they work, conduct research, or perform other professional activities. (*emphasis added*) (1996–2006)

Youth workers don't have an official organization that covers these kinds of professional activities. However, most denominations and ministry organizations have developed a set of standards. Each youth worker should know what those practices are; and if their ministry doesn't have any established guidelines, he or she should work with the appropriate legal and ministry leaders to develop a workable plan to protect the "safety, dignity, and privacy" of students (Council of the American Anthropological Association 1996–2006).

Because of the nature of youth work, privacy is a particular concern. Teenagers, parents, volunteers, and others come to the context of youth ministry with expectations regarding privacy. And though these expectations aren't often articulated, they're always present. What kind of privacy should be expected? Inherent in the notions of privacy are ideas about confidentiality. This section discusses confidentiality in youth ministry, focusing on defining appropriate expectations and when to break confidentiality.

As a guideline, there are two aspects to any formal policy of confidentiality. The first is a written statement that serves to inform volunteers and staff, as well as students and parents. It's recommended that the statement be posted prominently at the ministry site and regularly communicated to students, parents, and youth staff. The following is an example of a suggested statement:

> We, the adult staff of First Church Youth Group, desire to build strong relationships with students and invite you to share your lives with us. We will endeavor to treat any information you share with us with respect, always seeking what's best for you.
>
> We therefore promise to keep what you say confidential, promising not to share any information you give us with anyone else without your permission. The only exception to this promise is if there is a perceived risk of harm to you or anyone else.
>
> In instances where there is perceived harm, the staff of First Church Youth Group will not share such information with anyone without making every possible attempt to contact you first.
>
> At all times the staff promises to seek the benefit of the youth of First Church Youth Group.

There are some important points to keep in mind as you develop a policy of confidentiality and care for students. Confidentiality includes conversations among adult leaders. Team meetings and prayer times can be occasions when the latest gossip about youth is shared. Personal information that reveals the identity of the youth involved should never be shared with other staff without the student's permission. Even *with* a student's permission, youth workers need to be cautious about sharing personal information, remembering that students may feel pressured to share and that adults must act for the benefit of the student at all times. Being too quick to share what a young person has entrusted can lead a student to feel a sense of betrayal and foster a belief that the youth group and youth leaders aren't safe places to confide anything personal.

As youth workers develop a strategy for confidentiality that fits their ministry, they should also discuss possible scenarios and appropriate ways to respond. For example,

- A young man has shared something with you and asked you not to tell anyone. But then you discover he's shared the same information with a number of other staff members with no such requirement. Are you required to maintain confidentiality?

- A young woman shares intimate details with her small group. Are you, as the adult small group leader, obligated to maintain confidentiality?

- A student shares something with a volunteer and asks her not to tell anyone. Is the volunteer obligated to maintain confidentiality? Or is there a greater responsibility to share the information with a paid staff person?

- Does a student have to ask for confidentiality in order to expect it?

WHEN YOU MUST BREAK CONFIDENTIALITY

Unfortunately, there are times when it's necessary for youth workers to break confidence. Specifically, there are four instances that should motivate youth workers to divulge the confidences of their students.

To Get Expert Advice

Sometimes it's necessary and appropriate for youth workers to seek outside help in addressing their students' needs. For instance, seeking counsel from experts who deal with particular adolescent concerns and getting help in assessing the appropriate ways to support our students. In those cases where outside consultation is warranted, there are two different scenarios.

The first involves seeking professional insight and knowledge without revealing the identity of the student. In this case it might not be necessary for the youth worker to inform the student that he or she will be discussing the situation with an outside person. However, if a youth worker determines that the student *should* be told, then this adult leader should reassure the student that his or her identity won't be revealed.

The second scenario occurs when it's impossible to maintain the student's privacy. In those instances breaking the confidence should follow the guidelines suggested above—the student should be notified ahead of time.

To Make a Referral

When the situation warrants referring a student to a professional (such as a counselor or treatment center), a written consent form should be drafted for both the youth worker and student to sign. It need not be formal, just a brief statement that sets forth whom the youth worker will contact, what information will be shared, and the future contact that will take place between the counselor and the youth worker.

For Personal Support

Because of the nature of youth work, adult leaders often need to find their own place of support and confidentiality. The person with whom a youth worker confides shouldn't have a personal relationship with the youth worker or any familiar association with the youth ministry. The greater the distance, the better. Even when abiding by these guidelines, it's still important for the youth worker to maintain confidentiality by not sharing personal details that would unintentionally reveal the identity of the student(s).

A caution is warranted here: Youth workers often turn to people they're close to—spouses, boyfriends or girlfriends, fellow youth leaders, or close family and friends—to share the burden of their concerns for youth. But without a student's permission, it is a violation of that teenager's privacy and a break in confidentiality to share personal information in these settings. Additionally, these support people are oftentimes intimately familiar with the youth ministry, sometimes working in it as well. This presents a potential for harm to the student. Youth workers should find places to receive support in ways that don't violate the promise of confidentiality or raise the potential for harm of students.

Assessing Harm

In instances in which there is suspected abuse, harmful intentions, destructive patterns, or addictions, youth workers must act to protect students from harm. That means confidentiality often needs to be broken. When it does, students should, if at all possible, be a part of the process of divulging private information. For example, if a young person reveals instances of sexual abuse, the youth worker should immediately work with the student to develop an appropriate plan that protects her and still helps the youth worker to abide by the laws regarding the reporting of such abuse. Guidelines for mandated reporting will be discussed in the next section.

It is both a privilege and a responsibility to participate in the lives of teenagers. Youth workers must act with integrity regarding the information we learn and still treat our students with dignity and respect in how we protect or divulge such information.

MANDATED REPORTING

"Mandated reporting" is the legal term that covers instances when adults in a fiduciary responsibility to children and teenagers are legally obligated to report suspected abuse. Because youth workers work closely with young people, they're often the ones with whom teenagers share their stories of abuse. Again, there are ethical and legal issues to be considered whenever youth workers suspect abuse. And each state has its own guidelines for mandated reporting, so youth workers need to know what the specific laws and guidelines are in their own states. In many states the failure to report is considered a crime.

Members of the clergy are sometimes exempt from the laws of mandated reporting because of "clergy privilege," which means that information told to clergy in the professional execution of their duties is protected and cannot be revealed. Again, each state has its own guidelines that cover the parameters of clergy privilege, particularly regarding matters of abuse of a minor child or youth.

The list below, as of January 2008, identifies the privilege standing for clergy in each state. Each youth ministry should determine when privilege applies to their particular context. Again, youth workers shouldn't rely solely on this information but should work with appropriate ministry and legal professionals to understand what the best practices are in their state and ministry. It should also be noted that many youth workers aren't considered clergy, especially if they aren't ordained or don't work in a church. So without clergy privilege, the laws of mandated reporting apply.

	Privilege granted but limited to "pastoral communications"	Privilege denied in cases of suspected child abuse or neglect	Privilege not addressed in the reporting laws
Clergy enumerated as mandated reporters	Alabama, Arizona, Arkansas, California, Colorado, Illinois, Louisiana, Maine, Massachusetts, Michigan, Minnesota, Missouri, Montana, Nevada, New Mexico, North Dakota, Ohio, Oregon, Pennsylvania, South Carolina, Vermont, Wisconsin	New Hampshire, West Virginia	Connecticut, Mississippi
Clergy not enumerated as mandated reporters but may be included with "any person" designation	Delaware, Florida, Idaho, Kentucky, Maryland, Utah, Wyoming	North Carolina, Oklahoma, Rhode Island, Texas	Indiana, Nebraska, New Jersey, Tennessee, Puerto Rico
Neither clergy nor "any person" enumerated as mandated reporters	Virginia, Washington	Not applicable	Alaska, American Samoa, District of Columbia, Georgia, Guam, Hawaii, Iowa, Kansas, New York, Northern Mariana Islands, South Dakota, Virgin Islands

(U. S. Department of Health & Human Services 2008)

Who Is a Mandatory Reporter?

Any adult who works in a professional relationship with children or teenagers, including that professional's delegate (for example, an adult volunteer or an administrative assistant). This professional relationship includes those "engaged in the practice of healing arts, social services, hospital administration, psychological or psychiatric treatment, child care, education, correctional supervision, probation and correctional services or law enforcement," as well as members of the clergy (Sexual Violence Justice Institute 2003). Clergy are required to report as long as the information gathered is not "otherwise privileged" (Child Welfare Information Gateway 2008).

What Must Be Reported?

Typically, any kind of physical or sexual abuse or neglect is mandated to be reported. States have differing guidelines regarding the time frame of the abuse (for example, how long ago it happened). The emphasis here is not on actual evidence but suspected abuse. If a young person tells you that he has been abused, you have reason to believe or suspect that abuse has taken place (Sexual Violence Justice Institute 2003). That revelation is sufficient, in most states, to require reporting.

States also have differing guidelines about what constitutes sexual abuse, particularly regarding adolescent sexual relationships. In some states a case in which a 15-year-old female is in a consensual sexual relationship with a 17-year-old male would be considered sexual abuse because she's a minor and not considered old enough to give consent. Again, it's important that each youth ministry know the guidelines in their own states.

Where to Report?

Typically cases of suspected abuse or neglect should be reported to governmental welfare agencies (for example, Child Protective Services) or law enforcement authorities. Information about where to report should be made readily available to all youth workers in case it's needed.

When and How to Report

Most often, legal guidelines require youth workers to report immediately. And in many states, failure to report can result in criminal charges being levied against the individual youth worker who doesn't report in a timely manner. Again, know your state's laws concerning the time frame for reporting and whether it can be made by phone or by written report.

In speaking to the churches in Ephesus, the apostle Paul encouraged them to "be very careful, then, how you live—not as unwise but as wise, making the most of every opportunity, because the days are evil" (Ephesians 5:15-16). Being wise in the ways of youth culture will bring many opportunities to offer protection and care to teenagers. Youth workers must act in ways that ethically and legally protect their students, doing everything they can to avoid causing harm.

REFLECTION ACTIVITY (5 TO 10 MINUTES)

This chapter suggested that there is an unequal power dynamic between youth workers and youth. Consider this idea and reflect on whether you agree or disagree with this idea and why.

DIGGING DEEPER (10 TO 15 MINUTES)

Find out the confidentiality policy of a youth ministry with which you're familiar. How prepared are they to deal with matters in a confidential manner? Write a brief response on what you find, reflecting critically on how well this ministry is prepared to protect and care for students regarding matters of confidentiality.

- Youth workers have a fiduciary duty to care and act for the benefit of youth.

- Every youth ministry should have a written policy of confidentiality.

- Every state has legal guidelines regulating clergy privilege and the mandated reporting of abuse of a minor child or youth.

WORKS CITED

Bonhoeffer, Dietrich. 1978. *Life together: The classic exploration of faith in community.* New York: HarperOne.

Brown, K. M., P. Perlmutter, and R. J. McDermott. 2000. Youth and tattoos: What school health personnel should know. *Journal of School Health* 70 (9): 355–360.

Child Welfare Information Gateway. 2008. Clergy as mandatory reporters of child abuse and neglect. U. S. Department of Health and Human Services. *Child Welfare Information Gateway.* Current through January 2008. http://www.childwelfare.gov/systemwide/laws_policies/statutes/clergymandated.cfm.

Cornell Lab of Ornithology. 2009. Red-tailed hawk. *All about birds.* http://allaboutbirds.org/guide/red-tailed_hawk/id.

Council of the American Anthropological Association. 1996–2006. Statements on ethics: Principles of professional responsibility. Amended through November 1986. http://www.aaanet.org/stmts/ethstmnt.htm.

Day, Leslie. 1996. 79th Street Boat Basin Flora and Fauna Society. *NY Site.* http://www.nysite.com/nature/fauna/redhawk.htm.

Easterbrook, Frank H. 1993. Contract and fiduciary duty. *Journal of Law and Economics* 36 (1): 425–446.

Frankel, Tamar. 1998. Fiduciary duties. *The new palgrave dictionary of economics and the law.* Vol. 2, *E-O.* Ed. Peter Newman. Macmillan Reference.

Gerwig, Chuck. 2007. Tattoo and the Bible. SacredInk.net. http://www.sacredink.net/tattoo_and_the_bible.

Lack, Walter J., and Paul A. Traina. 2009. Fiduciary duties: What are they, when do they exist and why use them? Engstrom, Lipscomb & Lack. http://www.elllaw.com.

Lineberry, Cate. 2007. Tattoos: The ancient and mysterious history. History & Archeology. *Smithsonian.* http://www.smithsonianmag.com/history-archaeology/tattoo.html.

Merriam-Webster, Incorporated. 2009. Merriam-Webster Online Dictionary. http://www.merriam-webster.com/dictionary/subject.

Moschella, Mary Clark. 2008. *Ethnography as pastoral practice: An introduction.* Cleveland, OH: The Pilgrim Press.

Nouwen, Henri J. M. 1994. *The return of the prodigal son: A story of homecoming.* First Image Books ed. New York: Doubleday.

Pennsylvania State University. 2003. *The Virtual Nature Trail at Penn State New Kensington.* August 7, 2003. http://www.psu.edu/dept/nkbiology/naturetrail.

Reich, Alice. 1998. Anthropology as oxymoron. In *Field ethnography: A manual for doing cultural anthropology,* Paul Kutsche, 4–7. Upper Saddle River, NJ: Prentice Hall.

Sexual Violence Justice Institute. 2003. Mandated child abuse reporters: How to know when reporting is required for advocates. MN Coalition Against Sexual Assault. http://www.mncasa.org/documents/svji_fact_sheets/mandated.rptrfactsht.pdf.

Tierney, Gerry. 2002. Becoming a participant observer. In *Doing cultural anthropology: Projects for ethnographic data collection,* Michael V. Angrosino, 9–18. Prospect Heights, IL: Waveland Press, Inc.

Youth Culture. 2001. Special report on youth, piercing, tattooing and hepatitis C: Trendscan findings. Health Canada. Ontario, Canada. http://www.phac-aspc.gc.ca/hepc/pubs/youthpt-jeunessept/pdf/youth_piercings.pdf.

PART THREE

Ecologies of Culture

CHAPTER 9
The Need for an Ecological Understanding of Adolescent Development

LEARNING OBJECTIVE
When you've finished this section, you should be able to:

1. Articulate ways a young person's journey to adulthood is influenced by culture

Two adolescents may grow up in the same neighborhood, participate in the same church youth group, and attend the same high school; yet, we know they'll grow up to be very different individuals. Each will develop a particular understanding of life, as well as have a unique perspective of self and others. Even if these two young people have the same parents, the differences will be striking. The *developmental* process that all young people experience leads to different outcomes.

The dramatic changes (biological, psychological, social, and even economic) that take place during the adolescent years are well documented. Youth workers are intimately familiar with the dramatic pubertal changes that transform a young boy into a gangly, voice-cracking, awkward teenager seemingly overnight. That same young man can amaze adults with his insight and maturity one moment and leave them shaking their heads at his immaturity the next.

This period of transition between childhood and adulthood—adolescence—is a journey of moving away from immaturity to maturity; a sometimes bumpy, often messy, but always interesting journey (Steinberg 2005). In fact, the word *adolescence* is derived from the Latin word *adolescere*, meaning "to come into maturity" (Oxford University Press 2009).

Human beings in all societies negotiate this period of human development, though there are historical and cultural differences that shape the individuals' experiences. This section explores the relationship between adolescent developmental processes and culture, seeking to identify ways in which culture influences this teenage journey toward maturity. Using the lens of developmental psychology to understand youth culture, the goal in these next three chapters is to further broaden our abilities to evaluate and assess the influences of culture in the life of an adolescent.

Specifically, this section explores the work of Urie Bronfenbrenner and others regarding an ecological model of adolescent development—a model that views development through the network of relationships and interactions in the various contexts of an adolescent's environment. It's an interdisciplinary approach to understanding human behavior.

The field of *human ecology* is a branch of sociology in which the relationships between individuals and their natural and created environments are studied. *Developmental psychology* studies how a human being changes over the life span in all aspects of what it means to be human (cognitive, physical, emotional, spiritual, as well as one's personality). This inter-connection between the multiple cultures of an adolescent's world (human ecology) and the multiple transitions in which that same adolescent navigates toward adulthood (developmental psychology) will serve as the focal point for this section.

To that end, chapter 10 describes Bronfenbrenner's model of an ecological theory of development. Building on that model, chapter 11 looks more intently at the immediate (micro) contexts of adolescent relationships—the everyday circumstances of a young person's life. This text doesn't have the space to offer an in-depth look at all of the immediate contexts but will instead focus on the most significant for our vocation as youth workers—namely, family and peers. An underlying hope is that students will develop appropriate skills as they explore these contexts to enable them to critically analyze and evaluate other contexts.

The final chapter in this section examines the context of religious affiliation, particularly church and youth group contexts, and concludes with some practical application ideas for doing youth ministry as it relates to the culture of adolescents.

REFLECTION ACTIVITY (5 TO 10 MINUTES)

This chapter suggests that cultural experiences can shape a young person's journey into maturity. Consider in your own experience as an adolescent how this was true or not true for you.

DIGGING DEEPER (10 TO 15 MINUTES)

This chapter also suggests that there are historical factors that influence the way culture shapes the lives and identities of young people. Compare your experience as an adolescent with that of the teens you know today. Consider ways in which the influence of culture has changed, focusing on the differences in how young people might understand themselves. (Try to think of positive as well as negative influences.) Write down your responses.

- The journey of transitioning from childhood to adulthood (adolescence) is shaped by many processes: Biological, social, psychological, and environmental.

- Human beings in every culture navigate the transition from childhood to adulthood in ways that are particular to their historical and cultural context.

CHAPTER 10
An Ecological Model of Adolescent Development: The Influence on Culture and Experience

LEARNING OBJECTIVES

When you've finished this chapter, you should be able to:

1. Summarize the different cultural networks in an ecological model of development

2. Discuss the reasons culture is influential in the development of self and identity of an adolescent

3. Account for the significance of the interconnections between the immediate and personal cultural contexts in a young person's life

Any adult who regularly spends time with young people knows the significance of relationships to an adolescent. The developing teen is constructing a whole new world of relating. Relationships with parents and family are redefined and re-envisioned, their world of relating to friends outside the immediate context of family grows in significance and character, while their world expands to include new and different contexts from school networks, romantic relationships, work, and participation in broader society. These webs of relationships form cultural contexts in which an adolescent acts and interacts. These interconnections provide an environment in which the developing adolescent can construct an identity and better understand self.

This next section examines Urie Bronfenbrenner's theory of development, which sets forth a framework for understanding these relationship contexts and their influence in shaping the identity of young people.

PRELIMINARY CONCEPTS AND TERMS

The first step is to set forth some preliminary concepts. The term *adolescent development* is seldom defined, but it's frequently used to mean a variety of thoughts and ideas relative to how a person grows during the adolescent years. Urie Bronfenbrenner's definition for *development* provides a helpful framework for our discussion:

A "person's evolving conception of the ecological environment and his [or her] relation to it, as well as the person's growing capacity to discover, sustain, or alter its properties." (1979)

Adolescent development, then, is the process of evolving conception that takes place during the teenage years. This definition notes the *reciprocal* relationship between a young person and her environment, meaning there's a back-and-forth, give-and-take dynamic to the interactions she has with her environment. On one hand, the personal experiences and the feedback she receives in that environment, including growth in cognitive and emotional capabilities, shape how the young person conceives of her world. On the other hand, a young person also shapes the environment through her interactions, giving feedback and response in a variety of ways that meaningfully shape her surroundings.

URIE BRONFENBRENNER

Early on, Urie Bronfenbrenner caught the passion for scientific research and human development. Immigrating to the United States from his native Russia at the age of six, Bronfenbrenner grew up in a small New York community where his father was a clinical pathologist and research director for the state hospital for those with mental disabilities. Bronfenbrenner completed graduate degrees in developmental psychology—an M.A. from Harvard University and a Ph.D. from the University of Michigan. In 1948, he joined the faculty at Cornell University, serving there until his death in 2005.

During his professional career, Bronfenbrenner was motivated to do research in the developmental sciences and to bring that research to bear on public policy and private practice. That motivation fostered an activist spirit to help others understand the implications of developmental theory, as well as shape public response to the developing child and adolescent (Cornell University 2009).

Dr. Bronfenbrenner focused on research that fostered practices in society to encourage positive outcomes for children and adolescents. His research confirmed for him the immeasurable value of positive adult relationships, as well as formative contexts to encourage healthy development. He was cofounder of Head Start and is probably best known in the broader society for his belief that "every child needs at least one adult who is irrationally crazy about him or her" (Brendtro 2006).

Furthermore, there are two aspects of a young person's *environment*: Context and the self. External forces shape the immediate *context*. Namely, historical, economical, social, and cultural forces affect the contemporary world or context of an adolescent. The reciprocal relationship between environment and youth is evident in three ways:

- Interpersonal Relationships: The ways one interacts with others—speaking, acting, and being

- Activities: The kinds of things a person does or participates in

- Roles: Societal expectations about how a person should participate in his or her activities and interpersonal relationships (Bronfenbrenner 1979)

A person's environment also consists of the *self*. As adolescents are making sense of their surroundings, they're also making sense of their selves in relation to that context. The cultural contexts in which an adolescent exists help him discover answers to the "Who am I?" and "Why am I here?" kinds of questions. An adolescent cannot experience his or her context independent of self (Bronfenbrenner 1979).

Another concept in an ecological understanding of development is the process of *socialization*. As young people experience self and context within their environments, they're socialized in certain ways. A young person learns how to self-regulate, is prepared to adopt social roles, and gains knowledge about sources of meaning through interpersonal relationships in her environment. "Self-regulation is the capacity for exercising self-control in order to restrain one's impulses and comply with social norms" (Arnett 2007). Again, it's through a person's environment (via the reciprocal aspects of interpersonal relationships, activities, and the practice of role-taking) that a young person begins to assemble a system for engaging in the world. In effect, a young person's environment teaches her what's valuable in terms of social norms, roles, and meaning. "Should I say this? *Can* I say this?" "Can I get away with this behavior?"

All of this takes place as a young person is creating reality and understanding identity. Therefore, it's important to acknowledge, as Bronfenbrenner does in his theoretical model, that an adolescent's *perception* of what takes place in his environment is key to how he makes sense of his world. It isn't solely experiences but how each adolescent perceives those experiences that lead to formulated concepts of values, beliefs, self, and others.

As Bronfenbrenner states:

> [An ecological conception of development] emphasizes the evolving nature and scope of perceived reality as it emerges and expands in the child's awareness and in his [or her] active involvement with the physical and social environment. (1979)

Perception and experience are inextricably intertwined in the developing adolescent.

A final concept crucial to an ecological model of development is called *custom complex*. A custom complex "consists of a customary practice and of the beliefs, values, sanctions, rules, motives, and satisfactions associated with it" (Arnett 2007). These customary practices are experienced in a young person's local environment and are signifi-

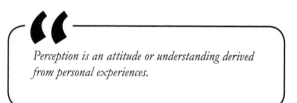

Perception is an attitude or understanding derived from personal experiences.

cant in the process of adolescent culture and development. Examples of adolescent custom complexes are dating (see page 140 for a discussion of the history of dating), prom, and some school sports programs. Every community has a variety of these customary practices, each with its own set of beliefs, values, and rules.

WHY CULTURAL BELIEFS ARE IMPORTANT TO ADOLESCENT DEVELOPMENT

Jeffrey Jensen Arnett, a developmental psychologist at Clark University in Massachusetts, identifies two reasons why cultural beliefs and values are important to the processes of development. First, the processes of socialization are essential components to development. Bronfenbrenner argued that development is, in part, about a "person's evolving conception of the ecological environment and his [or her] relation to it" (Bronfenbrenner 2005). That means development includes the work an adolescent engages in to develop appropriate self-control (self-regulation), understand appropriate cultural roles and one's reaction to those expectations (role preparation), as well as discover what's meaningful and purposeful (sources of meaning), all of which are processes of socialization and all of which involve learning what is valued in a culture. Thus, as Arnett states: "Cultural beliefs form the foundation for every aspect of socialization that takes place in a culture" (2007).

> ### Food for Thought
>
> *How have you noticed adolescents' perception of self and others compare to reality or to what you see as being reality? Consider ways in which your own perception of reality shaped your experiences as an adolescent.*

Second, in part because of the cognitive and emotional growth that takes place during the teenage years, adolescence is a time when knowledge of cultural beliefs "is communicated with special intensity" (Arnett 2007). Together, these two reasons underscore the importance of cultural beliefs and values in the developing adolescent.

BRONFENBRENNER'S ECOLOGICAL MODEL

In his ecological model of human development, Urie Bronfenbrenner proposed that there is both progressive and mutual "accommodation between an active growing human being" and the relating between that growing human being and the various settings in which such human being exists (1979). The interconnected relationship between culture and adolescent development can be described by looking at the different systems of networks or relating. Bronfenbrenner argued that differences in these networks create either cultural environments that promote healthy development or cultural environments that are at greater risk of fostering unhealthy development.

In Bronfenbrenner's model there are four contextual systems (Fig. 2), each offering different aspects of interpersonal relationships, role identity, and sources of meaning.[1]

---

1 Dr. Bronfenbrenner later added a fifth system, the chronosystem, to account for significant environmental events and transitions that influence across the life span. Additionally, following criticisms that his model didn't allow for biological and cognitive influences, Bronfenbrenner added these to his theory, although many argue that his theory still fails to give sufficient attention to those aspects of development.

A HEALTHY ECOLOGICAL ENVIRONMENT

A HIGH RISK ECOLOGICAL ENVIRONMENT

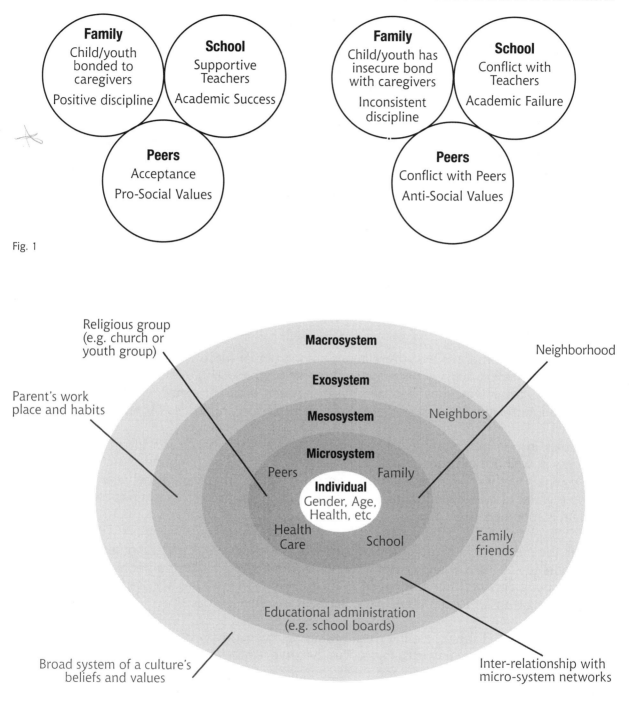

Fig. 1

Fig. 2

Micros

The micro-level of an adolescent's environment consists of her immediate surroundings and involves regular interactions in which the teen is an active agent. This includes the adolescent's usual places of interaction (context) and usual people and relationships (personal networks). For most young people, those particular people and places include family, peers, neighborhood (or a particular locale), school, and religious or church context.

On the chart (Fig. 3), "Health Care" is included in the list of personal networks. Others have also included this as a part of the microsystem network of relationships; and for many adolescents, their immediate context may include regular interaction within the world of health care (physical, mental, or emotional) (Santrock 2005, Arnett 2007). For others, however, this social network may play a minimal role in their immediate microsystem of relating. In addition, the context of the work environment may be a part of some teenagers' close, immediate social reality.

A microsystem is a pattern of activities, roles, and interpersonal relations experienced by the developing person in a given setting with particular physical and material characteristics. —Urie Bronfenbrenner, The Ecology of Human Development

Mesosystem

The mesosystem comprises the interrelations among two or more settings in the microsystem in which the adolescent actively participates (Bronfenbrenner 1979). *Meso,* meaning "in the middle," signifies the interactions that take place between different elements of the microsystem. And these interrelations consist of people, communications, and values (Arnett 2007).

Individuals in one microsystem network may relate to a young person in other microsystem networks as well (for instance, a high school teacher may attend the same church as a student). This system is further comprised of formal and informal communications between networks (for example, parent newsletters from church or school, and informal conversations between friends and family members).

As well, the mesosystem is comprised of each setting's values regarding the other settings. What do parents say about a young person's friends or other peers? What do people at school value about a young person's church connection? In addition, larger values about life that are learned in one setting transfer to and shape what happens in other settings.

As the chart in Fig. 3 shows, the interrelationships in this middle level can be viewed as a web of complex and interconnecting exchanges. This dynamic reinforces the significance of how an adolescent *perceives* his or her world and these complex networks of relationships affect the developmental journey.

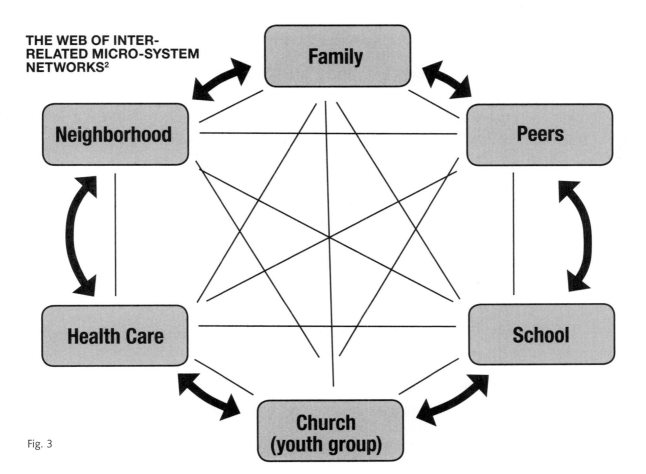

THE WEB OF INTER-RELATED MICRO-SYSTEM NETWORKS[2]

Family

Neighborhood

Peers

Health Care

School

Church (youth group)

Fig. 3

Exosystem

The next level of environmental contexts is the exosystem. *Exo*, meaning "outside," describes settings in which an adolescent doesn't participate regularly. But what happens in those settings has great potential to shape what happens in the micro or meso settings of the adolescent (Bronfenbrenner 1979). As noted in the Ecological Development chart, these settings may include parental workplaces and work habits, parental friend networks, educational administration settings (such as school boards), as well as church leadership (such as elder boards).

So, for example, the adolescent's microsystem settings are influenced when a mom's work requires her to spend several days a week traveling

> ## Mesosystem
>
> *A mesosystem comprises the interrelations among two or more settings in which the developing person actively participates (such as, for a child, the relations among home, school, and neighborhood peer group).*
> —*Urie Bronfenbrenner,* The Ecology of Human Development

2 See Urie Bronfenbrenner, *The Ecology of Human Development: Experiments by Nature and Design,* Cambridge, MA: Harvard University Press, 1979.

or, similarly, when a dad has a flexible work schedule that allows him to attend all of his daughter's track meets.

Macrosystem

This system refers to the way the institutional elements of the other systems (micro, meso, and exo) function consistently because of broader cultural beliefs, values, and patterns of behavior. Bronfenbrenner uses the analogy of a set of blueprints to describe the way this system functions. In any broader society, there are particular ways or expectations for how that society is conducted.

For example, as Bronfenbrenner states: "Within a given society... one crèche (nursery school), school classroom, park playground, café, or post office looks and functions much like another, but they all differ from their counterparts in [other societies]" (1979).

> **"**
> ### Exosystem
> *An exosystem refers to one or more settings that do not involve the developing person as an active participant, but in which events occur that affect, or are affected by, what happens in the setting containing the developing person.*
> —Urie Bronfenbrenner, The Ecology of Human Development

WEB OF RELATIONSHIPS

With his theory Bronfenbrenner sought to highlight the reciprocal notion of adolescent relationships. Behaviors aren't isolated acts but reciprocal transactions with other individuals in the context of a "child's life space" (Brendtro 2006). These ongoing connections and interactions between self and others construct a web of relating that helps a young person understand role expectations (what it means to be a man or woman, husband or wife, father or mother), learn how to conform to societal behavioral expectations, as well as discover meaning and purpose. These connection points are two-way interactions—the young person sends as well as receives. Behavior, then, is a manifestation of these transactions within these immediate circles of influence (Brendtro 2006).

> **"**
> ### Macrosystem
> *The macrosystem refers to consistencies, in the form and content of lower-order systems (micro, meso, and exo) that exist, or could exist, at the level of the subculture or the culture as a whole, along with any belief systems or ideology underlying such consistencies.*
> —Urie Bronfenbrenner, The Ecology of Human Development

In the almost 60 years of Bronfenbrenner's professional life, he observed significant changes in the circles of influence for many adolescents in American society—changes that resulted, in his estimation, in less positive environments for healthy youth development. Toward the end of his career, Bronfenbrenner called for:

Greater involvement by adults in the immediate circles of influence, "rather than...letting peer groups dominate youth development," along with greater involvement of youth in service to the larger community, "rather than having them grow up disengaged from the community without ever making contributions to others" (Brendtro 2006).

IT'S THE SAME, BUT NOT REALLY

One might think the menu at a McDonald's restaurant is universally the same. And there may be many things that carry over from one culture to the next (for example, the big yellow arches, and the red and yellow decor). But with 31,000 restaurants in 118 countries on six continents, great variety can be found—particularly on the menu (McDonald's 2007).

For example, if you visit a McDonald's in Uruguay, you can order a McHuevo. It's similar to a Big Mac, only it's topped with a poached egg. For a different "special sauce," you might order a Koroke Burger in Japan, which includes mashed potatoes and cabbage with a spicy, ketchup-based katsu sauce (Allrecipes.com 2009). The Big Mac in India's McDonald's—the Maharaja Mac—is made of lamb or chicken, while a regular burger in Greece— the Greek Mac—comes wrapped in pita bread. If you don't care for fries with your burger, perhaps you might enjoy Gallo Pinto (rice and beans) as a side dish, which is offered at McDonald's in Costa Rica (Adams 2007).

International travelers can count on some familiarity with the McDonald's menu; however, each culture has influenced and shaped its own particular menu. Tourists from the United States may be in for a shock when they enter a McDonald's in another country and expect the same experience as home.

REFLECTION ACTIVITY (5 TO 10 MINUTES)

The macrosystem refers to broader cultural values that shape a person's more immediate contexts (for example, the menu at McDonald's restaurants around the globe). Consider some of the everyday places of the adolescent. Now identify places and ways those places are shaped by larger macrosystem consistencies.

DIGGING DEEPER (10 TO 15 MINUTES)

This chapter identified examples of adolescent *custom complexes*, such as the prom and dating. Choose one of those youth practices or select one from your own experience. Describe the particular practice as you've observed it and summarize the "beliefs, values, sanctions, rules, motives, and satisfactions associated with it."

- An ecological model of human development integrates human ecology (the study of the relationships between individuals and their environments) and developmental psychology (the study of how human beings change over their life span) to understand the influences between adolescent development and adolescent culture.

- Bronfenbrenner's ecological model of development consists of four cultural contexts:

1. Microsystem: One's immediate environment, involving those regular and daily interactions in which the teen is an active agent.

2. Mesosystem: The interrelations among two or more microsystem settings in which the adolescent actively participates.

3. Exosystem: Settings in which an adolescent doesn't participate regularly. But what happens in those settings has great potential to shape what happens in the micro or meso settings of the adolescent.

4. Macrosystem: The way the institutional elements of the other systems (micro, meso, and exo) function consistently because of broader cultural beliefs, values, and patterns of behavior.

CHAPTER 11
The Cultures of Adolescent Relationships

LEARNING OBJECTIVES

When you've finished this chapter, you should be able to:

1. Discuss how family culture shapes the culture of peer relationships

2. Explain the different kinds of relationships in adolescent peer culture

3. Articulate ways that online relating influences peer friendships

4. Summarize the cultural changes regarding dating practices, including how romantic relationships shape adolescent developmental processes

It seems as if Jodi's always in touch with her group of friends. No matter what we're doing with her, her mind is with Leslie, Lindsay, and Sarah. If I'm driving her to soccer practice, she's texting. If we're trying to eat dinner together, I can count on having a fight with her about turning off her phone. Most of the time she's up in her room tex-ting, IMing, or visiting with her friends in some way. It seems like the four of them are attached at the hip. —Mom of a 14-year-old

I do everything with my two best friends, Jake and Shawn. We have most of our classes together at school, and we're all on the JV basketball team. When we aren't at practices or games, we just hang out together, either playing video games at the mall or watching TV, mostly at Shawn's house. —Josh, 15

Mostly I spend time with Luke, sometimes Allyson and Tracy, but mostly just Luke. There used to be a whole bunch of us from youth group that hung out together, but I don't have time to do that anymore. If I spend time with everybody else, I don't have time for just Luke and me, so..." —Emmie, 18

THE CULTURE OF ADOLESCENT PEER RELATIONSHIPS

As noted in the previous chapter, adolescence is a time of socialization—a significant time for learning the appropriate skills, values, and beliefs for functioning successfully in one's society. Culture is at the heart of socialization, which is the process of learning the norms of a culture—becoming *enculturated* into a society.

Because of the changes that occur during puberty, young people are ripe for learning the rules, norms, and standards being communicated through their interactions with family, friends, and communities. The pubertal and maturation changes in adolescence lead to a greater awareness of self and others, which in turn leads to a greater understanding of the values and beliefs of the groups within which young people interact.

In this chapter, we explore the changing dynamics of relationships during adolescence, focusing particularly on the changes in family and friend networks and how those cultural contexts influence how young people understand themselves.

FAMILY INFLUENCE ON THE CULTURE OF PEER RELATIONSHIPS

Long before a young person begins the transition from childhood to adulthood, the adolescent has had a long experience in the culture of his or her family. The developmental changes, along with the web of relationships in an adolescent's world, lead to transitions in the ways a young person relates within the family context. These transitions set the stage for less hierarchical relationships between parents and teens. This section briefly summarizes the culture of the family system, highlighting three dynamics that influence and shape an adolescent's network of relationships.

Standards, Norms, and Values

As an early adolescent becomes more aware of self and increasingly drawn to more intimate relationships with friends, he or she will bring to this new world the standards, norms, and values of the family. At the age of 11 or 12, she will already have working knowledge of what her family considers right and wrong. This set of values will include standards and norms for what it means to be independent. Has her family encouraged her to think for herself, or have they taught her to value being close with her family?

A young sixth grader will, often without much awareness, know what his family expects of him regarding achievement. Do they have high standards for him in school or in sports, or do they give him greater freedom to figure out on his own what's important? A person in this early stage of adolescence will also have a good idea about his or her parents' religious beliefs and how important it is to follow them in that regard.

Since birth, these young people have been learning the values and beliefs—the standards—of their culture. And for most, these cultural standards are their family norms, which have been shaping their ideas about who they are.

Young adolescents don't come to adolescent friendships or other relationship networks with a blank slate. They've been shaped by parents and family dynamics in a variety of ways that will, in turn, shape their world and identity. Parental impact is far-reaching, providing a framework for how a young person envisions relationships as a friend and romantic partner, to how one relates to teachers, coaches, and other adults. As Nancy Cobb (2004) states, "The sense of self that develops within the family prepares adolescents for friendships outside it" (see also Brown and Larson 2009).

Support

For most children, mothers and fathers are the first people they turn to when they're hurt or need support. Throughout a person's childhood, the child and his parents develop ways of relating and levels of expectations regarding the kinds of support that should be offered and can be counted on. Studies indicate that in homes where interactions communicate support, affection, and encouragement, young people show greater measures of self-esteem (Cobb 2004). During the transition from childhood to adulthood, young people shift from primarily looking to parents for support to seeking support in friendships outside the family network.

A study by Wyndol Furman and Duane Buhrmester (1992) found that for fourth graders, parents were the primary source of support. By the seventh grade, same-gender peer friendships were equal to parents in terms of being a source of support. And by tenth grade, same-gender friends had surpassed parents in being the primary source of support. Again, as we consider these transitions, it's important to bear in mind the interaction and connection between these immediate networks of relationships. As young people increasingly turn to peer friendships for support, there can be increased conflict between parents and teens as they navigate these transitions.

AN INDEPENDENT OR INTERDEPENDENT SELF

Societies place differing values on independence and connectedness, and these societal values influence the significance that families, and ultimately, young people, give to independence or personal autonomy within and outside the family context. Some cultures place a greater value on a collectivist spirit, that is, a commitment to support and nurture others (for example, family, community, the larger society) than to personal autonomy and independence.

American society values independence, highlighting its personal freedoms and achievements. Many Asian, African, and Latin American cultures, on the other hand, place a higher value on young people staying connected to their families and contributing to the support, encouragement, and well-being of the family as a whole. And oftentimes the responsibility to be interdependent is reciprocal: The young person commits to support and nurture parents and siblings, while the parents and broader family commit to provide mutual support and nurture to the young person.

In American society, families have a variety of expectations regarding independence. And conflict within the family network can result from the parent-adolescent relationship as the teenager negotiates between independence and interdependence (Arnett 2007, Cobb 2004).

Food for Thought

Families often have expectations for how their young person participates in church and youth group activities. How might these expectations cause conflict between parents and youth? How about between parents, youth, and youth leaders?

Closeness and Intimacy

The closeness between parents and teens diminishes during adolescence. But this diminished closeness is more about an adolescent's need for more personal space and privacy and fewer expressions of physical affection than it is a decrease in love and respect for the parents (Laursen and Collins 2009). There is additional research that indicates that distancing, particularly in the early years of adolescence, is a short-term change and that by the end of high school there is a return toward greater levels of intimacy and closeness (Steinberg 2005).

A study by Kenneth Rice and Patricia Mulkeen (1995) showed that high school seniors indicated having a greater level of intimacy with their parents than adolescents in eighth grade did. An adolescent's increased capability at engaging in close, intimate relationships from eighth to twelfth grade may encourage a closer connection with parents. Yet even as many adolescents report greater intimacy in their mid- to late-adolescent years, the overall "level of warmth and closeness between parents and adolescents declines" as young people increasingly move from the social world of their parents toward other relationship contexts outside the family network (Arnett 2007).

There is also a dramatic drop in the amount of time adolescents spent with their parents that influences perceptions of closeness. Studies have shown

CLOSENESS IS WHAT WE SAY IT IS

One of my assignments for first-year youth ministry students, typically 18-to-19-year-olds, is to sketch out their family systems. Students draw their family trees and then highlight the connections, conflicts, values, and expectations that exist within them. Each student then meets with me individually to discuss what she's learning about her own family microsystem and how that system may shape her in her future vocation as a youth worker.

One of the aspects of the family system that we discuss is closeness. Hardly ever does a student say that her family isn't very close. To the contrary, one of the first comments a student almost always makes is that her family is *very* close. When asked to describe what that closeness means, students give a variety of responses:

"My family and I do everything together."

"I know I can always count on them to be there for me if I need them."

"We can talk about everything. I never make a big decision without talking to my mom and dad first."

Family members learn what it means to have a meaningful relationship within the context of their own family system. Therefore, young people often perceive closeness based on what they've learned is meaningful. For example, if spending lots of time together is perceived as closeness in one particular family, then family members will perceive diminished levels of closeness if an adolescent begins spending less time with family and more time with people outside the family context.

Food for Thought

"Closeness" means different things to different people. What does closeness mean to you? How might your expectations about closeness affect your significant relationships or your relationships with youth?

that between fifth and ninth grades, the percentage of time spent with family decreases by about 50 percent, declining even more steeply between ninth and twelfth grades (Larson, Moneta, et al. 2002). For young males, time with parents is often replaced with time alone; for young females, time with parents is replaced with time alone and time with friends (Steinberg 2005). As Brown and Larson note, however, just because peers grow in significance and teens spend greater amounts of time with their peers doesn't automatically imply that parental significance diminishes in absolute terms (2009).

In this section, we've repeatedly addressed the issue of conflict between parents and adolescents. A general perception is that there is a significant increase in conflict between parents and teens and that it's unavoidable. While that may be the case in some families, research indicates there is typically only a slight increase in the amount of conflict—particularly in early adolescence.

For many families, though, rates of conflict aren't much higher than during the childhood years. And rather than large-scale conflicts, it's more likely to come about over daily incidental issues, such as cleaning their rooms and taking care of other chores (Steinberg 2005). Laursen and Collins note that the perception of conflict may increase as a young person matures, even as the rates of actual conflict diminish, "leaving families with the perception of worsening discord" (2009).

Mesosystem Dynamics: How the Family Network Shapes the Peer Network

Adolescents don't transition into adolescent peer relationships with a blank slate. They bring with them all of what they've learned from their families about cultural standards, norms, and values. Additionally, they bring many expectations about what it means to be in a close relationship with another person. These understandings learned in the family context shape the developing adolescent's peer networks in significant ways.

Briefly, there are three ways that family contexts shape friendship contexts. First, the strength of the parent-child relationship shapes the strength of adolescent friendships. Young people who have a strong, secure attachment with their parents typically form strong, secure attachments with friends (Ducharme, et al. 2002, Furman, et al. 2002, Santrock 2005, Brown and Larson 2009). And the opposite also holds true. Young people with unsecure attachments with their parents typically have unsecure attachments with friends (Allen, et al. 2003). Furthermore, "the more adolescents are able to trust and confide in their parents, the more likely they are to describe [those] same qualities in their relationships with their friends" (Arnett 2007). (See also Blain, Thompson, and Whiffen 1993, Raja, McGee, and Stanton 1992.)

Additionally, Brown and Larson (2009) note that parents directly influence peer friendships through the monitoring of an adolescent's activities. Establishing and monitoring curfews and setting guidelines concerning what social activities a teen may participate in are ways that parents condition the influence of peer relationships. Further, parents may exert influence through engineering or curtailing friendships, as well as providing advice and counsel about friendships.

A third way that families shape friendship contexts is more indirect. While families may have a less direct influence on friend selection during the adolescent years than during childhood, there are still a couple of ways that families can apply indirect influence. Generally, parents make the decisions regarding where to live, where to send adolescents to school, and the religious affiliation of the family, thereby limiting the pool of friend possibilities (Cooper and Ayers-Lopez 1985).

Additionally, the family has been the primary source of meaning. Whether families have placed an emphasis on athletics, academics, the arts, camping and outdoor adventures, or political, economic, and social values, young people carry those meanings with them into the world of their peers. "Like seeks like"; and since young people carry those family norms noted above, they often seek out peers who look like them, sharing a similar race or ethnicity, achievement values, risk behavior norms and beliefs, and even religious, political, and economic beliefs (Arnett 2007, Brown and Larson 2009, Cobb 2004, Steinberg 2005).

Again, noting the nature of adolescent cultural contexts, the influence of peers and parents on an adolescent's friendships is reciprocal. Peer friends may also exert influence on the family context by affirming or undermining parental authority, shaping parental behaviors, as well as serving as sources of encouragement (positive and negative) for changing the nature of the parent-adolescent relationship (Brown and Larson 2009).

THE CULTURE OF PEERS IN THE ADOLESCENT WORLD

Adolescence in the Westernized, particularly American, context covers a wide span of a person's life. The average individual will spend about 10 to 15 years as an adolescent. As has already been noted, there are many developmental changes taking place during this span of time. All that means is that the world of an early adolescent (roughly ages 11 to 15) is very different from the world of a late adolescent (roughly ages 19 to 25).

There are, however, some general aspects that have been identified relative to adolescent friendships. As we begin to explore these aspects, it's helpful to begin by defining what is meant by *peer* and *friend*. A *peer* is someone who has a similar status: Age, social class, and location. So, for example, the entire enrollment of students at a particular middle school would most likely be peers to each other, but they wouldn't all be friends. On the other hand, a *friend*, though certainly a peer, would be different because of the relational dynamics. A friendship signifies a dynamic interrelating, greater intimacy, trust, and mutuality between peers, and it would necessarily include engaging in close interaction (Arnett 2007).

During the early adolescent years, a young person learns the culture of peers, beginning with developing affiliation and belonging in a *group* context before moving on to deeper friend relationships. Certainly most early adolescents will have peer friendships, but gaining acceptance in the larger peer culture helps to facilitate more quality peer friendships later on.

At all ages, friendship is about developing *social competency*. But again, because of the developmental processes taking place during adolescence, there is greater significance for social competence. As Santrock notes, social competence includes, "prosocial behaviors, such as sharing, being cooperative and being trustworthy." These kinds of behaviors "are related to peer acceptance, as is knowing which strategies are appropriate for making friends and which ones aren't" (2005). In particular, social competency for an adolescent involves the bidirectional negotiation of friendships with peers and includes feedback, mutuality, and self-disclosure.

Feedback and Mutuality

As Newman and Newman have noted (2001), adolescents experience a greater need for connection and belonging with peers. This need is related to the psychosocial task of forming a group identity, an essential developmental task in early adolescence that prepares a young person for developing a cohesive personal identity. As young people reach out to other young people, they receive vital *feedback* that helps them navigate and sort through appropriate ways of relating. Peers serve as important sources of information concerning what is normative behavior.

Though adolescents come to this context with preconceived understandings of normative behavior based on family relationships, they try out these norms and receive reactions, both negative and positive, that help them make sense of appropriate and acceptable behaviors within the world of their peers. They're also giving response and reaction; there is *mutuality*. The process of feedback is very fluid and helps young people sort through who they are, where they fit, and who they fit with, preparing them for social relationships as adults (Cobb 2004; Pakaslahti, et al. 2002).

As noted earlier, adolescence is also a time in which self-regulation and self-control develops. Again, feedback within friend peer networks assists young people in understanding appropriate kinds of regulation and control (Arnett 2007).

Self-Disclosure

During adolescence, young people learn and develop an awareness of appropriate disclosure of personal information. As they become more adept at close friendship relating, they also learn when, where, how, and with whom to share their worries, fears, secrets, and embarrassing experiences. Studies indicate that adolescents, in general, report greater quality in the level of intimate relationships, including mutual self-disclosure. Young men typically report greater qualities of mutual self-disclosure with best friends, while young women typically report self-disclosure across their friend networks (Brown and Larson 2009).

Duane Buhrmester and Karen Prager (1995) identified five ways in which peer relationships encourage intimate self-disclosure. Through the context of peer friendships, adolescents can receive social validation, gain social control, clarify a sense of self, exercise self-expression, and enhance relationship development. It's in the positive feedback of these five aspects of peer friendships that self-disclosure is affirmed or, in negative instances, undermined.

Adolescent peer relationships further teach young people the basic aspects of friend relationships. As noted above, it's important for teens to navigate through connection in the larger peer context before exploring close friendships. "Only when issues related to affiliation and belonging have been resolved will they be ready...to engage in addressing issues of individual identity" and develop close personal friendships (Cobb 2004).

Later in this section we'll explore large group *friendships*. At this point, however, the emphasis is on the much larger *peer* context. As young people develop skills in abstract thinking, they're increasing their abilities to not only understand their thoughts and emotions, but also communicate them. This greater awareness fosters exploration of trust, intimacy, and self-disclosure. As adolescents begin to develop these personal attributes, feedback from peers leads to a greater awareness of self, which acts as impetus for forming friendships within their group of peers (Arnett 2007, Santrock 2005).

Gender Differences in Peer Friendships

Young women and men explore similar aspects of socialization and how friendships function. However, in our broader American social context, men and women explore aspects of peer relationships differently. There are pubertal dynamics that shape and influence these aspects of socialization (for example, women typically begin puberty earlier than men do). There are also ways that young women and men are socialized inside and outside the context of peers.

Typically, young men report closeness relative to having a friend to do something with, while young women report closeness relative to self-disclosure of feelings and emotions (Rice and Mulkeen 1995). Young men are often discouraged from showing their painful emotions and talking about their feelings, while young women are encouraged in that regard (Oransky and Marecek 2009). Young men tend to maintain their friendships longer than young women do, although young women typically rate their friendships more positively, seeing them as stronger, more supportive,

"Why do you want to do all of those 'boy things'?" —A comment by a young adult woman to a 12-year-old female after the adolescent shared about her passion for soccer and her desire to become a mechanical engineer so she could build cars.

"Come on now. It's just a little cut. Get up and go play. You can't let a little thing like that hold you back. You don't want others to see you crying, do you?" —Comment to a crying four-year-old boy

"Oh, come here and let me see. It's okay; it's only a small cut. It's going to be all right." —Comment to a crying four-year-old girl

(Both comments were overheard at a park playground within a span of five minutes.)

"If you live alone, who makes all the decisions? There's no man in your house." —A comment made by a five-year-old girl to a single female neighbor

Every culture develops different expectations regarding the appropriate ways for women and men to act in a wide array of customary practices, such as dating relationships, childrearing, vocations, as well as marriage and spousal practices. Through personal experience, observation, and imitation, children are conditioned regarding the expected behaviors for women and men in a society. Called *gender roles*, these expectations comprise the cultural guidelines that prescribe how males and females should think, act, and feel (Santrock 2005).

Interactions, particularly in the micro and meso contexts of adolescent relating, are powerful influences on gender attitudes and behaviors. Within these contexts especially, young people negotiate an understanding of their own identity while navigating experiences regarding gender, encountering culturally prescribed roles, and deciding whether to accept or reject them. Beyond the micro and meso contexts, other cultural influences, particularly the media, communicate influential messages regarding gender expectations. Nancy Cobb (2004) has noted that traditional roles for masculine gender and feminine gender are quite different from each other and are typically exclusive, meaning that cultural expectations assume that one individual cannot portray both masculine and feminine traits.

Traditional Societal Expectations[3]

Masculine Gender Roles	Feminine Gender Roles
Self-reliance	Sensitive to other's feelings
Self-sufficient	Affectionate
Able to defend their beliefs	Understanding
Make decisions	Warm
Take a stand	Patient
Be leaders	Tender
Risk takers	In touch with emotions
Assertive	Passive
Dominant	Childlike
Aggressive	Dependent

Scripture provides many guidelines for appropriate behavior for Christ's disciples (many of which are noted in the chart above), although they aren't strictly designated as being solely for men or women. Christians are called to be leaders, as well as being patient, kind, and gentle. The passage in Galatians 5 denotes characteristics that are evidence of the transforming work of the Spirit, behaviors that transcend cultural expectations.[4] In Jesus we see a truly human being, capable of being strong and soft, compassionate and firm, and exhibiting the full range of positive social behaviors in multiple ways.

> " *But the fruit of the Spirit is love, joy, peace, patience, kindness, goodness, faithfulness, gentleness and self-control.*
> —Galatians 5:22-23

3 Adapted from Nancy J. Cobb, *Adolescence: Continuity, Change, and Diversity*, New York: McGraw-Hill, 2004, 5th edition.
4 On one occasion I heard a speaker tell a group of 125 to 150 senior high youth that the characteristics described in Galatians 5 were feminine characteristics and certainly not what God intended for Christian men. Fortunately, that teaching does not predominate.

and more rewarding than young men do (Thomas and Daubman 2001; Brendgen, et al. 2001; Engels, et al. 2002).

How Peer Relationships Change from Preadolescence to Adolescence

"American society is very age segregated"; school friendships, extracurricular activities, and church groups are all "structured in a way that groups people together by age" (Steinberg 2005). This dynamic of age segregation, along with other changes during adolescence, serves to foster an adolescent culture that is predominated by peer and friend relationships. For most, the sheer number of friends dramatically increases during early adolescence (Cobb 2004, Steinberg 2005).

> The number of friends increases in adolescence, especially for girls. The percentage of these friends whom mothers know (40%) remains about the same as in childhood; however, because the circle of friends widens in adolescence, the actual number of friends whom mothers *do not* know increases substantially. (Cobb 2004) (*emphasis added*)

Peer friendships increase not only in quantity, but also quality—particularly over the span of adolescence. Peer friendships become more meaningful. And as adolescents mature, the friendships become more complex as well (Brown and Larson 2009).

Another significant change in the cultural context for American youth is the amount of time that adolescent peers spend with each other. In earlier times (and still today in other cultures), adolescents spent time with people across a wide age range from extended family settings to work and apprentice settings to larger multigenerational social settings (Larson and Verma 1999, Steinberg 2005).

Not only is there typically a significant increase in the amount of time young people spend with same-aged peers, but there's also a corresponding decrease in the amount of time spent with adults (Steinberg 2005). Until 1930, attending high school was a luxury and adolescents were generally working or at home, thereby spending greater amounts of time with other adults and young people of different ages.

For most American teens today, those settings are limited. Instead, young people spend huge chunks of time in large school settings in which interactions are limited to people their own age and a few adults. The dynamics of large high schools and middle schools often restrict the quality and quantity of adult interactions with young people (Steinberg 2005). One study showed that by sixth grade, only 25 percent of a young person's significant other social network includes adults. For many, the figure is only 10 percent, and it typically decreases as they transition to high school (Brown 1990).

Part of the reason for the decrease in time spent interacting with adults is the increase in time spent with peers without adult supervision. Young people spend greater amounts of time in peer-related activities at school, at home, and in leisure pursuits in which few or no adults participate (Brown 1990). It is this research indicating far less contact with adults in the adolescent years than during childhood that sparked Bronfenbrenner to argue for greater involvement by adults in the life space of adolescents (Brendtro 2006).

As an adolescent matures and gains greater skills in intimacy, trust, mutuality, and self-disclosure, the peer network will broaden to include greater numbers of opposite-gender peer relationships (Steinberg 2005). From here we will move on to a discussion of peer friendships, examining how the culture of friendships influences a young person's well-being, particularly looking at the dynamics between the two predominant contexts for peer relationships: Cliques and crowds.

THE CULTURE OF CLOSE PEER GROUPS: CLIQUES AND CROWDS AND ADOLESCENT WELL-BEING

Adolescent Well-Being

As noted above, not only do teenagers spend less time with adults and more time with their peers, but the quality of the relationships with peers also deepens. Young people depend more on their peers for companionship and intimacy (Furman and Buhrmester 1992, Arnett 2007). Friendships in adolescent culture function in ways beyond simply being playmates.

John Santrock (2005), citing the work of other researchers, identifies six categories of adolescent-friendship functioning:

1. **Companionship.** Adolescents seek to find partners with whom they share similar interests and activities. Increased time in a peer-dominated context means an increased reliance on peers as social companions—someone to eat lunch with, sit on the bus with, go to the mall with, and so on.

2. **Stimulation.** Young people look to friends for excitement, amusement, and to discover interesting information about their world.

3. **Physical Support.** Increasingly, young people turn to their friends for resources and assistance, looking for help with homework, lending each other money, and so on.

4. **Ego Support.** In addition to physical support, young people look to their friends for emotional support and encouragement. They provide consolation, help them cope during stressful life events, and encourage them to greater achievement. Peers also become a strong source of support in problem solving regarding other friends, romantic relationships, parents, or school situations.

5. Social Comparison. Closely related to ego support is social comparison, in which young people look to friends to give them feedback on relations with others—from parents to teachers and peers.

6. Intimacy and Affection. Friend relationships function to provide young people with warm, close, trusting relationships that include self-disclosure.

The quality of peer friendships shapes and influences the well-being of youth during adolescence and even into adulthood. The more positive a young person perceives his or her peer friendships to be, the greater the quality of the friendships and the more positive his or her self-concept will be (Cobb 2004).

Friends' influence, sometimes referred to as "peer pressure," is stronger in early adolescence, peaks in mid-adolescence, and declines in late adolescence (Berndt 1996). Typically, there are three ways in which friends can exert influence on the thoughts and behaviors of their peers.

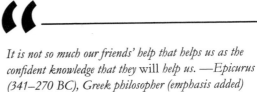

It is not so much our friends' help that helps us as the confident knowledge that they will *help us. —Epicurus (341–270 BC), Greek philosopher (emphasis added)*

First, friends frequently attempt to bring about certain attitudes or behaviors within the close friend network. There is interesting data relative to this kind of influence that shows both positive and negative influences in supportive friendships. Research has shown in a number of studies that young people with strong supportive friendships sometimes decrease their risky behavior (for example, low academic achievement, drug or alcohol abuse, and so on), but sometimes they increase it (Laird, et al. 2005, Arnett 2007). Some longitudinal studies suggest that friends are similar in risk behavior before they become friends (remember, "like seeks like"). "But if they stay friends, they tend to become even more similar, increasing or decreasing their rates of participation in risk behavior so that they more closely match one another" (Arnett 2007).

To like and dislike the same things, that is indeed true friendship. —Sallust (86–34 BC), Roman historian

A second way that friends exert influence on their peers is through the modeling of desirable behavior. Friends observe particular ways of acting in their friends or other peers and aspire to imitate them.

Third, friends and other peers exert influence through antagonistic methods—that is, through teasing, ridicule, or bullying. This form of influence can range from relatively harmless joking and cajoling someone to do something (and might even encourage pro-social behaviors) to negative and harmful forms of physical and verbal abuse.

The culture of peer relationships fosters an environment in which peer influence is reciprocal and may be unintentional (Brown 1990, Brown and Larson 2009). The perception of young people is significant. Therefore, peer influence isn't automatic, but it's contingent upon how open a young person is to being influenced. As Mitchell Prinstein and Kenneth Dodge (2008) have noted, young people who are uncertain in their self-concept are more likely to conform to another's influence. Additionally, a young person's perception of the one who's exerting influence impacts how the pressure is received. Adolescents accorded power and prestige typically have greater influence.

> ## Food for Thought
>
> *Teasing, joking, and ridiculing others is often a part of youth ministry relationships among youth, as well as between youth leaders and their students. How appropriate is this? Are there positive motivations for this kind of influence?*

Cliques

Cliques are small groups of friends, typically composed of three to eight people. An aspect of clique culture is the *perception* that all members feel they know each other well and think of themselves as a cohesive group. The clique is the "main social context in which adolescents *interact* 'with each other'" (Steinberg 2005, Feldman and Elliott 1990). This context is where most teens hang out, talk to one another, form close friendships, and get to know and be known by their peers. Generally a young person will express that she knows these friends better than others outside this small group context and, just as important, they know her better than other peers do (Brown and Larson 2009).

The most important influence on the composition of cliques is similarity. Cliques generally consist of youth who are the same age, race and ethnic background, and gender (at least this is true during early adolescence). They also share similar values and find meaning in similar activities (Arnett 2007, Brown 1990). Within cliques, one can observe a group of people who dress alike, listen to the same music, engage in similar types of leisure pursuits, and share similar patterns of drug use, as well as other life values regarding meaning and purpose (Brown and Larson 2009). Typically, norms and standards develop within the context of the clique (Feldman and Elliott 1990).

> *Tell me what company thou keepest, and I'll tell thee what thou art.* —Miguel de Cervantes (1547–1616), Spanish novelist

Close peer groups are essential in aiding healthy psychosocial development (Arnett 2007). There are three ways, in particular. First, experience within a clique provides a context for the development and expression of autonomy. As a young person moves away from the close authority and control of family and parents, friendship groups provide a "context for adolescents to test out decision-making skills in an arena where there are no adults present to monitor and control their choices" (Steinberg 2005).

The clique also plays a significant role in the development and understanding of intimacy. The peer group is the primary place in which young people develop a sense of trust, learn mutuality, and practice self-disclosure. The peer group is influential in the norms and understanding of what is appropriate in this regard. In addition, the peer group is typically where young people are socialized in understanding appropriate sexual behavior (Santrock 2005, Steinberg 2005).

However, as a young person matures and develops, the peer group may lose significance. In one study 75 percent of seventh graders were members of a clique, with a dramatic decline indicated for older teens. Even in the early adolescent years, not all teens will belong to a clique.

Researchers have identified two other designations regarding peer relating. *Liaisons* are youth who develop healthy relating with teens in more than one context, while not belonging to a clique themselves. *Isolates* are teens who seemingly don't have healthy relating patterns with any clique or peer group. More young men than young women are isolates, and more young women than young men become part of a clique network of peers (Steinberg 2005, Cobb 2004).

Crowds

Crowds are large groups of students, generally around 20 youth, based on similar stereotypes. As Arnett notes, crowds are "a particular cultural phenomenon of societies with large schools where students spend significant time with peers" (2007). Within the United States and Canada, for example, groups are identified with names such as "jocks," "druggies," "Goths," and so on. These perceptions and labels are typically imposed from the outside and reflect the image placed upon the group from other groups of peers (Feldman and Elliott 1990, Steinberg 2005).

Laurence Steinberg (2005) and others argue that crowds serve three broad purposes: (1) They situate students within the much larger cultural context of the school, (2) they guide students into affiliation with some peers and away from others, and (3) they provide places that affirm some groups and disparage others (Brown and Larson 2009).

The culture of the crowd context differs from the culture of the clique context in a number of ways. First, there typically isn't the same level of intimacy and self-disclosure within a crowd context. While there may be a level of familiarity, often based on shared common features like ethnicity, neighborhood, or a shared interest, teens don't feel as if they know each other well (Cobb 2004, Brown and Larson 2009).

A second contrast is that crowds tend to be environments that allow youth to try out new social skills and ideas regarding self-definition (Cobb 2004, Newman and Newman 2001). In the crowd context, a young person can lean pro-social behaviors, such as being a good friend, effective communication, or how to be a leader. As Cobb characterizes this distinction, clique activities serve as coaching sessions; crowd events are the game itself (Cobb 2004).

As with cliques, the culture of crowds changes during adolescence. While most young people are associated with at least one crowd, crowd identity is more differentiated in early adolescence and there is less movement between crowds. As teens mature and develop a more cohesive self-concept, crowds become less significant, more permeable, and less hierarchical (Steinberg 2005, Cobb 2004, Brown 1990).

MEDIA IN THE CULTURE OF ADOLESCENCE

In the years since Urie Bronfenbrenner first proposed his ecological model of human development in the 1970s, the amount of time adolescents spend with media has increased dramatically, along with the number of available media and electronic options. As youth workers conceptualize the immediate and personal contexts of teen relationships, there is a need to broaden our understanding of these relationships to include the influence of technology and how it shapes adolescent lives.

This next section briefly examines the role of media and technology in the lives of adolescents, specifically highlighting the role of the online world of adolescents and its significance for adolescent relationships. This isn't a comprehensive examination by any means, but a cursory sketch identifying positive and negative influences of this aspect of youth culture.

Media Use and Exposure

At the risk of stating the obvious, if young people are awake, they're most likely using some form of media and technology: Television, computer, cell phone, and the list continues. The data suggests that:

- The use of technology and multitasking increases during the adolescent years.

- Two-thirds of teens ages 12 to 17 have their own cell phones.

- The use of all screen media (television, video games, movies, and so on) declines with age.

- Throughout adolescence television dominates other screen media.

- Just over half of all teens, ages 12 to 17, have at least one profile on a social networking site such as MySpace and Facebook. (Roberts, Henriksen, and Foehr 2009, Valkenburg and Peter 2007)

Youth (and children) have become adept at using multiple forms of media simultaneously, also known as "multitasking." This capability makes it more difficult to analyze the influence and time spent using media. However, distinguishing between media *exposure* (the estimated amount of time spent with a particular media) and media *use* (the overall time using all forms of media) offers a clearer picture of media's influence.

Studies using these distinctions note that young people typically spend about one-quarter of the time using media multitasking. So a young person may watch a television sitcom while texting his friends and completing his homework on the computer. Allowing for multitasking, young people still spend around six hours engaged in media use each day (Roberts, Henriksen, and Foehr 2009).

The chart below provides a picture of the kinds of media use and the amount of time spent in each.

Average Daily Media Exposure[5]

	8-10 years	11-14 years	15-18 years
Television	3:17	3:16	2:36
Videos/Movies/DVDs	1:24	1:09	1:05
Audio (radio, CDs)	:59	1:42	2:24
Print Media	:44	:41	:45
Video Games	1:05	:52	:33
Computer	:37	1:02	1:22
Total Media Exposure	8:05	8:41	8:44
Total Media Use	5:52	6:33	6:31

THE ONLINE CULTURE OF ADOLESCENCE

It will come as no surprise to say that the Internet and electronic communication has become an integral part of youth culture. From homework assignments to texting with friends, to youth group Bible studies, to maintaining contact with parents, young people are online a significant part of every day. Researchers at Pew Internet Research, in a survey conducted in 2001, found that 17 million (or roughly 75 percent) of youth ages 12 to 17 regularly use the Internet (Lenhart, Lewis, and Rainie, Overview 2001). A subsequent study by Pew found that the number had grown to 87 percent by 2007 (Pew Research Center 2005).

In the 2001 survey, Pew found that 48 percent of young people said the use of the Internet improves their relationships with their friends, while 32 percent said the Internet helps them make new friends (Lenhart, Lewis, and Rainie, Teenage Life 2001).[6] A more recent study indicates that of those who use online communication to stay in touch with friends, 80 percent said they do so to keep in touch with friends they infrequently see, while 91 percent do so to keep in touch with friends they frequently see (Roberts, Henriksen, and Foehr 2009).

---

5 Adapted from Roberts, Henriksen and Foehr, 2009.
6 Their research also indicated that 64 percent of online teens said they believe the Internet takes them away from spending time with their families.

For most adults, the Internet is perceived as a negative aspect of youth culture, one that puts them at peril for negative relationships. But is that perception reality? This section looks at research on the online culture of teens and explores how the Internet shapes and influences adolescent relationships. First, a brief review of the literature as it relates to the use and function of the Internet as a means of communication by adolescents. Second, a consideration of the significance of key aspects of this data. And finally, a discussion of what this means for youth work, specifically the use of social networking sites as an aspect of ministry practice.

Review of the Research

In an article published in 2009, Valkenburg and Peter reviewed the breadth of research focusing on "the uses, functions, and consequences of online communication technologies." They identified three categories of research. One set of data focused on the use of online communication technology. The prevailing view of this research indicated that email and instant messaging (IM) was primarily used for maintaining *existing* social relationships.

A second set of data looked at differences between online and offline relationships. This category of research showed that online friendships were generally perceived as lower quality than offline friendships. But if the online friendship lasted for more than a year, the quality increased, becoming comparable to offline friendships. Additionally, this research showed that youth who had many offline friends found it easier to make friends online (Valkenburg and Peter 2009).

A third category of research examined the consequences of different types of Internet use on the quantity or quality of existing friendships. The studies in this category showed mixed results—some showed negative effects, while some showed minimal or no effects. As Valkenburg and Peter (2009) noted, the great majority showed positive effects on both quantity and quality of existing friendships.

Overall, the research seems to indicate that the Internet is frequently used as a means for facilitating and maintaining adolescent friendships. Further, the Internet influences both the quantity and quality of adolescent social relationships.

USES, FUNCTIONS, AND CONSEQUENCES OF ONLINE COMMUNICATION TECHNOLOGIES

This next section explores three hypotheses evaluated in research and their implications for adolescent social relationships.

The Reduction Hypothesis

Early research on online communication proposed the idea that the use of the Internet was "associated with subsequent reduction in family communication, declines in the size of social relationship networks, and increases in loneliness" (Blais, et al. 2008). This *reduction hypothesis* proposed that the Internet allowed for young people to communicate with strangers, to develop shallow and superficial relationships, and that the time spent in those relationships decreased the amount of time spent in more beneficial and rewarding relationships. Early research supported this hypothesis, showing that online communication impeded further development in preexisting offline adolescent relationships (Gross 2004). However, as Blais, et al. (2008) and Valkenburg and Peter (2009) have since shown, "[As] the Internet became more familiar to adolescents, later studies began to refute the early findings supporting the reduction hypothesis." (See also Valkenburg and Peter, "Preadolescents' and Adolescents' Online Communication and Their Closeness to Friends" 2007.)

Stimulation Hypothesis

More recent research has led to the development of the *stimulation hypothesis*, which proposes that use of the Internet may actually stimulate relationship formation with strangers *and* also improve the quality of preexisting social relationships. It's further hypothesized that the culture of online relationships may motivate development of friendship and greater closeness because of the "arm's-length" nature of online communication. Paradoxically, the distance created by online communication may actually foster more intimate self-disclosure, which leads to increased relationship quality with both strangers and existing friendships (Blais, et al. 2008).

Enhanced Self-Disclosure Hypothesis

The most recent hypothesis regarding online communication proposes that the Internet enhances intimate self-disclosure, which creates greater feelings of closeness and increases the quality of social relationships. Valkenburg and Peter (2009) define "intimate self-disclosure" as talking about "one's worries, fears, secrets, and embarrassing experiences." They contend that certain types of Internet communication foster intimate self-disclosure, and it's that dynamic that accounts for the greater quality of social relationships among adolescents in online relationships.

Recent research has examined adolescent social relationships in light of these three hypotheses and corresponding research, providing us with wonderful insights into the different aspects of Internet usage and the varied influences they have on adolescent friendships. This next section explores some of the different types of Internet communication and their influences on social relationships.

Positive Influences on Social Relationships

Best friends and romantic partners are important relationships in adolescence because they serve to provide emotional support to young people, while at the same time allowing for mutual self-disclosure. As was highlighted in the earlier section on the culture of friendships, support, trust, and mutual self-disclosure allow young people to experiment—to try on—identities and help them develop social strategies. The Internet is a likely place for teens to develop and experience these skills.

The research of Blais, et al. (2008) indicates that certain aspects of online communication do facilitate support, trust, and mutual self-disclosure, thereby fostering more quality friendships and romantic partners. Specifically, their research found that instant messaging provided two aspects of positive change in relationships.

First, IMing allows for greater opportunities for a young person to stay in contact with a best friend or romantic partner. Particularly for younger adolescents, for whom physically being in contact with a friend or partner might be difficult, IMing provides a way for friends to be in more regular contact than through offline contexts.

A second agent for positive change for teens using IM is that it allows for more intimate self-disclosure because it removes the physical aspects of communication. Frequently, it's asserted that online communication removes the visual dynamic of personal communication and is, therefore, a negative influence on social relationships. But Blais, et al. (2008) and others argue quite the opposite. Rather than being detrimental, the removal of "visual, auditory, and contextual cues, such as social status cues" leads to fewer concerns about how one is being perceived and fewer inhibitions, thereby increasing the likelihood of intimate self-disclosure (Valkenburg and Peter 2009).

Whether it's the removal of the cues of face-to-face interaction or other reasons that promote greater self-disclosure, it seems evident that there is increased self-disclosure in online relationships. Pew Internet Research (2009), for example, determined that one-third of IM users say they use IM to say things they wouldn't want to say face-to-face (for example, asking someone out or breaking up with someone). Schouten, et al. (2007) found that one-third of adolescents in online communication preferred IM for intimate self-disclosure to face-to-face interaction.

Mutual intimate self-disclosure in online communication positively influences adolescent social relationships in three ways. First, maintaining existing friendships, an important developmental aspect in adolescence, is positively influenced online. Second, because IM enables young people to "talk about more intimate things," the quality of their friendships is positively influenced. And third, there seems to be a "close-get-closer" effect produced by intimate self-disclosure in IM conversations. "Adolescents who disclose more online develop higher quality friendships," increasing the likelihood that those same adolescents will self-disclose to those same friends (Valkenburg and Peter 2009).

Negative Influence on Social Relationships

Other types of Internet communication tend to produce negative influences on adolescent friendships. For example, one study found that adolescent males who use the Internet to communicate with friends reported higher levels of support than adolescent males who did not.

However, that same study found that males who use the Internet to play games reported *lower* levels of social support than those who did not play games. This lower level of social support reflected a decrease in romantic relationship commitment and trust and communication. As well, use of the Internet for general entertainment reflected a negative influence on levels of commitment, intimacy, and companionship with best friends and romantic partners (Blais, et al. 2008).

Spending time in chat rooms was another type of Internet communication that had a negative influence on adolescent social relationships. Spending time in chat rooms was related to increased alienation and conflict and decreased intimacy and companionship with best friends. Additionally, time spent chatting was typically spent with strangers. It seems that part of the dynamic is that the more time adolescents spent in chat rooms (with strangers), the less time they spent communicating with preexisting friends or "known-others."

Blais, et al. (2008) also suggest that a dynamic of spending time in chat rooms with strangers is the contrast that develops between "more likeable strangers" and the flawed reality of people whom adolescents already know. This may, in turn, serve to move a young person away from known friendships to social communication with strangers.

The world of online communication is constantly changing, but it seems there are at least a few principles that one can take away from this look at online culture. First, the news is not all bad. There are many positive influences that the Internet affords a young person, particularly in the area of social competency. For example, online communication can serve to help young people

ARE TEENS OUR FRIENDS? THE ETHICS OF YOUTH WORKERS AND SOCIAL NETWORKING SITES

Social networking sites, such as Facebook and MySpace, make it easy for youth workers to stay in touch with the students in their youth groups, to post the latest photos of youth group outings, and to communicate the latest youth group news and activities.[7] The ease of an online connection, however, makes it easy to blur the lines between "friend" and "youth leader."

Furthermore, being online "friends" with teenagers poses ethical questions regarding the amount of information we share with one another. For example, what if one of your students, or one of their friends, posts photos showing the student engaging in inappropriate, illegal, or otherwise questionable behavior? What are your legal, moral, and ethical obligations regarding the information you received—whether it was received unsolicited or unintentionally?

7 There are a number of Christian social networking sites. Rachel D. Jackson identifies top sites for Christians who want to network on Christians-only sites: They include Tangle.com, Mychurch.org, FaithLight.com, and Loveandseek.com. (http://ezinearticles.com/?Top-5-Christian-Social-Networking-Sites&id=2490701).

Or, for another example, what if one of *your* friends posts photos of you that were personal or revealed something you didn't want your students to know? Even in cases where photos and conversations between adult youth leaders and their friends are above reproach, do you really want teenagers in the middle of your personal conversations? When we cross those boundaries, the ability to maintain a professional, adult relationship with the young people in our youth groups gets more complicated.

Education professionals have begun to develop suggested best practices regarding the use of social networking sites with students. These provide a helpful guideline for youth workers as they consider how to take advantage of the benefits of social networking, while still maintaining an appropriate relationship between adults and students.

Caroline Lego Muñoz and Terri L. Towner (2009) have put together "Best Practices Policies" for educators. Their suggestions have been adapted here to fit the youth ministry context. Their first suggestion is that professionals who work with students should maintain separate personal and public pages. Privacy settings should be implemented on the personal page, limiting this page to your own family, peer friends, and acquaintances. Then on the public page, publish the specific contact information that would be appropriate for students to use to contact you. They further suggest that the public page have some personal information so students can get to know you, but make sure it's information that *you* select and monitor.

As Muñoz and Towner (2009) state: "Tidbits of personal information can lead to positive [youth worker]-student interactions," but it is "important to maintain a level of professionalism that does not cross the boundary of the [youth worker]-student relationship."

A second suggestion is to promote your networking site with students, but allow them to initiate inviting you to be their friend, rather than you inviting them. That way, students can peruse your site if they choose to without feeling pressured to be your "friend."

Previously, chapter 8 discussed ethical issues of confidentiality. On social networking sites, the issues of confidentiality are blurred as well. Youth workers need to establish and communicate their policy for viewing posted information. Muñoz and Towner (2009) suggest that a policy be established not to view students' profiles and that the policy be communicated to students. Since many sites now allow users to put people on a limited profile list, they also suggest that adults ask students to limit youth leaders' access to their personal profiles.

Social networking sites can be a tremendous benefit to relationship building, outreach, and overall communication with students. As well, they can be a means for increasing teaching and learning, inviting small-group discussions, and creating safe environments where students can engage adults in some of the deep theological questioning that takes place during the teen years. The responsibility belongs with youth workers to consider the implications for youth worker-student boundaries to ensure ethical practices and safekeeping of young people.

Food for Thought

A youth intern shared that a 15-year-old student in her youth group had posted photos of herself and a group of friends, and it was clear they'd been drinking. What are some of the ethical and legal dilemmas for this intern? How would you respond in a similar situation?

navigate and develop peer-friend relationships as it allows them to develop skills of intimate self-disclosure. As youth workers, perhaps it would be advisable to talk about the pros and cons of intimate self-disclosure both with youth and with parents.

Second, online relationships can be a means for dealing with anxiety and loneliness, as well as help teens with poor social skills. As the online world functions as a safe place for teens, young people can practice relating with their peers, thereby developing better social skills that can be transferred into offline relating (Roberts, Henriksen, and Foehr 2009).

Third, there are potential negative influences that we should be aware of as well. Understanding the different dynamics in friendship relationships and stranger relationships online, as well as the potential detrimental effects of chat rooms, should be a part of training and teaching in our youth group settings.

ROMANTIC RELATIONSHIPS

Adolescence, with all of its physical and sexual maturation and heightened peer and friendship relating, brings, for the first time in a young person's life, desires for romantic relating. Jennifer Connolly and Caroline McIsaac (2009) identify this aspect of adolescent relating as the link between passionate feelings for relationship with sexual desire. This section briefly explores the culture of peer romantic relationships. Specifically, we'll consider the characteristics of romantic relationships, including the quantity, quality, and function.

Quantity of Romantic Relationships

Throughout the adolescent years, young men and women engage in romantic relating with frequency increasing over the span of adolescence. A national study indicated that one-fourth of 12-year-olds in the United States had been in at least one romantic relationship within the previous 18 months. That number increases to over two-thirds by the age of 18 (Connolly and McIsaac 2009).

Adolescent Romantic Relationships[8]

	Experienced first-date	In a romantic relationship within last 18 months	Typical duration of romantic relationship	Most often reported closest relationship
12-14 year-olds	25%	25%	Few weeks	Mother[9]
15-16 year-olds	75%	50%	6 months	Same gender friend
18 year-olds	100%	70%	1 year or more	Romantic partner

Quality of Romantic Relationships

As one might expect, the quality of romantic relationships increases over time as well. One indicator of the quality of romantic relationships is reflected in their duration. Connolly and McIsaac's research (2009) revealed that the typical romantic relationship for a young adolescent lasted only a few weeks and seldom longer than four months. As adolescents mature and increase their skills at intimacy, trust, and self-disclosure, the duration of their romantic relationships increases as well. By the age of 18, the typical romantic relationships last a year or longer.

Thus far, no attention has been given to same-gender romantic relationships. There is significant research to indicate that many young people experience same-gender romantic and sexual attraction during adolescence. A recent study reported that five percent of adolescents report same-sex attraction or a non-heterosexual orientation. That same study also revealed that those reporting same-sex attraction or a non-heterosexual orientation reported having as many romantic experiences as other adolescents (Connolly and McIsaac 2009).

Though the research is sparse to date, when acknowledging the quantity and duration of romantic relationships (particularly in early adolescence), consideration must be given to the influence of romantic breakups. Zimmer-Gembeck (2002) notes that romantic relationship breakups can "challenge adolescents' coping skills and self-concepts." While little is known about the negative or positive effects, one may surmise that greater incidents of romantic breakups may foster a context for greater feelings of depression, as well as anxiety and lower feelings of self-worth (Connolly and McIsaac 2009).

---

8 Adapted from Melanie J. Griffith Zimmer-Gembeck, "The Developing of Romantic Relationships and Adaptions in the System of Peer Relationships," Journal of Adolescent Health, 31, No. Suppl. 6, December, 2002, and Jennifer Connolly and Caroline McIsaac, "Romantic Relationships in Adolescences," in *Handbook of Adolescent Psychology*, Vol. 2, Ch. 4, 104-151, Richard M. Lerner and Laurence Steinberg, eds., Hoboken, NJ: John Wiley & Sons, Inc., 2009.
9 The age group reporting mother as closest friend were at the high end of this age range, mostly 14 year-olds.

Function of Romantic Relationships

As "The Art of Dating" sidebar details, in contemporary American adolescent culture, more than any other, the practices of dating and romantic relationships are detached from traditional practices of courtship without expectations of marriage. Instead, the culture of romantic relationships and its associated practices typically serve different functions for today's adolescent.

Romantic relationships serve as significant sources of support, providing places of safety and trust where young men and women can practice intimate self-disclosure as well as "developing a sense of caretaking and trust" (Connolly and McIsaac 2009, Furman et al. 2002). Further, romantic relationships can function as contexts for developing greater strengths in intimacy and self-disclosure, as well as teaching young people how to deal with conflict and how to get along with others.

Additionally, for many young people, romantic relationships can become a substitute for the peer friend context, such that there is a tendency for young people to curtail time spent with friends in order to accommodate romantic relationships. Thus, they're looking to their romantic partners to fulfill many of the relationship functions previously achieved in the peer friendship context (Zimmer-Gembeck 2002).

It should also be noted that research indicates there is an association with lower future goals and negative affect or low feelings of self-worth and self-concept in young women who report high rates of dating, greater experience with sexual activity, or low quality of romantic relationships (Zimmer-Gembeck 2002). Additionally, a function that's controversial for Christian youth workers is that romantic relationships in contemporary youth culture often serve as a context for exploring and experimenting with adult sexual roles (Cobb 2004, Santrock 2005).

At the beginning of the twentieth century, the primary system of courtship in middle-class America

THE ART OF DATING

As Rebekah and her sister, Elizabeth, washed dishes after Sunday lunch, they talked excitedly about Rebekah's news. After weeks of working up the nerve, she'd finally given Andrew her calling card after Sunday worship and invited him to call on her the following Saturday afternoon. He'd accepted her card and agreed that he'd like to call. Rebekah, at the age of 20, was excited about the possibility that Saturday's visit at her home, in the not-so-private world of her family, would lead to something more permanent—a marriage proposal. This was the beginning. (circa 1900)

Daniel was a high school senior who worked after school at the local drugstore. He'd finally saved up $8.00, which was a lot of money from his hourly wage of just $ .75. Eight dollars should cover dinner for two at the neighborhood diner and a movie. He might have just enough to spring for a malt afterward. Daniel's father had agreed to lend him the family car. Now all he had to do was get Kathy to say yes. He was planning on asking her out at school tomorrow. (circa 1950)

Nora was both excited and anxious. After weeks of arguing with her parents, they'd finally agreed that she could go on a date with Tim. Her parents were concerned that she was too young to be dating. But at 12 1/2, she'd already waited longer than any of her friends to start dating. As soon as her parents agreed she could go, she texted Tim and told him she'd meet him in an hour at the mall. (circa 2009) was *calling*. Whiting and Child refer to typical practices and associated beliefs, values, rules, motives, and satisfactions as a *custom complex* (Santrock 2005). Such practices and accompanying beliefs aren't universal but arise out of the meaning-making of particular cultures. The practices of courtship, in this case dating in the United States, would be an example.

Beth L. Bailey, in her significant work on dating practices in twentieth-century America, refers to these customs as "conventions," public sets of rules and understandings that provide a framework for public and social activity. These public codes of behavior "may not *determine* actions," but they do *structure* experience. They provide a basis for understanding what is appropriate, normal, and expected (Bailey 1988).

The conventions of calling were extensive and elaborate. Calling practices will be briefly outlined here, although it's important to note the detail of calling practices, the ways in which culture reinforced and reiterated the rules of calling, and the shifts that transpired resulting in the demise of calling as a practice of courtship.

Calling Practices

Calling during the late nineteenth and early twentieth centuries wasn't solely a courtship phenomenon but a broader aspect of the social life of middle-class Americans. The family's social activities were structured around issuing invitations for others to *call* on specific dates and times. It was the means of arranging one's

Courtship

In the last few years, many youth workers have urged parents and youth to return to the days of courtship when a young man courted a young woman. As is often the case, when we begin to wax nostalgic for the good ol' days, we tend to have more of an ideal in our minds than factual history.

Courtship, a romantic relationship between young people prior to marriage, has taken many forms within American culture, never mind across cultural contexts. We probably draw upon aspects of courtship from different time periods when we wistfully think about courtship traditions of the past. As we consider the culture of courtship of today's youth, it's helpful to explore the historical traditions and consider where we've come from, how we got here, and what the future might look like.

In the years following World War II, 13-year-old girls who hadn't begun to date were considered late bloomers. "A 1961 study by Carlfred B. Broderick, professor of family relations at Pennsylvania State…found that 40 percent of the fifth graders in one local middle-class district were already dating" (Bailey 1988). Dating as a primary aspect of romantic courtship is a particular American phenomenon. Though countries in Western Europe also have patterns of dating, none has so passionately embraced dating as a primary cultural experience of youth as has the United States.

As Windy Sombat (2000) notes,

> Few other countries carry on this practice with as much fervor as Americans do. Then again, few other countries have the same social conditions as America. Since the turn of the century, there has been a greater freedom between men and women, for example, both attend the same schools with the same classes. Both sexes become accustomed to the other at early ages, which is very conducive to the practice of dating.

This has not always been the case.

social calendar. Callers would arrive at a home, present their "calling card" to the maid or house-keeper, and wait to be received. The home was the focal point for social life and considered the realm of women, who controlled the family social calendar. Men, in this context, functioned and had control and authority in the public realm.

Courtship began once a young woman "became of age" (Bailey 1988). Typically a young woman around the age of 20 would be allowed to invite a young man to visit her at her home—to *call*, in other words. As a young woman became close to marriageable age, her family would begin to consider possible suitors—young men who shared similar traits such as age, education, back-ground, social class, and future prospects. Initially, a young woman's mother would arrange for young men to call on her daughter at their home. Gradually, a young woman would take over that responsibility, but still under the supervision of her parents, particularly her mother.

Once an invitation to call was issued, there were appropriate and expected behaviors. When a young man called on a young woman, she'd entertain him in the family parlor or a similar room, often playing the piano for her guest. The time together was structured regarding whether refreshments would be served, the topics of conversation, the length of time of the call, and even how the couple should part at the end of the visit. All of this took place under the watchful eye of a young woman's family in this private setting.

The young woman and her family had the responsibility for initiating courtship and thus had the power and control over every aspect. Calling was serious business. If a young man called on a young woman, it was understood that his acceptance implied a serious move toward a possible marriage proposal (Bailey 1988, Arnett 2007, Santrock 2005).

As noted, a young woman typically began receiving callers when she was around 20. Young men would have been a similar age, perhaps a year or two older. The expectation was that within a short period of time, a young woman would move from courtship to marriage. The average age of marriage for young men back in 1900 was 25.9 years, and 22 for young women.[10] (U.S. Census Bureau 2006).

This kind of romantic courtship was reserved for middle-class and affluent youth who had the ability to entertain callers in their homes. Poorer youth and youth of color most likely wouldn't have had the private space, piano, or even maid and housekeeper to entertain callers in this man-ner. So the courtship took on a different dynamic. These young people created their own form of courtship, which involved meeting others in more public spaces. These practices became the precursor to the move away from calling as a primary means of romantic courtship to contem-porary dating practices. The culture of courtship among poor youth, along with other cultural changes, influenced the practices of dating by the mid-twentieth century (Bailey 1988, Sombat 2000, Merrill 1959).

---

10 The average age of first marriage in 1950 was 22.8 for men and 20.3 for women; by 2003 the average age of first marriage had risen to 27.1 for men and 25.3 for women (U.S. Census Bureau 2006).

A number of cultural shifts influenced the changing landscape of courtship in middle-class America during the last half of the twentieth century. First, greater numbers of families lived in urban, rather than rural contexts. Homes were typically smaller and didn't always have the separate rooms for entertaining callers. Additionally, the urban context afforded greater opportunities for social activities in the public arena and away from the supervision of parents.

Second, the creation of the mass-produced automobile meant many families now had access to transportation that further facilitated opportunities for young women and men to engage in courtship in public spaces.

Third, telephones were commonplace in many homes, easing the need to physically "call" on someone to arrange a meeting. As others have noted, the environment of courtship that evolved in the 1940s and '50s was radically different from calling, and it changed patterns of behavior relating to roles, responsibility, and authority for men and women both inside and outside the home (Bailey 1988).

By the middle of the twentieth century, dating had replaced calling for most young people. The onus shifted from a young woman and her family issuing an invitation, to a young man asking a young woman to go out on a date with him. Sombat (2000) notes that popular places for dates were "ice cream parlors, pizza parlors, drive-ins, bowling alleys, coffeehouses and record shops." Movies were also places for cheap entertainment. At a movie, teenagers "could be immersed in the dark with their date, enjoy a snack, and be entertained for a while."

Dances were also a large part of the dating scene in the '40s and '50s. These social activities were a far cry from the polite, well-mannered conversations between a young couple in the parlor of a young woman's home.

The shift in courtship had economic implications as well, particularly for young men. Obviously, dating in the public realm and going to dances, movies, and diners increased the economic expense of courtship. Young men were expected to pay for the costs of dating, thereby encouraging expectations regarding what should be given in return. These expectations—along with couples dating without the supervision of a young woman's mother—gave dating couples greater opportunities for sexual exploration and experimentation.

The amount of time spent in school had lengthened, with most middle-class young people going to high school and often college—a new phenomenon brought on by economic changes. Additionally, many young people no longer worked the long

> "
> *Girls who [try] to usurp the right of boys to choose their own dates [will] ruin a good dating career...Fair or not, it is the way of life. From the Stone Age, when men chased and captured their women, comes the yen of a boy to do the pursuing. You will control your impatience, therefore, and respect the time-honored custom of boys to take the first step.* —Beth Bailey, From Front Porch to Back Seat: Courtship in Twentieth-Century America, *20*

hours associated with running the family farm, and leisure time increased. These significant cultural changes fostered an environment in which teens at younger ages were going out on dates.

As noted earlier, girls as young as 13 were dating. Though the age of marriage did decline during the 1940s and '50s, the early age of dating meant that young people dated for many years before considering marriage, and marriage as a primary focus for courtship disappeared (Bailey 1988, Sombat 2000).

Dating served to function mainly as a form of recreation, a place where young people could learn how to relate to others—particularly those of the opposite gender—as well as a context for sexual experimentation and exploration (Santrock 2005).

Today the dating scene has shifted once again, though there are still some similarities to dating in the 1950s. One significant change is the number of years spent dating. A typical young woman in America will start dating around the age of 12 to 13. The average age of first marriage, though, has continued to rise. Most young women, if they marry, will marry around the age of 25; for young men the age is even higher. You can do the math: That means young people have the possibility of dating for 13 years or more. Dating still functions as a form of recreation and helps to socialize youth into appropriate ways of interacting with other young people. As such, dating functions to help adolescents negotiate and understand aspects of their identity.

Other things have changed as well, even as some things have remained the same. For example, while dating primarily still takes place in public spaces among young teens, the young man isn't expected to bear the economic expense of dating. There are many occasions when each person will pay or the young woman might cover the costs.

Finally, the whole concept of dating, particularly among younger youth, is being re-envisioned and reinterpreted because of the Internet and other forms of technology that shape how people relate to one another. What does dating look like in the new public spaces of the twenty-first century? Can you have a date on Facebook or MySpace?

REFLECTION ACTIVITY (5 TO 10 MINUTES)

Consider your friendships during adolescence. How did your family context influence the friends you chose and the character of those friendships?

DIGGING DEEPER (10 TO 15 MINUTES)

Ask a group of young people to write down the names of their three closest friends. What patterns can you identify regarding cliques? Write a brief analysis of your findings.

- Family standards, norms, and values give adolescents the foundation for constructing adolescent peer relationships.

- Adolescent peer friendships encourage the development of social competencies.

- During adolescence, peer friendships increase in quantity and quality.

- Crowds facilitate identity processes; cliques provide places of belonging.

- Online relating can provide positive and negative benefits for the developing adolescent.

- The culture of romantic relationships and their primary functioning have changed from a means of finding a marriage partner to a form of recreation.

CHAPTER 12
The Culture of Church and Religious Affiliation

LEARNING OBJECTIVES

When you've finished this chapter, you should be able to:

1. Articulate the distinctions between religiosity, spirituality, and faith

2. Understand the ways that religious connections provide protection from risky behaviors and promote positive social development in adolescents

3. Summarize the different contexts of religious culture

Bronfenbrenner doesn't directly address the microsystem context of church, church youth group, or other religious affiliation. But since Bronfenbrenner's time, other developmental psychologists have acknowledged the influence of the cultures of church and religious affiliation in young people who participate in those contexts. A number of studies indicate the majority of young people in North America consider religion and spirituality important to their lives.[11] This chapter explores those influences.

Though there are significant gaps in the research regarding adolescent religiosity and church participation, there is also important data accumulated over the past few decades that provides insight into the influence of religious environments. In discussing this research, this chapter highlights why religiosity is particularly salient during the adolescent years, looks at what the research indicates regarding the promotion of positive behaviors and protection from risk behaviors, examines the character of the religious environment, and concludes with questions and suggestions for contemplating youth ministry practice.

As we begin, it's important to clarify what is meant by *religiosity, spirituality,* and *faith. Religiosity* is the measure of a person's religious commitment. Van Dyke and Elias (2007) noted four similar definitions:

> *For most U.S. teenagers [religion has] quite a small place at the end of the table for a short period of time each week (if that).* —Christian Smith, Soul Searching, 161

---

11 A Search Institute study from 1989 indicated that 95% of young people believed in a deity, 75% believed in a personal God, and 70% were church members. A study of Canadian youth revealed similar findings: 79% identified with an organized religion, 81% believed God exists, and 80% believed in the divinity of Jesus. (See Carol A. Markstrom, "Religious Involvement and Adolescent Psychosocial Development," *Journal of Adolescence* 22 (1999): 206–221.) In Christian Smith, et al.'s study (2005), 84% of 13-to-17-year-olds reported they believed in God, 65% prayed at least once a week, 52% attended religious services at least twice a month, while 38% were involved in a youth group. (See Christian Smith and Melinda Lundquist Denton. *Soul Searching: The Religious and Spiritual Lives of American Teenagers.* (New York: Oxford University Press, 2005).)

1. "Acceptance of and a level of practical commitment to a religious tradition"

2. "Allegiance to a particular system of faith and worship"

3. "Adherence to a set of sacred doctrines or membership in a body of people, who share similar beliefs about God, holy observance, and morality"

4. "The individual and corporate search for the sacred that has been formalized into an institution"

Generally speaking, religiosity refers to a commitment to a set of beliefs and the informal and formal practices associated with that set of beliefs. These can be either private (for example, prayer, meditation, and so on) or public (for example, attending corporate worship).

Spirituality concerns the aspect of a person's identity that addresses issues of the transcendent and questions about ultimate meaning in one's life. Many developmental psychologists assert that spirituality is the capability of a person to act beyond or outside of self to connect with the Divine or another human being. This spiritual searching can be evidenced in religious practice, but not necessarily or solely so (King 2003).

Faith speaks of the level of personal trust and devotion that a person places in God. Christians often talk about their "faith" or lack of faith. Typically, these kinds of statements refer to one's belief in and devotion to Jesus Christ and reflect a person's commitment to a particular set of spiritual beliefs about Jesus as the divine Son of God and his relationship to that person. As our society reflects, Christians can and do practice their faith through a variety of religious traditions and in a wide range of religious practices. As well, Christians (and others) may have differing levels of religious commitment to those beliefs and practices.

THE SALIENCE OF RELIGIOSITY DURING ADOLESCENCE

Carol Markstrom cites three reasons why issues of religion and spirituality are sharpened during adolescence. First, cognitive development promotes a greater ability to consider the abstract concepts of spirituality and God. The ability to engage in the big questions of life (Who am I? Why am I here? Who is God? Where is God?, etc.) can "serve as catalysts for adolescent pursuits for deeper meaning" (1999).

Second, adolescence is a pivotal period for exploring personal identity, and the spiritual dynamic is an essential and important element of identity formation.

Third, Markstrom (1999) notes teenagers' self-concept, or feelings of self-worth, and the connection between those feelings and their perceptions of God. These dynamics lend themselves to young people seeking greater connection to religion and spirituality, as well as supporting the notion that religious environments are significant sources of influence in shaping an adolescent. This influence can be seen in the data on how religious contexts can offer protection from risk behaviors, as well as provide an environment for promoting positive behaviors.

Protection from Risk Behaviors

There has been a wealth of research into religiosity and at-risk behaviors of adolescents. It should be noted, though, that part of the difficulty in conducting this kind of research is the difficulty in measuring religiosity. Since much of religiosity has to do with personal religious practices, it's often more difficult to determine the influence. Typically, the data measures frequency, as in, how often do you pray and how many times do you attend church or participate in a Bible study?

That said, the data is strong in showing that young people involved in greater levels of religiosity are less likely to engage in some risk behaviors than are young people with lower levels of religiosity. In particular, the research indicates that higher levels of religiosity provide a measure of protection against several health-related behaviors (Nonnemaker, McNeely, and Blum 2003).

Regarding substance abuse behaviors, higher levels of religiosity, such as participation in a Bible study group and youth group, were associated with lower levels of cigarette use, alcohol use and abuse, marijuana use, and other illicit drug use (Nonnemaker, et al. 2003; Smith 2003; King and Furrow 2004). Additionally, young people indicating high religious involvement were less likely to engage in steroid use or to drive under the influence of alcohol (Regnerus 2003, Steinman and Zimmerman 2004).

There have also been studies that found a connection between greater levels of religiosity and reduction in substance abuse, as well as lower rates of delinquency and violence (King and Furrow 2004, Smith 2003, Van Dyke and Elias 2007).

Nonnemaker, et al. (2003) and others have found that higher levels of religiosity act as a buffer against depression, suicidal ideation, and feelings of hopelessness. (See also Wright, Frost, and Wisecarver 1993, Van Dyke and Elias 2007.) Though further research needs to be conducted, the data regarding religiosity and sexual practices is mixed. For example, Ball, et al. (2003) in their study of African-American female, urban adolescents found that more frequent church attendance was associated with lower frequency of sexual activity.

> ## Food for Thought
>
> *Why might religious environments be associated with both positive (lower frequency of sexual activity and greater sexual responsibility) and negative (unprotected sex and lack of birth control methods) outcomes?*

Similarly, Nonnemaker, et al. (2003) reported frequent church attendance and personal devotion were associated with greater sexual responsibility. However, they (and others) also found that higher levels of religiosity were associated with unprotected sex and lack of birth control methods (Nonnemaker et al. 2003, Miller and Gur 2002).

Promoting Positive Development and Behaviors

Regular participation in a religious context offers an environment for promoting positive development and behaviors in the developing adolescent. Particularly, higher levels of religiosity promote healthier psychological functioning. Studies show that attending religious services and participation in Bible studies and youth group are associated with higher levels of general self-esteem, more positive self-concept, as well as a more positive future orientation (Markstrom 1999, Van Dyke and Elias 2007, Ball et al. 2003).

Moreover, there is also a connection between school self-esteem and religiosity—that is, higher levels of religiosity reflected greater academic competence and academic achievement (King and Furrow 2004, Smith 2003, Markstrom 1999).

Greater religious participation reflected more pro-social values and behaviors as well. *Behaviors* such as helping others, volunteering, involvement with their families, and a greater ability to cope effectively with stress have all been found to be associated with greater religious participation. *Values* associated with most positive outcomes, such as a strong sense of personal meaning, beliefs in supporting community and society, and civic and political involvement, were also connected to greater religious participation (King and Furrow 2004, Smith 2003).

Additionally, King and Furrow found that greater religious participation was associated with greater evidence of thriving—that is, the "absence of problem behaviors and the presence of healthy behaviors" (2004).

Pamela King and Robert W. Roeser (2009), in a recent review of the literature on religiosity, spirituality, and adolescence, identified three key aspects to the cultures of religious environment that have significant potential for shaping youth.

Ideological Context

As noted in chapter 3, ideology refers to a set of concepts concerning human life and culture. A church or youth group provides opportunities in which beliefs, values, and goals are *explicitly* communicated and is, thereby, a context rich for instilling religious and spiritual ideologies.

Further, the religious context provides opportunities for adolescents to "reason critically and skeptically" about such beliefs, values, and goals. As well, the religious environment provides not only opportunities to wrestle with new ideas and concepts, but also a place to think through and question "previously held beliefs" (King and Roeser 2009).

An additional way the church or youth group functions as an ideological context is the opportunity to develop relationships with parents, friends, and adults outside their family who share a similar set of beliefs and values. As young people engage in these close friendships and relationships as they share in religious experiences, a sense of shared beliefs and values is constructed (King and Roeser 2009).

Social Context

The church or youth group culture also serves as an influence in adolescent social relationships. Specifically, the religious context can offer social experiences that foster positive self-concepts, as well as providing an environment in which young people can experiment with or practice those concepts (Markstrom 1999, King and Furrow 2004). In addition, as King and Roeser note (2009), the social experiences of the religious context may afford young people opportunities to activate certain "aspects of their identity" not readily activated in other contexts (for example, leadership, service, and compassion) (King and Furrow 2004). Finally, the social dynamics of religious contexts can foster greater levels of intimacy and trust with parents and close friends, as well as other adults.

Dworkin, et al. (2003) have also noted that participation in youth activities such as youth group (as well as sports and extracurricular activities) provides young people with opportunities for developing social skills such as teamwork, leadership, and the capacity to direct attention toward a challenging goal.

Though the influence in all three categories is important, fostering stronger relationships between youth and other adults is particularly important since environments in which young people are encouraged to develop close, positive relationships with adults have increasingly diminished in the last few decades.

Spiritual Context

Religious environments can also foster positive spiritual development in adolescents. As highlighted at the beginning of the chapter, spirituality relates to the developmental processes in which a young person searches for meaning and purpose and wrestles with questions of the transcendent. A church or youth group can facilitate this time of questioning, as well as provide a faith community and a sense of belonging (King and Roeser 2009).

Further, religious ritual experiences and connection to a community of relationships can facilitate a sense of connectedness with the Divine (King and Furrow 2004). A sense of belonging and connectedness to peers, parents, other adults—and ultimately, God—can have a profound impact on aspects of self-worth and self-concept (King and Roeser 2009).

Finally, as highlighted earlier, adolescent peer influences can serve to influence desirable modeling of behavior. (See chapter 11 on peer influence.) In a similar way, the culture of the religious environment promotes "observational spiritual learning," meaning the religious context can encourage young people to emulate spiritual role models, whether peers or adults. Thereby, as King and Roeser (2009) note, "engaging in behaviors that emulate spiritual models may enable youth to integrate abstract ideology into their self-concept."

REFLECTION ACTIVITY (5 TO 10 MINUTES)

What connections have you observed between religious practices and the social health of young people?

DIGGING DEEPER (10 TO 15 MINUTES)

Other than the research on sexuality, there was little data regarding potential negative effects of the religious environment for adolescents. How might the influence of religious environments, in particular, be harmful for a young person?

- Spirituality concerns the ways all human beings pursue an understanding of ultimate meaning and purpose.

- Religious environments, such as churches and youth groups, are particularly influential during the adolescent years.

- There are three aspects to the cultural environment of the religious context: (a) Ideological, (b) Social, and (c) Spiritual.

WORKS CITED

Adams, Beatrice. 2007. *McDonald's strange menu around the world. Trifter.* Budget Travel. July 19, 2007. http://www.trifter.com/Practical-Travel/Budget-Travel/McDonalds-Strange-Menu-Around-the-World.35517.

Allen, Joseph P., et al. 2003. A secure base in adolescence: Markers of attachment security in the mother-adolescent relationship. *Child Development* 74 (1): 292–307.

Allrecipes.com. *Tonkatsu/Katsu Sauce.* 2009. http://allrecipes.com/Recipe/Tonkatsu--Katsu-Sauce/Detail.aspx.

Arnett, Jeffrey Jensen. 2007. *Adolescence and emerging adulthood: A cultural approach.* 3rd Ed. Upper Saddle River, NJ: Prentice Hall.

Bailey, Beth L. 1988. *From front porch to back seat: Courtship in twentieth-century America.* Baltimore: The Johns Hopkins University Press.

Ball, Joanna, Lisa Armstead, and Barbara-Jeanne Austin. 2003. The relationship between religiosity and adjustment among African-American, female, urban adolescents. *Journal of Adolescence* 26 (4): 431–446.

Berndt, T. J. 1996. Transitions in friendship and friends' influence. In *Transitions through adolescence: Interpersonal domains and context.* ed. J. A. Graber, J. Brooks-Gunn, and A. C. Petersen, 57–84, Mahwah, NJ: Erlbaum.

Blain, Michelle D., Janny M. Thompson, and Valerie E. Whiffen. 1993. Attachment and perceived social support in late adolescence. *Journal of Adolescent Research* 8 (2): 226–241.

Blais, Julie J., Wendy M. Craig, Debra Pepler, and Jennifer Connolly. 2008. Adolescents online: The importance of internet activity choices to salient relationships. *Journal of Youth and Adolescence* 37 (5): 522–536.

Brendgen, Mara, Dorothy Markiewicz, Anna Beth Doyle, and William M. Bukowski. 2001. The relations between friendship quality, ranked-friendship preference, and adolescents' behavior with their friends. *Merrill-Palmer Quarterly* 47 (3): 395–415.

Brendtro, Larry K. 2006. The vision of Urie Bronfenbrenner: Adults who are crazy about kids. *Reclaiming Children and Youth: The Journal of Strength-based Intervention* 15 (3): 162–166.

Bronfenbrenner, Urie. 1979. *The ecology of human development: Experiments by nature and design.* Cambridge, MA: Harvard University Press.

Brown, B. Bradford. 1990. Peer groups and peer cultures. In *At the Threshold: The developing adolescent,* S. Shirley Feldman and Glen R. Elliott, 171–196. Cambridge, MA: Harvard University Press.

Brown, B. Bradford, and James Larson. 2009. Peer relationships in adolescence. In vol. 2 of *Handbook of adolescent psychology: Contextual influences on adolescent development,* 74–103. 3rd ed. Ed. Richard M. Lerner and Laurence Steinberg. Hoboken, NJ: John Wiley & Sons, Inc.

Buhrmester, Duane, and Karen Prager. 1995. Patterns and functions of self-disclosure during childhood and adolescence. In *Disclosure processes in children and adolescents,* ed. Ken J. Rotenberg, 10–56. Cambridge: Cambridge University Press.

Cobb, Nancy J. 2004. *Adolescence: Continuity, change, and diversity.* 5th ed. NY: McGraw-Hill.

Connolly, Jennifer A., and Caroline McIsaac. 2009. Romantic relationships in adolescence. Vol. 2, chap. 4 in *Handbook of adolescent psychology: Contextual influences on adolescent development,* 104–151. 3rd ed. Ed. Richard M. Lerner and Laurence Steinberg. Hoboken, NJ: John Wiley & Sons, Inc.

Cooper, Catherine R., and Susan Ayers-Lopez. 1985. Family and peer systems in early adolescence: New models of the role of relationships in development. *The Journal of Early Adolescence* 5 (1): 9–21.

Cornell University. 2009. Bronfenbrenner Life Course Center. About Us, Mission and History page. http://www.blcc.cornell.edu/about_mission.html.

Ducharme, Jennifer, Anna Beth Doyle, and Dorothy Markiewicz. 2002. Attachment security with mother and father: Associations with adolescents' reports of interpersonal behavior with parents and peers. *Journal of Social and Personal Relationships* 19 (2): 203–231.

Dworkin, Jodi B., Reed Larson, and David Hansen. 2003. Adolescents' accounts of growth experiences in youth activities. *Journal of Youth and Adolescence* 32 (1): 17–26.

Engels, Rutger C. M. E., Maja Dekovic, and Wim Meeus. 2002. Parenting practices, social skills and peer relationships in adolescence. *Social Behavior and Personality* 30 (1): 3–18.

Feldman, S. Shirley, and Glen R. Elliott. 1990. *At the threshold: The developing adolescent.* Cambridge, MA: Harvard University Press.

Furman, Wyndol, and Duane Buhrmester. 1992. Age and sex differences in perceptions of networks of personal relationships. *Child Development* 63 (1): 103–115.

Furman, Wyndol, Valerie A. Simon, Laura Shaffer, and Heather A. Bouchey. 2002. Adolescents' working models and styles for relationships with parents, friends, and romantic partners. *Child Development* 73 (1): 241–255.

Gross, Elisheva F. 2004. Adolescent Internet use: What we expect, what teens report. *Journal of Applied Developmental Psychology: An International Lifespan Journal* 25 (6): 633–649.

King, Pamela Ebstyne. 2003. Religion and identity: The role of ideological, social, and spiritual contexts. *Applied Developmental Science* 7 (3): 197–204.

King, Pamela Ebstyne, and James L. Furrow. 2004. Religion as a resource for positive youth development: Religion, social capital, and moral outcomes. *Developmental Psychology* 40 (5): 703–713.

King, Pamela Ebstyne, and Robert W Roeser. 2009. Religion and spirituality in adolescent development. Vol. 1, chap. 13 in *Handbook of adolescent psychology: Individual bases of adolescent development*, 435–478. 3rd ed. Ed. Richard M. Lerner and Laurence Steinberg. Hoboken, NJ: John Wiley & Sons, Inc.

Laird, R. D., G. S. Pettit, K. A. Dodge, and J. E. Bates. 2005. Peer relationship antecedents of delinquent behavior in late adolescence: Is there evidence of demographic group differences in developmental processes? *Development and Psychopathology* 17 (1): 127–144.

Larson, Reed W., and S. Verma. 1999. How children and adolescents spend time across the world: Work, play, and developmental opportunities. *Psychological Bulletin* 125 (6): 701–736.

Larson, Reed W., Giovanni Moneta, Maryse H. Richards, and Suzanne Wilson. 2002. Continuity, stability, and change in daily emotional experience across adolescence. *Child Development* 73 (4): 1151–1165.

Laursen, Brett, and W. Andrew Collins. 2009. Parent-child relationships during adolescence. Vol. 2, chap. 1 in *Handbook of adolescent psychology: Contextual influences on adolescent development*, 3–42. 3rd ed. Ed. Richard M. Lerner and Laurence Steinberg. Hoboken, NJ: John Wiley & Sons, Inc.

Lenhart, Amanda, Paul Hittlin, Mary Madden. 2005. http://www.pewinternet.org/Reports/2005/Teens-and-Technology.aspx, July 27, 2005.

Lenhart, Amanda, Oliver Lewis, and Lee Rainie. 2001. *Teenage life online: The rise of the instant-message generation and the Internet's impact on friendship and family relationships.* June 21, 2001. http://www.pewinternet.org/Reports/2001/Teenage-Life-Online.aspx.

Markstrom, Carol A. 1999. Religious involvement and adolescent psychosocial development. *Journal of Adolescence* 22 (2): 206–221.

McDonald's Canada. 2007. FAQs. http://www.mcdonalds.ca/en/aboutus/faq.aspx.

Merrill, Francis Ellsworth. 1959. *Courtship and marriage.* New York: Holt Publishing.

Miller, Lisa, and Merav Gur. 2002. Religiousness and sexual responsibility in adolescent girls. *Journal of Adolescent Health* 31 (5): 401–406.

Muñoz, Caroline Lego and Terri L. Towner. 2009. Opening Facebook: How to use Facebook in the college classroom. *Paper presentation, Society for Information Technology & Teacher Education International Conference 2009. Charleston, South Carolina.*

Newman, Barbara M., and Philip R. Newman. 2001. Group Identity and Alienation: Giving the We its Due. *Journal of Youth and Adolescence* 30 (5): 515–538.

Nonnemaker, James M., Clea A. McNeely, and Robert Wm. Blum. 2003. Public and private domains of religiosity and adolescent health risk behaviors: evidence from the National Longitudinal Study of Adolescent Health. *Social Science & Medicine* 57 (11): 2049–2054.

Oransky, Matthew, and Jeanne Marecek. 2009. "I'm not going to be a girl": Masculinity and emotions in boys' friendships and peer groups. *Journal of Adolescent Research* 24 (2): 218–241.

Oxford University Press. 2009. AskOxford.com. http://www.askoxford.com/concise_oed/adolescent.

Pakaslahti, Laura, Anu Karjalainen, and Liisa Keltikangas-Järvinen. 2002. Relationships between adolescent prosocial problem-solving strategies, prosocial behaviour, and social acceptance. *International Journal of Behavioral Development* 26 (2): 137–144.

Prinstein, Mitchell J., and Kenneth A. Dodge. 2008. Current issues in peer influence research. Chap. 1 in *Understanding peer influence in children and adolescents.* Ed. Mitchell J. Prinstein and Kenneth A. Dodge, 3–13. New York: The Guilford Press.

Raja, Shyamala Nada, Rob McGee, and Warren R. Stanton. 1992. Perceived attachments to parents and peers and psychological well-being in adolescence. *Journal of Youth and Adolescence* 21 (4): 471–485.

Regnerus, Mark D. 2003. Moral communities and adolescent delinquency: Religious contexts and community social control. *The Sociological Quarterly* 44 (4): 523–554.

Rice, Kenneth G., and Patricia Mulkeen. 1995. Relationships with parents and peers: A longitudinal study of adolescent intimacy. *Journal of Adolescent Research* 10 (3): 338–357.

Roberts, Donald F., Lisa Henriksen, and Ulla G. Foehr. 2009. Adolescence, adolescents, and media. Vol. 2, chap. 9 in *Handbook of adolescent psychology: Contextual influences on adolescent development*, 314–344. 3rd ed. Ed. Richard M. Lerner and Laurence Steinberg. Hoboken, NJ: John Wiley & Sons, Inc.

Santrock, John W. 2005. *Adolescence.* 10th ed. NY: McGraw-Hill.

Schouten, Alexander P., Patti M. Valkenburg, and Jochen Peter. 2007. Precursors and underlying processes of adolescents' online self-disclosure: Developing and testing an "Internet-attribute-perception" model. *Media Psychology* 10 (2): 292–315.

Smith, Christian. 2003. Religious participation and network closure among American adolescents. *Journal for the Scientific Study of Religion* 42 (2): 259–267.

Sombat, Windy. 2000. Teenage dating in the 1950s. *HONR 269J: The beat begins: America in the 1950s.* http://www.honors.umd.edu/HONR269J/projects/sombat.html.

Steinberg, Laurence. 2005. *Adolescence.* 7th ed. NY: McGraw-Hill.

Steinman, Kenneth J., and Marc A. Zimmerman. 2004. Religious activity and risk behavior among African American adolescents: Concurrent and developmental effects. *American Journal of Community Psychology* 33 (3-4): 151–161.

Thomas, Jennifer J., and Kimberly A. Daubman. 2001. The relationship between friendship quality and self-esteem in adolescent girls and boys. *Sex Roles* 45 (1-2): 53–65.

U.S. Census Bureau. 2006. Estimated median age at first marriage, by sex: 1890 to present [2005]. U.S. Census. http://www.census.gov/population/socdemo/hh-fam/ms2.pdf.

Valkenburg, Patti M., and Jochen Peter. 2007. Preadolescents' and adolescents' online communication and their closeness to friends. *Developmental Psychology* 43 (2): 267–277.

Valkenburg, Patti M., and Jochen Peter. 2009. The effects of instant messaging on the quality of adolescents' existing friendships: A longitudinal study. *Journal of Communication* 59 (1): 79–97.

Van Dyke, Cydney J., and Maurice J. Elias. 2007. How forgiveness, purpose, and religiosity are related to the mental health and well-being of youth: A review of the literature. *Mental Health, Religion & Culture* 10 (4): 395–415.

Wright, Loyd S., Christopher J. Frost, and Stephen J. Wisecarver. 1993. Church attendance, meaningfulness of religion, and depressive symptomatology among adolescents. *Journal of Youth and Adolescence* 22 (5): 559–568.

Zimmer-Gembeck, Melanie J. 2002. The development of romantic relationships and adaptations in the system of peer relationships. *Journal of Adolescent Health* 31 (6): 216–225.

PART FOUR

Theologies of Culture

CHAPTER 13
Paul Tillich: Religion and Culture

LEARNING OBJECTIVES
When you've finished this chapter, you should be able to:

1. Discuss Tillich's definition of *religion* and how his definition differs from a traditional understanding

2. Describe "ultimate meaning"

3. Articulate Tillich's argument for the function of the Church in culture

INTRODUCTION

In seeking to develop a critical approach to culture, it's essential to consider a theological understanding of culture. Simply put, theology is the study of God and God's relationship with the world. In that sense, a theology of culture seeks to understand God and his relationship with humanity and human culture. This section explores twentieth-century theological perspectives regarding human culture. More specifically, it takes a closer look at the work of three theologians—Paul Tillich, Richard Niebuhr, and Karl Barth—who primarily wrote from a modern understanding and approach to culture. This section concludes by exploring Kathryn Tanner's critique of a modernistic understanding of culture, followed by a review of a theological model that starts with culture.

> *The problem of religion and culture has always been in the center of my interest. Most of my writings...try to define the way in which Christianity is related to secular culture. —Paul Tillich,* Theology of Culture, *iv*

PAUL TILLICH

In the years since his first public address on a theology of culture back in 1919, Tillich refined his thinking and theology about culture. After spending many decades as a teacher of systematic theology, Paul Tillich wrote the above words in the foreword to his book *Theology of Culture* (1959). In this book Tillich offers a thorough definition of *culture* and suggests ways that Christians should think about and respond to culture (as the Church). Our discussion will therefore focus on Tillich's definitions. In particular, this chapter provides a framework for exploring the four aspects of Tillich's argument: Religion, Time and Space, Culture, and the Role of the Church in Human Society.

Defining Religion

Tillich begins his argument by presenting an unorthodox definition of *religion*. In his estimation, it's an erroneous assumption to conclude that religion is solely about humanity's relation to the Divine. Moreover, he contends religion isn't simply some special function of a person, such as being moral or gaining knowledge about God or even having feelings about God. The basis of Tillich's argument is that religion is an aspect of the human spirit. Religion is at the core of all human activity—spiritual and cultural. He goes on to say that this aspect of the human spirit is the *"depth of all functions of [one's] spiritual life"* (Tillich 1959, 7, *emphasis added*). That is, religion is the deepest expression in all aspects of a person's spirit and encompasses the totality of the human spirit.

[One] who can read the style of a culture can discover its ultimate concern, its religious substance.
—*Paul Tillich*, Theology of Culture, *42-43*

Tillich uses three characteristics to further define what he means by "depth." First, depth is that reality that is *ultimate* reality. By this, Tillich contends that religion is that part of a person's spirit that attests to the best, the definitive, and the authoritative reality.

Second, depth is that reality that points to the infinite. We'll explore Tillich's understanding of time and space in the next section. But for now, it's sufficient to state that, for Tillich, humanity and our world is finite, while the deepest part of each individual demonstrates a reality that's *infinite*. Ultimate reality is manifested in the "ground of all being"—the "infinite Truth that is self-evident and pre-supposed in all thought and meaning" (Bulman 1981).

And third, depth refers to the idea of ultimate reality that is unconditional. The depth of a person's spirit attests to the ultimate reality of a God who is unconditioned—a being that transcends conditioned humanity and the cultural activities of humankind.

Tillich brings together these three characteristics of religion (as the depth of the human spirit) by stating that the depth of a human being's spirit (i.e., religion) is truly about ultimate concern or ultimate meaning. As Tillich reiterates, religion is not a special, separate function; but religion as ultimate concern "is manifest in all creative functions of the human spirit" (1959, 8).

Out of the very nature of humanness, individuals are motivated to seek true meaning. This depth of being is evident in human strivings and cultural activities. Tillich offers, as examples of this depth, three connection points:

- In the moral sphere of life, ultimate concern is apparent as the "unconditional seriousness of the moral demand." In striving to be moral and ethical people, there is the acknowledgment of the rightness of such actions.

THE MORAL DEMAND
Sara Shady[1]

Going all the way back to the ancient Greeks, a central philosophical question has been: "What is the nature of the good life?" Philosophers from different historical time periods, cultural backgrounds, and religious perspectives have asked what we ought to do to be moral, as well as how to have a good society. These are basic ethical questions. Although there are many different answers, the fact that these are perennial questions suggests that human beings, generally speaking, continuously make judgments about what is right and wrong. And, for the most part, they also try to defend their actions as right.

For example, it's hard to imagine a person saying she's completely neutral about whether or not it's good to torture an innocent child. Rather, most people will have a strong opinion about this issue. Certainly we won't all agree regarding the reasons *why* we shouldn't torture innocent children. And we also know that having reasons for why something is wrong doesn't automatically prevent us from doing an immoral action. But it's important to realize that thinking about morality is part of what it means to be human.

The drive to be moral transcends history, culture, and religion. Although it is evident that people have different views about morality, we shouldn't ignore the fact that we still have a lot in common. First of all, our actions may vary by culture, but there are several cases in which we share core moral values and principles. For example, a Hindu person may not use a cow for food, while most Americans really enjoy a good hamburger. But as philosopher James Rachels puts it, "The difference is in our belief systems, not in our values. We agree that we shouldn't eat Grandma; we simply disagree about whether the cow *is* (or could be) Grandma" (1993).

Second, we should avoid believing that only religious people think about and practice morality. There are countless examples of "secular saints" throughout history. And, on the other hand, we need to remember that lots of immoral things have been done in the name of religion.

> ## Food for Thought
> *Can human beings do good things apart from God? Or should the question be, "Can human beings ever truly be apart from God?"*

Third, the fact that moral norms change throughout history is itself a reason to believe there's something fundamentally human about being moral. We now recognize that slavery is morally wrong and should be abolished, and we can critique the moral judgments of previous societies for condoning slavery. But the fact that American plantation owners enslaved hundreds of thousands of Africans doesn't mean they weren't thinking about ethics. In fact, historical documents—*including sermons!*—contain several arguments *for* the morality of slavery. This isn't to say that those were good arguments. What we can recognize, however, is that people throughout time have acted on an internal drive to be moral by practicing moral reasoning.

Living a good life means we must think critically about our actions and have good reasons for what we believe is right and wrong. This is something that transcends history, culture, and religion.

---

1 Sara Shady is associate professor of philosophy at Bethel University in St. Paul, Minnesota.

- In the realm of knowledge, ultimate concern is apparent in the "passionate longing for ultimate reality." In the desires to gain greater and deeper knowledge, there is the acknowledgment of humanity's activity toward greater knowledge outside of self.

- In the realm of aesthetics or the artistic, ultimate concern becomes apparent in the "desire to express ultimate meaning." (1959, 8)

Tillich cites examples only in these three aspects of humanity. However, one might extend his argument to also include the physical and sexual aspects of human beings. In both humanity's physicality and sexuality, ultimate concern is manifest in the longing for ultimate reality and desire to express ultimate meaning.

To carry his argument to its conclusion, Tillich must necessarily address why religion has become a separate sphere from the rest of a person's existence and within culture, as well. He argues that religion has become a "special sphere among others, in myth, cult, devotion, and ecclesiastical institutions," because of the estrangement of humanity's spiritual life from its spiritual depth. There is a "fundamental ontological estrangement at the heart of the human condition" (Bulman 1981).

Raymond Bulman, in his examination of Tillich's theology, provides an extensive quote from Tillich's *Systematic Theology*. "The universal tragic condition of human estrangement is overcome in the new God-human relationship established in Jesus as the Christ:

> The biblical picture of Jesus as the Christ confirms his character as the bearer of the New Being or as the one in whom the conflict between the essential unity of God and [humanity] and [humanity's] existential estrangement is overcome. Point by point, not only in the Gospel records but also in the Epistles, this picture of Jesus as the Christ contradicts the marks of estrangement that have been elaborated in the analysis of [humanity's] existential predicament. (Bulman 1981)

Ultimate meaning cannot be found in strictly secular culture but is inherently connected to the depth of being afforded by the work and character of Jesus Christ.

Defining Time and Space

At this juncture in human history, in the context of humanity and its estrangement from its spiritual depth, human beings are in a struggle with the powers of time and space. The present victory of time and space is the human struggle regarding the process of life. Life goes from birth to death, growth to decay. There is no possibility of reversal of that process, only the possibility of the process being repeated by other individuals. So the cycle continues even as individuals continue to succumb to death and decay.

>
> *Religion is the* substance *of culture, culture is the* form *of religion. —Paul Tillich,* Theology of Culture, *42 (emphasis added)*

Though humankind is conditioned by time and space, humanity's victory over time and space is the possibility for individuals to "act towards something beyond" their death (Tillich 1959, 31). In this discussion Tillich builds on his contention that religion is the depth of every aspect of a human spirit. Ultimate meaning—ultimate concern—is possible when a human being engages in acting towards something beyond the inevitability of one's own death and decay. True religion, then, is being ultimately concerned about that which one should be concerned about. For Christians, "faith is the state of being grasped by an ultimate concern," which takes us beyond and out of the power of time and space (Tillich 1959, 40).

Defining Culture

As Tillich begins his discussion defining culture, he does so by highlighting his foundational principle for the relationship between Christians and culture. If, as he argues, true religion is about a person's spirit being in pursuit of ultimate concern, then the separation of culture into secular and spiritual realms is not possible. Spiritual and secular cannot be separated because they're inextricably intertwined; every aspect of life is sparked with ultimate concern.

As such, in every aspect of life, ultimate concern is present, consecrating even the most ordinary. Humanity's estrangement, though, works to separate the sacred from the secular and puts them in competition with each other. The sacred seeks to consume the secular. The secular seeks to consume the sacred.

According to Tillich, the ultimate concern of religion is expressed in the form of culture. Culture entails those symbols, rituals, and behaviors (whether or not they're an aspect of organized religion) that give form to the religious dynamic of humanity. Therefore, "culture is the totality of forms in which the basic concern of religion expresses itself" (1959, 42). So whether it's a reflection of the moral, intellectual, or aesthetic aspects of a people, the style of a culture reflects the expression of their ultimate concern. By reading the style of a culture, one is able to discover the ultimate concern of its people.

> *The universe is God's sanctuary. Every work day is a day of the Lord, every supper a Lord's supper, every work the fulfillment of a divine task, every joy a joy in God. —Paul Tillich,* Theology of Culture, *41 (emphasis added)*

The Function of the Church

In writing about Tillich's theology of culture, Raymond Bulman explains that Tillich's definition of religion is "intentionally directed toward" ultimate meaning. Culture, on the other hand, is directed toward ultimate meaning in substance ("culture is the form of religion") but not necessarily in intentionality. While culture may be rooted in ultimate meaning, it's often "directed toward conditioned forms" as a result of humanity's estrangement from God. Therefore, it's essential that the Church act within culture to help direct culture toward God or, as Tillich might say, toward ultimate meaning (Bulman 1981).

As such, Tillich concludes his argument about the basic considerations of culture and Christianity by suggesting some functions of the Church. First, he states that the primary function of the Church in the world is to answer the question regarding the meaning for human existence. He further argues that the Church should proclaim a message of meaning and healing. In his estimation a message of "any kind of healing that promises success" is the wrong message. Instead, a message of ultimate concern is one that proclaims "the good news of the conquest of the law by the appearance of a new healing reality" (Tillich 1959, 50). In Christ, the universe has been redeemed and saved. There is now the possibility of a new reality.

> *Christianity is the message of a New Reality which makes the fulfillment of our essential being possible. Such being transcends all special prohibitions and commands by one law which is not law, namely love.* —Paul Tillich, Theology of Culture, *211*

Second, Tillich contends that the Church—in seeking ultimate concern—should pursue the transformation of culture. This transformation, however, is not one that seeks to establish the realized kingdom of God, nor does it seek to establish perfect social structures. Instead, the Church *participates* in culture—sometimes in a leading role, but always acknowledging that change occurs within the "inner dynamics of culture" and with the Church acting as a "cultural force beside others" (Tillich 1959, 50).

Finally, the Church should seek to function in a prophetic role within culture. It can do this in three ways. First, by acting as a guardian and pointing out structures in culture that don't appropriately express ultimate meaning and concern. Second, by acting as a protector against the demonic power within those structures. And third, by acting as judge of culture, which includes judging the Church itself.

As Tillich astutely notes, culture shapes the forms of the Church. Therefore, they're subject to the same estrangement as other forms of culture. He also wisely notes that the prophetic voices of culture don't always come from the Church. Part of the prophetic witness of the Church is to rightly judge those prophetic voices that are outside the Church.

Tillich concludes *Theology of Culture* with a few words of encouragement and admonishment for the Church and its relationships in culture. Tillich states that the Church is not just

> *The Church is the Community of the New Being.* —Paul Tillich, Theology of Culture, *212*

an institution, organized religion, hierarchical authority, or even a social organization. The Church "is primarily a group of people who express a new reality by which they have been grasped" (Tillich 1959, 212). It is as this new reality that the Church can and must engage culture.

PAUL JOHANNES TILLICH

Paul Tillich was born in eastern Germany in 1886. He grew up in a conservative Lutheran church where his father was the pastor. Tragically, Tillich lost his mother to cancer when he was only 17. As a young man, Tillich was ordained as a Lutheran minister, but also completed his Ph.D. in theology from the University of Breslau in 1911. He taught at various German universities until he emigrated to the United States in 1933.[2]

During World War I, from 1914 to 1918, Tillich served as a chaplain in the German army. He was deeply influenced by his time spent on the front lines with German soldiers. And this experience served to raise doubts and questions about human existence and divine revelation. As Raymond Bulman writes,

> Tillich's pastoral duties during the war, which brought him into close contact with soldiers from all the social classes, convinced him of the terrible class divisions in German society and especially of the great chasm that separated the church from the industrial masses. (Bulman 1981)

While Tillich was a professor of philosophy at the University of Frankfurt, he came into conflict with Hitler. In public lectures he gave throughout Germany, Tillich opposed Nazism. And shortly after Hitler became chancellor of Germany in 1933, Paul Tillich was dismissed from his university post.

During a visit to Germany, Reinhold Niebuhr (Richard Niebuhr's brother) invited Tillich to join the faculty at Union Theological Seminary in New York City. So Tillich and his family left Germany and emigrated to the United States. He taught at Union Theological Seminary until 1955.

Dr. Tillich then joined the faculty at Harvard Divinity School as professor of theology. He later moved to the University of Chicago in 1962 and served there until his death in 1965.

Key to Tillich's work and theology was his belief that "theology formulates the *questions* implied in human existence, and theology formulates the *answers* implied in divine self-manifestation under the guidance of the questions implied in human existence. This is a circle which drives [humanity] to a point where question and answer are not separated. This point, however, is not a moment in time" (Tillich 1951) (emphasis added). (See also Wildman 1994–2009, Tillich 2000, and Bulman 1981.)

REFLECTION ACTIVITY (5 TO 10 MINUTES)

Paul Tillich argued that ultimate reality is the "infinite Truth that is self-evident and presupposed in all thought and meaning." How might this idea impact how youth workers approach the critique and evaluation of the movies that students (and youth leaders) watch?

---

2 http://voxtheology.wordpress.com/2008/06/26/voices-paul-tillich/

DIGGING DEEPER (10 TO 15 MINUTES)

Paul Tillich contends that the Church has a prophetic role to play in culture. Based on Tillich's three aspects of a prophetic role (guardian, protector, and judge), write a short response for how a youth ministry might function as prophet in a church and community.

> • Tillich defined *religion* as the core of all human activity, manifested in all "creative functions of the human spirit."

CHAPTER 14
H. Richard Niebuhr: On Christ and Culture

LEARNING OBJECTIVES

When you've finished this chapter, you should be able to:

1. Elaborate on and discuss Niebuhr's definitions of Christ and of culture

2. Articulate the five different typologies of a Christian response to culture

3. Critique each of the five typologies, noting the strengths and weaknesses of each

H. Richard Niebuhr was probably the most renowned theologian of the twentieth century on the topic of Christians and culture. His book *Christ and Culture*, which was first published in 1951, has been in almost continuous print since that time, with a fiftieth anniversary edition released in 2001.

In it, Niebuhr tackles the dilemma all Christians face: The enduring problem of how to appropriately respond to both Christ and culture. He begins this work by identifying two foundational principles by which he constructs his discussion.

First, Niebuhr was motivated in his own struggle with this question by a "conviction that Christ as living Lord is answering the question in the totality of history and life in a fashion which transcends the wisdom of all his interpreters yet employs their partial insights and their necessary conflicts" (Niebuhr 1951, 2).

In every cultural context since the beginning of the Church, Christians have responded to this dilemma. The wisdom that Christ offers his followers regarding how they should respond to culture encompasses all of human existence and experience. Limited by our finite nature and particular cultural context, humanity has only "partial insights." Any response that a person or group makes is, at best, a flawed effort. Niebuhr contends that any and every Christian response proves itself inadequate. As the quote above indicates, Niebuhr was convinced that Jesus Christ provided answers that encompassed the totality of history and life and that Christians' best efforts to respond appropriately to Christ or culture came out of their inability to gain full and complete insight into either Christ or culture.

Second, as Niebuhr further argues, throughout the history of Christianity, there's been no agreed upon Christian perspective for responding to culture. Differing Christians in differing times and differing contexts have chosen differing ways to answer the question of how to respond to culture. It's on the basis of these two points that Niebuhr begins his essay in which he identifies five types of Christian responses to Christ and culture.

As we examine these five types, it's important to also include Niebuhr's definitions of Christ and culture.

CHRIST

Niebuhr begins his definition of Christ by highlighting people's different views about what it means to be a Christian. Some hold that a Christian is "one who believes in Jesus Christ"; others believe it's one who claims to be a "follower of Jesus Christ" (Niebuhr 1951). He continues with other descriptions and concludes by stating that the variety of definitions one might hold about what it means to be a Christian come down to the authority one is willing to give the person of Jesus Christ. Is he a great teacher, a prophet? Is his character manifested in love or judgment or humility?

For Niebuhr, the Christ of the New Testament is one who without hesitation or wavering is convinced of the sovereignty of God. As the Son of God, Jesus' radical and complete loyalty to the Sovereign God of all things leads him to "point away from the many values of [humanity's] social life to the One who alone is good" (Niebuhr 1951, 28). By his very *nature*, Jesus points away from the finite world and social context of created humanity to the eternal God of the universe. By his very *nature*, Jesus creates a dichotomy between himself and human culture. He is not compatible with fallen, human culture. Yet, Christ is mediator between God and culture and is always pointing away from culture to God.

God's relationship to humanity and culture through Jesus Christ means Christians, in Niebuhr's words:

> Are forever being challenged to abandon all things for the sake of God; and forever being sent back into the world to teach and practice all the things that have been commanded them. (Niebuhr 1951, 29)

CULTURE

Next, Niebuhr offers his definition of *culture*. He doesn't stray too far from the anthropological definitions highlighted in the first chapter of this text. Noting what many of the New Testament writers referred to as the "world," Niebuhr states that "culture is the 'artificial, secondary environment' which [humanity] superimposes on the natural" (1951, 32).

Quoting one of the well-known anthropologists of his day, Bronislaw Malinowski, Niebuhr concludes that culture is composed of "language, habits, ideas, beliefs, customs, social organization, inherited artifacts, technical processes, and values" (1951, 32). In other words, all the creative activities of humanity in social context.

He further highlights what he considers to be the chief characteristics of culture. A synthesis of his list follows:

- Socially constructed and organized. Culture is always socially constructed and transmitted and social organization is always a form of culture.

- Human achievement. Culture is the creative work of human beings, which gives rise to human achievement. Culture encompasses all within the natural world that is humanly constructed.

- World of values. What human beings have constructed "is intended for a purpose; it is designed to serve a good" and is, therefore, a thing of value (34). As Niebuhr further argues, the values of human achievement are predominantly concerned with what is "good for [humanity]," and all that is cultural is directed toward the realization and preservation of what is valued (35).

- Pluralistic. Cultures are highly complex, with myriad values and possibilities present at any given moment. Moreover, individuals within a culture have their own interests, values, and claims, such that there is a never-ending flux of competing values and possibilities. As Niebuhr describes: "Societies are always involved in a more or less laborious effort to hold together in tolerable conflict the many efforts of many [people] in many groups to achieve and conserve many goods" (38).

At this point in Niebuhr's dialogue, he's created a distinctive contrast between Christ, who demands complete loyalty to the sovereign God, and culture, with its humanly constructed system of competing values and ideas (including those of the kingdom of God). Thus, the Christian is caught in between these two competing ideals—Christ and culture—and, by necessity, must respond. It's at this point that Niebuhr introduces his five typologies of the ways Christians respond.

NIEBUHR'S TYPOLOGIES

There are two points that will frame this discussion. First, as Niebuhr clarifies in his text, typologies are artificial constructs that serve to frame perspective and discussion. Though types are inadequate to fully explain how any one person or group might respond to culture, they're helpful in providing a framework for gaining insight into the question of Christ and culture.

Second, Niebuhr follows a three-point structure in describing each of the types. He begins by offering a definition of each type, followed by Scripture and historical figures that provide concrete examples for each type. And finally, he concludes by suggesting weaknesses of each type. We'll follow a similar pattern here.

Type 1: Christ against Culture

Niebuhr begins with a response to the question of Christ and culture that draws the starkest distinction between the two. In this answer, Christ is viewed as embodying absolute truth and, as such, sole authority over culture. This response rejects culture's claim of loyalty over the Christian. Culture, on the other hand, is acknowledged to be under the rule of evil. Thus, there is a clear line of distinction between Christ and culture. Christians are left to choose their allegiance: The world and the things of the world, or Christ—there is no middle ground. As Gordon Lynch states in *Understanding Theology and Popular Culture*:

> Christians adopting this approach have therefore tended to emphasize an either/or choice between following Christ or engaging in contemporary culture. At times this can take the form of a physical separation of Christian communities from the wider culture (e.g., in the case of some Anabaptist communities), or more commonly a sense of psychological and spiritual differentiation between God's people and the "world." (2005, 100)

As concrete examples of this type, Niebuhr cites the book of 1 John and the second-century Christian writer and apologist Tertullian, as well as the nineteenth-century Russian writer of *War and Peace* and *Anna Karenina*, Leo Tolstoy. In the book of 1 John, Niebuhr draws on the teachings that highlight how Jesus' disciples are to love one another and resist the world. Though Tertullian's and Tolstoy's practice of their beliefs and convictions about Christ and culture were fraught with inconsistencies, each espoused a view of a Christian response to culture that rejected culture's claims in politics, philosophy, the arts, and often churches and religious institutions as well (Niebuhr 1951).

It is those inconsistencies that highlight for Niebuhr the major weakness in this response. As Niebuhr rightly attests, this position "affirms in words what it denies in action; namely the possibility of sole dependence on Jesus Christ to the exclusion of culture" (1951, 69). Human beings are products of culture, from the language one uses to the processes with which one constructs an idea or response. Human beings are shaped by context and experience, history and achievement. As such, it's impossible for anyone to escape the influence of culture.

Do not love the world or anything in the world. If you love the world, love for the Father is not in you. For everything in the world—the cravings of sinful people, the lust of their eyes and their boasting about what they have and do—comes not from the Father but from the world. The world and its desires pass away, but whoever does the will of God lives forever. —1 John 2:15-17

Type 2: Christ of Culture

Niebuhr's second type is the polar opposite to the first. This answer to the dilemma of Christ and culture is a far more positive view than the radical position of "Christ against Culture." Niebuhr drew this description from the prevailing liberal Protestantism of his time. He labels this response the *accommodation* response; that is, Jesus Christ is "the fulfiller of [culture's] hopes and aspirations, the perfecter of its true faith, the source of its holiest spirit" (1951, 83).

In this perspective, there is no tension between Christ and culture. Proponents of this view see in Christ and his teachings the most positive elements of culture, and vice versa. Thus, certain aspects of culture, from democratic institutions to philosophers and artists, affirm and reflect humanity's ability to achieve moral perfection. As Niebuhr highlights:

> Jesus Christ is the great enlightener, the great teacher, the one who directs all [people] in culture to the attainment of wisdom, moral perfection, and peace. Sometimes he is hailed as the great utilitarian, sometimes as the great idealist, sometimes as the man of reason, sometimes as the man of sentiment. But whatever the categories are by means of which he is understood, the things for which he stands are fundamentally the same—a peaceful, co-operative society achieved by moral training. (1951, 92)

In support of this type, Niebuhr highlights the teachings of Gnosticism and Peter Abelard. Niebuhr contends that though many consider Gnostics to be heretics, Jesus was at the center of their thought and teachings. For Gnostics, "Jesus Christ was an individual and spiritual matter, which had its place in the life of culture as the very pinnacle of human achievement" (1951, 88).

Abelard was a medieval French philosopher and theologian. In his writings there is a positive ideal regarding the ability of Christians to attain moral achievement and be part of a moral culture. In other words, there is no conflict with culture. In Abelard's understanding, a clear picture of Christ would lead to a church moving culture toward a higher moral plane.

Niebuhr cites two weaknesses of this approach to Christ and culture. In his words, it is "impossible to remove the offense of Christ and his cross." Therefore, there is an inevitable tension between society and Christ. A second critique is the accommodation that Gnostics, Abelard, and Liberal Protestants of his day engage in to create the Christ of this view. As such, they tend to focus on a small segment of Scripture (for example, the Sermon on the Mount) to create a moral Christ and a high, positive view of the possibilities of culture to attain moral perfection.

Type 3: Christ above Culture

These next two views fall in the middle between the radicalists—Christ against Culture—and the accommodationists—Christ of Culture. This third type, Christ above Culture, which Niebuhr refers to as the *synthetic* view, doesn't see Christ and culture as an either-or dynamic. And while

GNOSTICISM

Gnosticism refers to a number of mystical religious movements that arose during the time of the early church, perhaps having their strongest presence during the second century AD. Not limited to Christianity, Gnosticism drew on Greek philosophy and thought, as well as Eastern religious traditions. Gnostics "believed in a heavenly redeemer, who came into the world to save people from bondage to the material world by giving them divine knowledge (from the Greek *gnosis*, meaning knowledge)" (Marshall, Travis, and Paul 2002).

Dualistic in nature, Gnosticism separated the spiritual, which was good, from the material or physical, which was evil. Within the physical world, there was no possibility of good overcoming evil. Salvation, therefore, was the release of the physical body (and its lusts and desires) from the world to the heavenly spiritual realm of the Divine (Elwell 1988).

> *We know that "We all possess knowledge."* But knowledge *puffs up while love builds up.*
> —1 Corinthians 8:1b (emphasis added)

Christian Gnostics emphasized knowledge over faith and believed that some had been given special knowledge. Two central themes within Gnosticism were:

1. "The divine Christ would not possibly get himself entangled with human flesh, which is inherently evil," thus the belief that he wasn't really human.

2. Since salvation meant the release from all things physical and material, no importance was attached to ethical or moral behavior. (Marshall, Travis, and Paul 2002)

Though it seems that Gnosticism was not a very developed movement during the time of the New Testament, some of Paul's letters, as well as John's, address some of the beliefs of the Gnostics. (See 1 John, 1 Corinthians, and the letters to Timothy and Titus.)

Food for Thought

Can you identify elements of Gnosticism in present-day youth ministry or youth culture?

---

it resists the Christ of Culture approach, it affirms that both Christ and culture confess the sovereignty of God. This view is held by some Catholics and Anglicans, who believe "culture to be a mediator of truth and grace, but [who] ultimately locate this truth and grace as gifts of God rather than in human achievement" (Lynch 2005, 100).

As Niebuhr states, culture is:

> both divine and human in its origin;
> both holy and sinful,
> a realm of both necessity and freedom,
> and one to which both reason and revelation apply. (1951, 121)

As Christians endeavor to live and act rightly within culture, they recognize that Christ reigns within and above culture.

As proponents of this view, Niebuhr looks to Clement of Alexandria and Thomas Aquinas. Clement, a Greek theologian of the second century, highlighted two key attributes of the Christians that correspond to this view. First, Christians are to espouse Christ's love in a sacrificial witness. Second, they are to exercise great care in the material and cultural attainments of society. Drawing upon his Greek philosophical roots, Clement contends it's a life of love and goodness—a "life of love of God for His own sake, without desire of reward or fear of punishment" (Niebuhr 1951, 127). Such a life isn't caught up in the rewards or attainments of this life, but in the desire for and realization of a future hope beyond this present life.

St. Thomas Aquinas was a philosopher and theologian in the thirteenth century. Niebuhr argues that Thomas was the greatest synthesist of all of Christian history. It's every Christian's responsibility to discipline him or herself to be a person of high moral character and to effect influence on the institutions of family, state, and church. The possibility of moral goodness in humankind invites the responsibility of humankind on culture and all of its human institutions. This kind of life isn't possible without the activity of the Spirit (through Jesus Christ) in a person's life. In this way, Christians have the possibility of affording a foretaste of the fullness of God promised—in Jesus—to their culture (Niebuhr 1951).

The biggest weakness in this response is the tendency to become a cultural Christian. The greater the emphasis on restoring culture, the less likely one is to experience tension between Christ and culture. On the other hand, the other extreme is to institutionalize Christ and the gospel. Again, this is the tendency as the focus leans toward ensuring that institutions are a model of Christ (Niebuhr 1951).

Type 4: Christ and Culture in Paradox

Niebuhr refers to the second of his two in-the-middle types as the *dualist* position. This type is characterized by a conflict between the righteousness of God and the unrighteousness of self. At one pole stands God (in other words, God in Christ and Christ in God); at the other stands humanity and all human activity (for example, culture). The beginning point for the dualist's response to the dilemma of Christ and culture is the extension of God's grace to humanity through Jesus Christ's act of reconciliation and forgiveness. Thereby, humanity has the possibility of hope and the assurance of salvation.

The emphasis is on God's grace and God's activity in contrast to humanity's sinfulness. All of humanity's works and activity—culture—are "pitifully inadequate" and "sordid and depraved" (Niebuhr 1951, 152). Niebuhr further argues that before the holiness of God there is little distinction between any person's actions—all culture is corrupt. "All human action, all culture, is infected with godlessness, which is the essence of sin" (1951, 154).

Unlike the accommodationists, the dualist realizes her inability to get out of culture, acknowledging the inevitability of being a part of culture, sinful though it is, and that God in his sovereignty sustains culture. The dualist lives in a perpetual state of paradox—living in sinful creation, yet also living in God's grace.

Niebuhr goes on to highlight the different paradoxes:

THE PARADOXES

Under law	yet,	Under grace
Sinner	yet,	Righteous
Believer	yet,	Doubter
Assurance of Salvation	yet,	Insecure
All things new	yet,	Everything as it was
God revealed in Christ	yet,	God hidden in Christ
Believer knows God	yet,	Walks by faith

(Niebuhr 1951)

Niebuhr uses the apostle Paul and Martin Luther as the primary examples of this type. He concurs that Paul's writing can be used to support many of the five types. Yet, in support of the dualist position, Niebuhr highlights Paul's argument that the greatest issue for a believer is the conflict between the righteousness of God and the unrighteousness of humankind. Christ's work revealed the unrighteousness of every human and human work; yet because of God's grace and forgiveness, every aspect of human activity is also subject to God's redemptive work. It's impossible to escape that tension. It seems that a justification for a Christian culture exists in this type, as the dynamic of Christian activity within a society works as a preventative to the destructive nature of sin.

As a further example, Niebuhr highlights the teachings of Martin Luther. Niebuhr underscores the distinctions in Luther's writings between the temporal and spiritual worlds, the external and internal, the body and the soul. Though humanity has been redeemed and there is the promise of a future hope, we now live in the between-the-times.

Niebuhr highlights two major weaknesses to this type. First, he contends there is the tendency for some who hold this conviction to be led into antinomianism—the belief that because salvation comes by faith, we aren't bound by moral laws (Niebuhr 1951). If there cannot be any bringing together of both Christ and culture—if they are truly in paradox—then what is to prevent believers from living a life without consideration of sin? This is what Paul responds to in his letter to the Christians in Rome:

What shall we say, then? Shall we go on sinning so that grace may increase? By no means! We are those who have died to sin; how can we live in it any longer? (Romans 6:1-2)

A second weakness of this type is the tendency toward cultural conservatism—the tendency to avoid addressing inequities within society. Again, Niebuhr highlights Paul and Luther as examples. While both Paul and Luther were concerned with bringing change to the church and its institutions, they seemed less concerned with addressing and opposing some of the cultural issues of their times—slavery and social stratification, for example (Niebuhr 1951).

Type 5: Christ the Transformer of Culture

Niebuhr presents his fifth typology in a different manner than the previous four types. He doesn't indicate a preference for any one of the types explicitly (quite the opposite). But implicitly, it seems evident that Niebuhr leans toward this type. Those who believe in this kind of response—Christ the Transformer—are referred to as *conversionists*.

Without the usual introductory explanation of the type, Niebuhr jumps right into the three theological convictions that he believes are the basis for this type. First, a key theological theme is a particular vision of creation. The context for all human thought and function is God's created world and the creative activity of God. As such, there is a creative ordering and power that serves to define and shape human response.

Further, this created order is under the rule of Christ. In all of human history and creativity, there is the acknowledgment that Christ has been a participant—past, present, and future. As Niebuhr states: "The Word that became flesh and dwelt among us, the Son who does the work of the Father in the world of creation, has entered into a human culture that has never been without his ordering action" (1951, 193). This understanding of creation and human activity and response forms the basis for this typology.

A second theological conviction centers on an understanding of humanity's fall and the disordering of creation. When sin entered the world, there was a radical change and distortion of God's created world and order. The resulting corruption has come about because of human activity. All the goodness of God's creation is now marred, corrupted, "warped, twisted, and misdirected" (Niebuhr 1951, 194). There is a subtle but important distinction here regarding the view of humanity's fall from grace compared to other views that hold a stark image of the fall. "It is perverted good, not evil; or it is evil as perversion, and not as badness of being" (Niebuhr 1951, 194). The conversionist isn't calling for the replacement of evil creation with a new, good creation. Rather, the conversionist holds that, at its essence, creation (and humanity) is good, but it needs to be restored to its original goodness.

Third, the conversionist approach to Christ and culture holds to a particular view of human history and God's participation in it. That is, rather than a Christ beyond human history or a "between-the-times" understanding, this view holds more to a "now" dynamic of God's participation. The premier concern is with the renewal of God's creation now, rather than a future eschatological moment. The present is eschatological. As Niebuhr states:

> The conversionist, with his view of history as the present encounter with God in Christ, does not live so much in expectation of a final ending of the world of creation and culture as in awareness of the power of the Lord to transform all things by lifting them up to Himself. (1951, 195)

In support of this typology, Niebuhr relies primarily on John's Gospel and Augustine. Niebuhr argues that in the book of John, one can see elements of the present as eschatological theological conviction. For example, Jesus is the Word who became flesh, who entered the "now" of humanity—time and space. As well, we find the idea that God's judgment is on the world "now." Calling to mind Jesus' interaction with the Samaritan woman, Niebuhr reminds his readers that John's Gospel tells us that the time is now for worshippers to worship "the Father in spirit and in truth" (1951). Though Niebuhr allows for other views in this Gospel, he contends that the conversionist's approach can be clearly seen as well.

One argument that supports the notion that this is the view Niebuhr favored is the fact that this is the one typology for which he doesn't include a section highlighting its weaknesses. However, Niebuhr argues that the typologies can overlap and that time, history, and place often dictate the appropriate response to Christ and culture. Further, he argues that each Christian has a personal responsibility to think and respond in his or her context and understanding. As he concludes his text, Niebuhr states that to make decisions out of one's faith in Christ:

> Is to make them in view of the fact that Christ is risen from the dead, and is not only the head of the church but the redeemer of the world. It is to make them in view of the fact that the world of culture—humanity's achievement—exists within the world of grace—God's kingdom. (1951, 256)

REFLECTION ACTIVITY (5 TO 10 MINUTES)

Niebuhr said Christians "are forever being challenged to abandon all things for the sake of God; and forever being sent back into the world to teach and practice all the things that have been commanded them" (1951, 29). Consider his quotation in light of your experience in youth ministry and the culture of youth. In what ways have you seen this tension exemplified?

H. RICHARD NIEBUHR

H. Richard Niebuhr was one of the most influential American theologians of the twentieth century. The youngest of five children in a German immigrant family, Richard was born in Missouri in 1894, and his father was a minister in the Evangelical Synod of North America. Three of the five Niebuhr children, including Richard, grew up to be acknowledged theologians. Richard was himself ordained in the Evangelical Synod in 1916, after completing degrees at Elmhurst College (1912) and Eden Theological Seminary (1915).

While serving as a pastor in Missouri, Niebuhr obtained a master's degree from Washington University in St. Louis (1918). From 1922 to 1924, he studied at Yale University, completing a bachelor of divinity degree in 1923 and his Ph.D. from Yale Divinity School in 1924.

In 1919, Niebuhr joined the faculty of Eden Theological Seminary, teaching there from 1919 to 1924, and again from 1927 to 1931. In the interim period, he served as president of Elmhurst College (1924–1927). In 1931, Niebuhr was invited to join the faculty of Yale Divinity School, where he taught until his death in 1962.

H. Richard Niebuhr's life, and consequently, his writings and teachings, were greatly influenced by the events of his day. As a young theologian, Niebuhr's thoughts and ideas about the gospel and the kingdom of God were greatly influenced by the social gospel movement, which gained prominence in the mid-nineteenth to early-twentieth centuries. According to William M. King, the "fundamental premise of the social gospel was the belief that social change should be controlled and directed through the rational application of religious ideals" (King 1983). That is, proponents of a social gospel believed that salvation and good works were inextricably intertwined.

Imbued with optimism, followers of this movement responded to the social plights of nineteenth-century industrialization (for example, urbanism, poverty, education, health issues, and so on) by calling for social justice and believing that the kingdom of God would be ushered in as social issues were addressed and reformed. Niebuhr's enthusiasm and optimism were tempered by the global pain and suffering brought about by the two World Wars.

Out of his studies and life experiences, several themes became prominent. Niebuhr held these two ideas in contrast to each other: The sovereignty of God and the difficulty of human beings to fully understand God outside of their own context and personal experience (historical relativism). Human beings, bound by history and culture, are thereby limited in their capacity for comprehending God—the sovereign, transcendent God who reigns above and beyond history.

Another major theme for Niebuhr was how human beings relate to each other, to God, and to culture. Though an author of numerous books, he's best known for *Christ and Culture*, in which he sets forth his "five-part typology" for "understanding the options by which faith and secular culture, ideal and material forces, could be interrelated" (Hartford Institute for Religion Research 1998). More than 50 years after it was written, *Christ and Culture* remains a significant force in the dialogue of the relationship of Christians to Christ and culture.

DIGGING DEEPER (10 TO 15 MINUTES)

Write a brief response in response to the following question: Of Niebuhr's five typologies, which one best fits your perspective regarding an appropriate response to culture? Give reasons for your choice.

- Niebuhr's five typologies of response to Christ and Culture:

1. Christ against Culture—Radicalist. Christ is absolute truth and authority over culture. Culture is under the rule of evil.

2. Christ of Culture—Accommodation. Jesus Christ is the perfecter of culture.

3. Christ above Culture—Synthetic. Both Christ and culture confess the sovereignty of God, though culture is sinful.

4. Christ and Culture in Paradox—Dualist. Characterized by conflict between God's righteousness and humanity's unrighteousness, culture (and humanity) is in a perpetual state of paradox.

5. Christ the Transformer of Culture—Conversionist. Culture (and humanity) is good and needs to be transformed through Christ and restored to its original goodness.

CHAPTER 15
Karl Barth: Bearing Witness to Culture

LEARNING OBJECTIVES

When you've finished this chapter, you should be able to:

1. Articulate Barth's definition of free culture

2. Express how culture, creation, and covenant are intertwined in Barth's theology

3. Convey the task of theology in relation to culture

4. State the role of the Church in bearing witness to culture

Unlike Paul Tillich and Richard Niebuhr, Karl Barth doesn't pursue a specific theology of culture. He does, however, develop his theology regarding the relationship between the secular (for example, culture) and the church, and as such has much to contribute to our discussion.

In attempting to synthesize Barth's theology of culture into a brief description from the wealth of writings he produced, particularly his *Church Dogmatics* (Volumes 1-4) and his commentary on Romans (*The Epistle to the Romans*), there is the danger of oversimplification. So with the acknowledgment that Barth's theology is quite complex and broad ranging and that any attempt to present a brief survey will fall short, we now engage in this task.

First, to understand Barth's perspective on culture, one must consider the context within which his theology developed. Throughout Barth's works, one theme is revealed as having greatly influenced his perspective on humanity and culture. Many of his peers espoused the conviction that humanity could bring about God's kingdom via a movement toward God. Proponents of the liberal Protestantism of his day argued that humanity, and thereby culture, was on a trajectory of realized perfection, and as social organizations pursued God, God's kingdom would become a reality. In reaction against this liberal Protestant movement, Barth resisted the idea that humanity could bring the reality of the kingdom of God. Further, he believed the notion that humanity could bring about God's kingdom had fueled a deification of humanity and human culture, resulting in a culture in which God was less than God and humanity was greater than humanity (Metzger 2003).

A second theme that stands out in Barth's understanding of culture is that Christians must act within culture to bear witness, though he gives few particulars on *how* they are to do this. The Church has a special role of critique and judgment and should act on behalf of culture even as it functions within culture itself (Palma 1983). These two themes shape Barth's understanding and theology. As we briefly examine Barth's theology of culture, we'll explore his understanding in four areas.

First, this chapter begins with an examination of what is foundational to Barth's theology of culture: His understanding of God's relationship to humanity and God's divine "Yes" and "No." The conversation then turns to a discussion of Barth's definition of culture, which includes a look at the three categories of creation, covenant, and culture.

Building on this definition, the next section explores Barth's understanding of the call of humanity to a free culture and looks at the characteristics of a free culture, as well as the enslavement of humanity in a culture that isn't free. An essential tenet of Barth's theology of culture was his conviction that *all* of culture is given the task to bear witness.

The next section outlines his understanding regarding the task of all humanity, but particularly the Church, to bear witness to "humanity's ultimate concern, the manifestation of the Logos in human history" (Metzger 2003).

Finally, our discussion of Barth's theology of culture concludes with an analysis of Barth's definition of the task of theology and the basis for his call to critique and judge culture.

> **Food for Thought**
>
> *What do you think about Barth's belief that human beings can't help establish the kingdom of God? What role does or can humanity play, if any?*

GOD'S DIVINE "YES" AND "NO"

Central to Barth's theology of culture is his understanding of the relationship between God and humanity. One of his concerns with his contemporaries was the notion that humanity could reach out and up to God. As noted above, he felt the church and many leading theologians espoused a theology that inflated the authority and possibility of human activity, while at the same time it diminished the authority, sovereignty, and nature of God.

In Barth's estimation, humans couldn't reach up to God; only God could descend to humans. "God is not acknowledged as God and what is called 'God' is in fact [humanity]. By living to ourselves, we serve the 'No-God'" (Barth 1933). God is wholly other, and any attempts for humanity to span the divide between God and his created beings are futile. Sin and evil, brought upon God's creation by humanity, had created a division between humanity and God leading to God's divine "No," or rejection of humanity. Thus, humanity and human culture are alienated from God.

Humanity is not, however, left with the divine "No" from God, thanks to God's gift of mercy and grace. In Jesus Christ, God has spoken his divine "Yes" of grace and mercy and descended into the realm of humanity and human culture to redeem those whom he loves and has created. The sovereign God speaks "Yes" as revealed to humanity in the work and life of Jesus Christ. It is this understanding of God's all-encompassing, radical love for his creation that Barth builds upon as he considers an appropriate response to culture.

God's Revelation

God has elected to reveal himself in the form of humanity through the person of Jesus Christ. Again, as noted above, this revelation comes from God *to* humanity. Jesus, as divine person within the godly Trinity, "takes a concrete human nature to himself in becoming incarnate as Jesus Christ" (Metzger 2003).

Paul Metzger, in discussing Barth's theology of God's revelation, identifies four components of this revelation in Jesus Christ (2003):

1. God's revelation occurs in and through the veil of humanity in a physical, human body. As such, the divine nature of God comes to human beings indirectly. Humanity is able to know God in and through this revelation, *but only as God reveals himself through the person of Jesus Christ.*

2. As such, humanity never has direct access to the revelation. God's revelation is hidden in the person of Jesus Christ. "Christ is the point of contact between God and humanity". Thus, our struggle to understand God begins and ends with the revelation within the person of Jesus Christ.

3. The Word (Jesus Christ) is of one nature with the Father (divine) and also of one nature with humanity. Here, Barth makes a careful distinction. As Metzger states, "Christ is not a human person, but a divine person who is human; his human nature 'has its personhood in the divine person.'"

4. The divine and human natures relate to one another indirectly. That is, "the divine is capable of the human, the human is not capable of the divine."

It is this foundational understanding of the revelation of God in Jesus Christ that sets the stage for his articulation of a theological response to culture.

God's "Yes/No" and Humanity's "Yes/No"

As Sovereign Lord and Creator God, God is able to speak a definitive "Yes" or "No" to humanity and human culture. God, in his sovereignty, says "No" to anything in his creation that is in contrast with his nature. Thus, in God's nature, he is able to speak with exactitude. On the other hand, humanity is, at best, able to speak only partially "Yes" or "No." Humanity offers its "Yes" or "No" based on its knowledge and understanding of God and its ability to perceive and act or "speak" to culture out of that knowledge and understanding.

As created beings, humans have limits in their understanding of God's revelation and their capability to speak rightly. God's "Yes" and "No" is determinative of humanity's ability to speak rightly its human "Yes" and "No." It is this limited ability to respond that is the impetus for Barth's call for the task of theology (Palma 1983). We will return to these ideas regarding the need for an appropriate and right theology in the section regarding the rightness of human culture.

BARTH'S DEFINITION OF CULTURE

In Robert Palma's book on Barth and culture, he quotes Barth's son, Markus, in providing a definition for Barth's understanding of culture:

> Culture is "the summit of human possibilities for which we yearn, which we can never define, which occurs in a great work of art, or in Mozart, or in great persons." (1983)

This definition of culture is the goal of true humanity. As Palma describes, culture "is the task set through the Word of God for achieving the destined condition of many in unity of soul and body" (1983). What one discovers in a study of Barth's work regarding culture, though, is that the above definition is his understanding of the truly human possibilities of culture. The reality, however, is that the wider experience of culture is one that, for Barth, encompasses the definition of many of the anthropologists of his day. That is, culture refers to the totality of human existence. It is this broader understanding of culture that Barth most often addresses. There is a tension between these two definitions of the reality and the ideal, the flawed and the renewed.

There are two foundational elements of Barth's understanding of culture: Creation and covenant. First, creation is the basis for the relationship between God and humanity. Creation is the stage upon which redemption—God's revelation activities—is accomplished. Though creation doesn't serve as a witness in the same way the Word of Christ does, creation does have the ability to function as a mirror into God's nature through its very nature as a reflection of God's creativity, care, and compassion.

In Barth's estimation, the nature of creation is to glorify God as it does what it does. That is, "creation glorifies God by being what it is in the freedom of its limits" (Metzger 2003). With a theology of culture grounded in the doctrine of creation, along with the "investigation of science and the...development and enjoyment of human life, including the arts...there is space for cultural creativity that is pleasing, not only to its human creation, but also to the divine creator" (Metzger 2003).

A second premise is the covenant of reconciliation between God and humanity. Creation and covenant are interrelated in that creation serves, according to Barth, as the external basis for

God's covenant of reconciliation. Both in the acts of creation and redemption, the person of Jesus Christ is central; therefore, creation cannot exist independently of Christ. Further, in Barth's understanding, humanity has no existence independent of a covenant relationship with God.

As we conclude this section, we see that Barth's perspective of culture is, therefore, grounded in the dynamic interrelationship of creation, covenant, and culture (Palma 1983, Metzger 2003). It is on this basis that Barth puts forth an understanding of human culture and the place of the church.

FREE CULTURE

As noted above, Barth identifies two kinds of culture. The first arises out of humanity's alienation from God—what is often called *secularization*. Humankind does not exist in the freedom with which it was originally created. It is this kind of culture that God has emphatically rejected (the divine "No").

The second is culture that has as its goal the manifestation of the Word of God. Barth calls this second kind of culture *free culture*. Out of God's divine "Yes" to his creation, humanity has the possibility of true freedom as persons and in culture. "Free culture is human activity which reflects genuine human freedom and is grounded in God's own freedom and humanity" (Palma 1983). The notion of free culture begs the question, "Free from what?" Barth responds with two categories of response: Culture that is free *from*, and culture that is free *for*.

Free From

Marred by the fall and sin, humankind and human culture need to be set free so they can fulfill God's commands in the sphere of culture. For culture to be truly free, humanity must be liberated from its fall and alienation from God. Humanity needs to be liberated from its quest to be autonomous and absolute. This desire to be like God and act for one's own self-interests has invoked the divine "No" of God and alienated humanity from its Creator and sovereign Lord. More will be said about this in the section on the task of theology. Specifically, though, perverted attitudes toward God, neighbor, and self have led humanity, and thereby human culture, to be enslaved.

Free For

In contrast with a culture that enslaves, free culture liberates humanity to experience life in its fullness and the full experience of God's creation, which God has entrusted to humanity. Specifically, there are six characteristics of a free culture that liberates. Persons and culture are liberated for:

1. *God.* Free culture, grounded in the mercy and grace granted to humanity in the person of Jesus Christ, liberates persons for a restoration of the relationship with the Trinitarian God. God has freely acted in grace toward humanity and, thereby, offers the possibility for humanity and human culture to respond positively to God's freedom, receiving the gift of God's freedom within the limits and constraints of our humanity.

2. *Obedience to God and his commands.* It's in this freedom that humanity has the capacity to choose and act in right ways toward God and his commands. Barth is careful to note that humanity's ability to choose and make decisions is a freedom granted by God, but it's limited. Humanity in no way has the freedom to choose and act as God does. God freely gives and freely acts; and in giving freedom to humanity, God does so with constraints. And humanity is free to act out of gratitude with obedience to God.

3. *God's cause in the world.* As Palma (1983) contends, Barth argues that the cause of God is the cause of humanity. Since God has chosen to reveal his divine personhood in and through the human person of Jesus Christ, God's cause is humanity. Thus, humanity that is free is free to serve the cause of Christ, which is humanity. As such, Barth says:

   > "God wants light, not darkness. He wants cosmos, not chaos. He wants peace, not disorder. He wants man to administer and to receive justice rather than to inflict and to suffer injustice." (Palma 1983)

Free culture is a light for peace and justice.

4. *Being fit and ready instruments for God's use.* Humanity and human culture that's been freed from idolatry, self-centeredness, "injustice and falsehood," is free to serve God and to be used in appropriate ways to mirror God's nature and self (Palma 1983).

5. *Responsible and appropriate human behavior.* Here, Barth is again careful to note that cultural products result from the actions and freedom of humanity. As such, "cultural products can be said to have been given a definite direction in terms of which they can be said to be free or unfree, right or wrong" (Palma 1983). It is in God's liberation of humanity that humanity is then free to choose responsible and appropriate human behavior that rightly reflects the nature of God.

6. *Being a true witness.* Jesus Christ is the greater light of witness, and humanity is the lesser light of witness. All cultural activity has the potential to become sign and parable for the kingdom. The lesser lights (humanity) bear witness to the greater light.

THE RIGHTNESS OF FREE CULTURE

In all human cultural pursuits (theology, politics, science, art, and so on), Barth contended for the production of right ways. Primarily, this meant production and evaluation of what was right in human motivation, objectivity, signification, proper critical response, the ordering of human life, and human goals and results (Palma 1983). A life of faith and obedience means freedom to work for rightness and production of right cultural acts and products.

Human Motivation

God's grace and mercy and the knowledge that humankind has been liberated calls for a human response of gratitude and obedience. This two-fold basis of gratitude and obedience provides the motivation for a right response in human culture. "Faithful correspondence to God's own being and acts as expressed in Jesus' words and deeds" gives rise to the rightness of our cultural activity (Palma 1983).

Objectivity

Objectivity in whatever arena of culture we participate results in rightness when what is acted upon and produced is in "right subordination, placement, and response" to God (Palma 1983). That is, in all that we are, do, and produce, God is the object of our actions and being. Further, our objective as we act is to acknowledge our rightful place in the Divine-human relationship.

True Signification

True signification or meaning implies that any representation of God, Jesus Christ, humanity, or the world is analogous to what God has revealed concerning the same realities. Anything that is spoken or acted upon must, to have true signification, correspond to what God has revealed.

Proper Critical Response

In light of God's Word and his revelation, truly free culture will offer a proper critical or evaluative response regarding "human acts, historical events, social movements, human ideas, and the like" (Palma 1983). So rightness doesn't solely encompass right meaning but includes right evaluation. Such an evaluation is based on God's Word in Scripture, church dogmas and doctrine, and the character of the fruit that such events bear.

Right Ordering and Right Goals

Finally, all cultural acts and products, in whatever arena they're produced, should be nothing less than an instrument for the praise of God (Palma 1983). Right goals and results serve to dispel darkness. As human beings work within culture to dispel darkness, such actions will lead to faith, repentance, obedience, love, gratitude, and praise of God.

Though Barth talks about the secularization of culture, meaning the alienation of humanity from God, he doesn't discard the idea of the secular. On the contrary, his understanding of secular culture was one that acknowledged the possibility for places of rightness and righteousness and opportunities to bear witness to the Divine. He called for Christians to look for places in the secular to recognize and praise the rightness of culture. Barth suggested secular culture might be an expression of "free" culture in any cultural activity in which genuine praise and gratitude for the Creator are present. In his estimation, culture that is secular could also exhibit signs of God's grace and kingdom.

He further argued that true words—words that bear witness to God's revelation—could be found both within and outside the church. Furthermore, any cultural activity that produced "good fruits in keeping with God's good will and purpose" were aspects of truly human or free culture (Palma 1983). Barth often pointed to the music of Mozart as an example of these kinds of free cultural expressions.

THE TASK OF THEOLOGY

The task of theology is essential, particularly in light of Barth's discussion of rightness and righteousness, because it's only in the rightness of theology (anchored as it is in culture) that culture can be rightly understood as an expression of God's grace and kingdom. The basis for evaluating culture is the determination of whether any cultural act or product "represents actual fulfillment of the cultural task set forth and determined by the Word of God" (Palma 1983). In this statement, Barth isn't holding out Scripture as the definitive word for all cultural activities (for example, science, politics, art, and so on). What he's suggesting is that, as was stated at the beginning of this section, the motivation for all cultural activities and the means for our evaluation is: "Do they bear witness to the manifestation of the Logos in human history?"

Paul Metzger, in his work on Barth, identifies four criteria for evaluating and critiquing culture:

1. Have they (fruits and words) led to people's greater freedom or their greater bondage?

2. Have they uplifted people a little or thrust them deeper into the mire?

3. Have they united people or divided them?

4. Have they built up or thrown down, gathered or scattered, quickened or slain? (2003)

KARL BARTH

In 1886, Karl Barth, a Swiss reformed theologian, was born in Basel, Switzerland, the oldest of five children. His father, Fritz Barth, was a New Testament professor and early church historian. Barth initially began his university education at the University of Bern, where he found orthodox Calvinism to be stifling. He shifted to the University of Berlin to study under Adolf Harnack. It was there that he came into contact with progressive liberalist theology. As noted elsewhere, Protestant liberalism espoused the belief that "church and state would work hand in hand for humanity's final victory over nature, and the eventual establishment of the kingdom of God on earth" (Time.com 1962).

In 1908, Barth was ordained in the reformed church by his father and served two positions: An assistant pastor in a church outside of Geneva (1909–1911) and pastor in a small mill town in northern Switzerland (1911–1921). In 1913, he married Nelly Hoffman, a violinist. They had five children (Time.com 1962, BookRags.com 2009).

> "
> *[Barth] advised young theologians to "take your Bible and take your newspaper and read both. But interpret newspapers from your Bible." —"Witness to an Ancient Truth," Time.com*

During his time as a pastor, Barth grappled with the optimistic liberal theology of his university professors. The wealth and prosperity of his parishioners stood in stark contrast to the economic inequality and exploitation of low-wage workers. As *Time Magazine* noted in "Religion: Witness to an Ancient Truth," an article highlighting his first trip to the United States:

> Shocked by the low wages paid to [Switzerland's] textile workers, Barth became an active socialist, earned the nickname of "the Red pastor" for his role in organizing unions, and for such deadpan japes as passing out free frankfurters to rich and poor alike one Christmas morning at church. (Time.com 1962)

Barth was further disillusioned when many of his professors supported Adolf Hitler's rise to power. When the German church initially supported Hitler's war policies, Barth became more discouraged. Looking to the Scriptures, he became convinced that the Bible spoke of a God who revealed himself to humanity and that God defied humankind's "efforts to reach him through inner emotion or reason" (Time.com 1962). For Barth, three things became preeminent in all of his theology: The Bible, faith, and God's revelation.

In the early 1930s, Barth, while teaching at the University of Bonn, refused to take an oath of allegiance to Hitler and was eventually deported from Germany. After World War II, during which time Barth volunteered in the Swiss army, he returned to the University of Basel, where he taught until his retirement in 1962. Barth died December 10, 1968, at the age of 82.

THE ROLE OF THE CHURCH

The Church doesn't exist independent of secular culture, nor does it have a different motivation than to bear witness to the manifestation of the Logos in human history. Existing within culture, the Church—because of its special relationship in its knowledge of God's revelation in Jesus Christ—bears witness to the reality of Jesus Christ through which all humanity has been reconciled to God (Metzger 2003). Though the Church and culture stand in a distinct, yet inseparable, relationship to one another in and through the Word of God, the Church has a special responsibility to act on behalf of culture. The Church, "as the one who participates in Christ…is to turn to the world and bear witness to the world of the objective reconciliation of all humanity in Christ" (Metzger 2003).

Barth contends that even in instances when the Church must go against culture, it does so with the motivation of exhorting culture to be fully human—what its Creator calls it to be (Metzger 2003). Even as the Church stands against culture, it does so with the acknowledgment that it exists *for* the world.

Barth further argues that it's the responsibility of the Church to speak and act God's message of reconciliation within culture. In the dynamic personal relationship with God, the Church is able to hear and speak in culture. God, in his grace and freedom, has acted to redeem his humanity. It is in God's grace, freedom, and sovereignty that the Church is able to receive God's message of redemption and reconciliation. As the Church hears and obeys the Word of God, it is then able to act with greater knowledge and understanding in being a light of God's testimony to the world. Through the Church's activity in culture, it serves as a sign of God's revelation and a witness of the redeeming work of Jesus Christ. Thus, there is an inextricable relationship between the secular and the sacred.

REFLECTION ACTIVITY (5 TO 10 MINUTES)

Paul Tillich had a unique definition of religion: "The deepest expression in all aspects of a person's spirit and encompasses the totality of the human spirit." Karl Barth had a unique definition of culture: "The summit of human possibilities for which we yearn, which we can never define, which occurs in a great work of art, or in Mozart, or in great persons" (Palma 1983). Reflect on each of the above statements and consider what each theologian is saying about humanity and human culture. How are they similar or dissimilar?

DIGGING DEEPER (10 TO 15 MINUTES)

Choose one of Niebuhr's five typologies and write a brief response comparing and contrasting Niebuhr's typology to Barth's theology of culture.

- God has said "No" to sinful humanity and culture but has spoken a divine "Yes" to humanity and human culture in Jesus Christ.

- In Jesus Christ human beings have the possibility of true freedom in culture.

- God sets humanity free to serve humanity by being a witness of the divine Word of Jesus Christ in culture.

- The task of theology is to evaluate the rightness of cultural acts of humanity.

- The Church exists in the world to bear witness to God's message of reconciliation.

CHAPTER 16
Kathryn Tanner: A Postmodern Response to a Theology of Culture

LEARNING OBJECTIVES

When you've finished this chapter, you should be able to:

1. Summarize Tanner's critique of modern cultural perspectives

2. Communicate how a postmodern context gives shapes to culture and cultural influences

3. Articulate ways that a postmodern culture shapes youth cultures

The previous theologians we've surveyed in this book all considered theology and culture during the twentieth century and most definitely framed their thinking from a modernist conception of culture. As societies have become increasingly connected—politically, economically, and electronically—with other societies on a global scale, the modernist concept of culture has been called into question. The notion that cultures are rigidly bounded systems of beliefs, values, and ideas fails to account for the fluid exchange and interaction both from within and without cultures.

Theologians from a variety of perspectives now challenge many of the ideas and assumptions of a modern approach to culture. In particular, Kathryn Tanner, in *Theories of Culture: A New Agenda for Theology* (1997), sets forth a solid critique and offers a framework for re-visioning culture from a postmodern perspective. She identifies six principles for critiquing a modern understanding of culture.

Tanner specifically targets the work of anthropologists, but her discussion provides a helpful framework for outlining ways in which a modern understanding of culture doesn't fit well in our twenty-first century world. The "reconstruction" she offers at the end of her critique will also be sketched here as we continue our discussion of understanding the influences of youth culture.

TANNER'S CRITIQUE OF A MODERN UNDERSTANDING OF CULTURE
Historical Process

As noted in chapter 1, Ruth Benedict asserted that culture develops out of a society's "consistent pattern of thoughts and actions" (1934). Further, as we've also studied, anthropologists tend to approach the study of culture with the premise that culture is an already established construct. Implicitly, in these ideas of culture is the notion that culture is a static, completed form that can be analyzed objectively and thoroughly without regard for the processes that bring one to the exact point in time of a particular culture. Operating from this kind of assumption leads to often erroneous conclusions because it fails to appropriately consider the question: "How did this culture (or artifact or group) come to have this particular shape or character?" It fails to consider the contributions of people—what Tanner calls "the agency of human actors"—that have historically shaped and produced the current culture "on the ground" (1997).

So, for example, as youth workers contemplate the overabundance of cell phones among their middle school youth, they need to consider not only what historical processes helped give rise to the accumulation of cell phones, but also the historical (and developmental) processes that have encouraged teenagers' needs to be in constant communication with their peers. While this makes the task of cultural analysis a messier endeavor, it will also guard against too-easy answers.

> ## Food for Thought
>
> *In your estimation, what ways has the history of youth culture been shaped by the accumulation and use of cell phones?*

Culture as an Internally Consistent Whole

A second faulty assumption, which often builds on the first assumption that says culture is a completed form, is that all persons within a given cultural context experience culture and its system of values, beliefs, and meanings in similar ways. Simplistically, it's easy to assume that the larger values of a culture are communicated and received by every person within that culture; the reality, though, is quite different. As Tanner states: "Culture never appears as a whole for the participants in it. No one is likely to know it [culture] all, and the whole of it is never mobilized on any particular occasion" (199).

This working assumption leads youth workers (and others) to make statements such as: "All teens are…," "All youth today are…," "All seventh grade boys…," "All fifth grade girls experience…." These generalizations belie the reality of adolescents' experiences in culture. As stated earlier, people are both culture bearers and culture makers. That implies that adolescents are always on the receiving end of cultural messages, yet they're also continuously responding and reacting to those messages in ways that are quite varied.

Consensus

It naturally follows that if one is unable to claim that culture is an internally consistent whole, then one is also unable to claim that every person within a culture holds the same cultural understandings. It's often argued that in our historical past there was greater consistency of values, beliefs, and meanings. There are those who contend the rightness and wrongness of that argument.

It's safe to say, however, that there is little argument regarding the lack of a consensus on beliefs, values, and meanings in the twenty-first century, Westernized world. As Tanner notes, as an outsider observing a culture (which is the place of all youth workers in an adolescent's world), the tendency is to see a consistency that isn't there.

While youth may talk about similar things and use a shared vocabulary, such that there's a "surface appearance of consensus," the reality is quite complex. While there may be core ideals that most share, there is a strong likelihood that individual teenagers will interpret and articulate those core ideals in very different ways. As Tanner contends:

> Shared elements are prone to be vague and unelaborated in and of themselves, more a matter of form than of substance, more a matter of vocabulary and manner of expression than articulated belief or clearly defined sentiment. This very lack of definition is what enables them to be shared, to be the focus of interactions among a whole group of differently situated people. (1997)

Principle of Social Order

Tanner argues that the idea of culture functioning as a principle of social order (as modern anthropologists hold) cannot be upheld in contemporary cultural contexts in which cultural consensus is lacking. She argues against the notion that the presence of a social order can be directly and causally connected to cultural consensus—that is, consensus developed out of a common agreement with a set of core ideals, values, and beliefs. Tanner doesn't deny the presence of social order within cultures; however, she contends that the impetus behind such order can be attributed to other factors.

Explicitly, a modern approach to social order often leads one to ignore or be dismissive of factors such as societal and governmental practices that encourage conformity to certain beliefs and values or, as Tanner claims, "the distractions of consumerism, or the inability of the general populace to figure out what is going on and mobilize action accordingly..." (1997).

Further, she questions the efficacy of norms (for example, customs, laws, rules, and regulations) as "constitutive principles of social action" arguing instead that they're more likely functioning as "secondary regulative principles" and depend in large part on whether such norms are advocated in social institutions, such as education, media, and the like (1997).

Tanner again cautions that a simplistic notion that culture serves to establish social order belies human agency and historical factors that contribute to or impede order. Social order comes about as human beings within a society struggle to make sense of cultural forces and values in a fluid, continuous manner.

Primacy of Cultural Stability

In this dynamic of culture, stability no longer is primary; change is constant. As Tanner aptly states:

> Historical processes that bring with them the constant possibility of change are the baseline against which stable, established cultural forms are measured, and not the reverse. (1997)

What that means is that as one seeks to understand cultural contexts and cultural forms, one must recognize that the presence of change is primary. Culture and society no longer correspond totally.

Sharply Bounded, Self-Contained Units

Cultural forms and cultural boundaries no longer exist within sharply bounded and divided social groupings. That is evident as one looks within and without cultures. The most visible evidence of this dynamic of cultures is electronic media—from the Internet to movies to television. A person can be in her apartment in Tashkent, the capital of Uzbekistan, watching American television. One can visit a Somali neighborhood and sit down in a restaurant for a traditional Somali meal in the heartland of North America. Cultural norms travel along the Internet superhighway, unbounded by national boundaries. There is no longer the ease of sharp divisions between this culture or that one.

Additionally, within societies the notion of sharply divided, easily identifiable cultures has faded and become more blurred. On almost any city street in any country, one can find any number of cultures represented.

> [In] today's world "social and cultural boundaries coincide less and less closely (because) there are Japanese in Brazil, Turks on the Main, and West Indian meets East in the streets of Birmingham—a shuffling process which has of course been going on for quite some time…but which, is by now, approaching extreme and near universal proportions." (Tanner 1997)

SO WHAT?

So what are we to make of Tanner's argument that before us is a new landscape of culture—one that requires a new set of eyes with which to see? A second "So what?" question would be, "Why is this important for youth workers to consider as we seek to understand the lives of young people?" Tanner concludes with some fresh ideas for how we can explore cultural norms and products (for example, the lives of teens).

First, she reiterates that the ideas of culture (as understood by modern anthropologists) haven't been completely thrown out, although they've been redefined with greater attention to historical processes and human agency.

She then explains how this cultural redefinition can now be understood as we look at cultures. Instead of assuming that cultures function as internally consistent wholes, we must recognize that cultures are more like Swiss cheese. Consistency may exist, but it's certainly not uniform. Perhaps cottage cheese is a better metaphor. Large curds, small curds—there is some consistency, and it's all cottage cheese, but nothing seems to hold it all together.

There is an ongoing process of cultural consolidation, giving rise to conflicts over power, as well as contradictions over and resistance to meanings. Tanner also concludes that consensus-building is an element of culture, though it's as likely to be a source of conflict and tension as it is the "basis for shared beliefs and sentiments" (1997).

Finally, in a world in which cultural boundaries are less sharply defined, so that cultural difference isn't marked by boundaries of self-contained cultures, distinctive cultural identities become more a matter of how cultural elements are used by particular social groups (Tanner 1997).

For example, as noted in chapter 5, the global phenomenon of hip-hop culture serves as evidence of this point. Historically, hip-hop culture and rap music were cultural products of African Americans. During the last three decades, aspects of hip-hop have been appropriated by white, middle-class Americans, and the influence of hip-hop culture has spread across the globe. Different groups have adopted the elements of hip-hop music—dress, language, and so on—and infused them with their own values and meanings, changing them and re-envisioning them with their own messages.

In this very different, multilevel, multivaried cultural landscape, we now turn to another theological perspective of culture. Though contextual theology has a long history of theological thought, it's become particularly salient in our contemporary global context.

REFLECTION ACTIVITY (5 TO 10 MINUTES)

This chapter argues that "generalizations belie the reality of adolescents' experience in culture." Consider the ways you've experienced this tendency to generalize regarding youth behaviors, beliefs, and values. Write down your thoughts about how these generalizations accurately and inaccurately portray the lives of youth.

DIGGING DEEPER (10 TO 15 MINUTES)

Consider the global context of youth culture. Identify ways in which differing cultural experiences and beliefs, values and norms, "butt up" against each other, resulting in conflicts and misunderstandings. Write down your response.

> • Historical processes are sources of influence that shape culture, along with the influences of groups and individuals within a culture.

CHAPTER 17
Contextual Theology: Theology That Starts with Culture

LEARNING OBJECTIVES

When you've finished this chapter, you should be able to:

1. Understand how context shapes our understanding of the world

2. Discuss ways in which theology is necessarily contextual

3. Articulate the components of a contextual theology

4. Demonstrate knowledge of the historical Christian traditions that encourage contextual theology

Yolanda is a bright 17-year-old woman living in an urban metropolitan neighborhood. She has two sisters—one older, one younger. Their dad left when Yolanda was five, and their mom died from complications of diabetes when Yolanda was 14. For a couple of years, she moved between foster homes. Once she was 16, however, she was emancipated from social services. Since then, she's bounced between the homes of friends and extended relatives, sleeping on sofas, the floor, wherever she can find a spot.

Yolanda is part of a group of young people called "sofa surfer" homeless.[3] She tries to stay in school but finds it difficult with no permanent address and little money for transportation or anything else. Her part-time, minimum-wage job barely covers the basics, let alone rent and other living expenses. Yolanda occasionally attends a local church youth group, but she feels her life is so different from everyone else's that they share little in common.

Just five miles away from Yolanda's neighborhood, Patrick (also 17) attends school at a private Catholic high school. He excels academically, plays varsity football, and is

---

3 The category of "sofa surfer" homeless isn't an official category in federal statistics, though some agencies do attempt to gather information on it. Because this group of individuals is very transient, moving from one temporary living space to another, there is little way to get an accurate estimate of the numbers. A quick Google search, however, indicates how common it is for families, children, and teens to find themselves looking for a sofa on which to sleep on a regular, if not daily, basis. In Toronto, Ontario, there are an estimated 5,000 street homeless, with more than twice that many estimated to be sofa surfers, many of them adolescents. In Oklahoma there are close to 6,000 children homeless, many of them teens living on each other's sofas. In both Dallas and Ft. Worth, journalists report around 1,000 teens relying on the charity of friends and family on any given night because they've either run away, been kicked out of their homes, or "graduated" out of the social service system. (See http://newsok.com/youth-couch-surfers-seeking-help/article/3362655; http://www.dallasnews.com/sharedcontent/dws/news/localnews/stories/110307dnm etsofasurf.2c86c31.html; http://www.insidetoronto.com/News/York/article/11919; http://www.examiner.com/x-8648-Fort-Worth-Parenting-Tweens—Teens-Examiner~y2009m5d27-The-invisible-plight-of-homeless-teens.)

a leader in his parish youth group. At the moment, Patrick is overwhelmed with his Advance Placement (AP) calculus and physics courses. He also feels the pressure of completing college applications and the accompanying tests and essays. His parents want him to attend a private Catholic university close to home. Patrick, however, wants to attend the state university five hours away, where many of his friends plan to go. He knows he'll have a number of options, which is part of the reason he sometimes feels overwhelmed. There are so many expectations for what he'll do and what he'll become. He sometimes wishes life were simpler.

Ruth, another 17-year-old, lives in a tight-knit Asian neighborhood. Her family immigrated to the United States when Ruth was four. Though her parents struggle with language skills and seldom speak English at home, Ruth's English is flawless. In Ruth's family, it's understood that the children will do well in school. In fact, three expectations are stringently enforced in her family and neighborhood: (1) Be a good student, (2) Respect your family, and (3) Work hard. Most afternoons, Ruth and her siblings help out in the family business before settling down to do their homework. Weekends are typically spent with extended family and friends from the neighborhood.

Ruth has been accepted at four different universities, with one granting her a full scholarship, although it's 500 miles from home. Ruth is ambivalent about leaving for college and being so far away from her family. She feels a sense of responsibility to her younger siblings and for helping out at home and at her parents' work. On the other hand, she's excited about the possibilities that college will bring.

Each of these young people is experiencing some of the typical aspects of being a 17-year-old in American society. However, life for each of them is unique. As noted in the previous chapter, in this very different, multi-level, multi-varied cultural landscape there is a need for a theology of culture that takes into account these multiple perspectives.

In this chapter we'll explore a theology of culture that focuses on context. Contextual theology has a long history of theological thought, and it's particularly salient in our contemporary global cultural experience to help youth workers consider the significance of youth culture for shaping the lives of adolescents.

In exploring this theology, there are two objectives. First, where one sits in a culture shapes one's perspective of self and cultural values. So how a person receives what a culture communicates is filtered through specific personal contexts. Likewise, different individuals and groups will hear the same message differently because of their positions in society and their personal experiences. Our first task, then, is to consider how our context shapes our own theological response to culture.

Second, as a diligent discerner of culture, one must consider the place of young people. Knowing that cultural influences shape young people in a variety of ways, exploring these different types of theologies will help us better understand the possible lenses with which youth view their culture and cultural experiences. Further, it will help us to understand the different kinds of responses teens make. In other words, it will give us insight into how they are culture bearers and culture makers.

Additionally, this exploration will encourage us to develop appropriate ways of response—how to challenge, guide, and instruct adolescents and help them make sense of their worlds. After all, our goal in becoming students and learners of youth cultures is to more clearly speak the good news of the kingdom and to become experienced guides to young people in their journeys as disciples.

In this chapter, we'll look at how one might engage in the practice of theology in our postmodern context, using Tanner's arguments as a framework. Drawing on the work of Stephen Bevans and his book *Models of Contextual Theology*, this chapter examines the components of a theology that is contextual, along with the aspects of our Christian faith that demand a contextual theology. As always, the goal is to move us closer to being good students of culture.

> *In the West, we tend to think of our interpretations as so normal and universal in Bible study that we often call American theology "theology," while we give every other form of theology a qualifier such as "Asian theology" or "African theology."*
> —*Ed Cyzewski*, Coffeehouse Theology, 146

DOING THEOLOGY THAT IS CONTEXTUAL

There is no such thing as "theology," there is only *contextual* theology—*feminist* theology, *black* theology, *liberation* theology, *Filipino* theology, *Asian-American* theology, *African* theology, and so forth. The contextualization of theology—the attempt to understand Christian faith in terms of a particular context—is really a theological imperative (Bevans 2006).

Some contend that the work of theology is and always has been contextual. Only in the last few decades, however, has that been acknowledged and encouraged. Traditional or *classical* theology is the work to understand one's Christian faith in light of Scripture and church tradition. Classical theology is sometimes viewed as objective, meaning that the work of theology is and can be done outside of cultural and historical processes. The reality, however, is that all theology, as Bevans notes above, is contextual. All theology is anchored in the history and the culture of the theologian (Bevans 2006).

Contextual theologians seek to first acknowledge this point—that theology, because it's a human activity, cannot be divested of the experience and tradition of the theologian. And, second, that theology that's often attributed as *classical* is anchored in its own history and cultural context.

As Bevans argues in *Models of Contextual Theology*, theology is by nature subjective. He's not arguing here for a relativistic, individual theology but acknowledging that human experience (for example, society, culture, history) functions as a boundary for the work of theology. The task of theology is to describe reality—divine and human reality in relation to the Divine. Human experience is the source for understanding that reality. Bevans is careful to draw a distinction between human experience and reality. Human experience is not true and full reality, but it's the source for understanding that reality.

> **Food for Thought**
>
> *Can you identify ways in which some of your theological beliefs are anchored in your cultural experience? (For example, perhaps how you see God, Christ, or the kingdom?)*

As Bevans, quoting Charles Kraft, states:

> God, the author of reality, exists outside any culture. Human beings, on the other hand, are always bound by cultural...and psychological conditioning to perceive and interpret what they see of reality in ways appropriate to these conditionings. Neither the absolute God nor the reality [God] created is perceived absolutely by culture-bound human beings. (2006, 4)

Context, therefore, shapes our understanding of God and the expressions of our faith. In other words, "reality is mediated by meaning" (2006, 4).

This is why Bevans makes the strong statement highlighted at the beginning of this chapter, that the "contextualization of theology...is a theological imperative." A twenty-first century understanding of culture is one in which a person is understood to be "cultured by being socialized into a particular context. Culture is not something 'out there,' but something that everyone participates in" (11).

Two things must be taken into account in engaging in the process of contextual theology. First, as we engage in understanding Scripture and tradition, we must acknowledge the influence of context on both. Scripture records the faith experiences of people in very real and quite varied contexts, as well as the revelation of God in and through those people. Further, the history and tradition of the church has also been a process elaborated in context. As we do theology, it's important to acknowledge this and to wrestle with what's been "kept alive, preserved, defended—and perhaps even neglected or suppressed—in tradition" (Bevans 2006, 5).

Second, while we need to be faithful to the past—to tradition—we also need to recognize that in the experience of the present, we must make faith our own. As Bevans aptly states: "The received tradition must...pass through the sieve of our own individual and contemporary-collective experience" (2006, 5).

COMPONENTS OF A CONTEXTUAL THEOLOGY

Contextual theology embraces five different aspects of human experience in the task of theology. First, contextual theology involves considering all aspects of life experiences of a person or group. This aspect builds on the understanding that life experiences function as the frame for understanding true reality. Therefore, in developing theological understanding, one must consider all aspects, whether traumatic or celebratory, mundane, profane, or sacred.

> *In those days* Caesar Augustus issued a decree that a census should be taken of the entire Roman world. (This was the first census that took place while Quirinius was governor of Syria.) And everyone went to their own town to register. So *Joseph* also went up from the town of Nazareth in Galilee to Judea, to Bethlehem the town of David, because he belonged to the house and line of David. He went there to register with *Mary*, who was pledged to be married to him and was expecting a child. *While they were there, the time came* for the baby to be born, and *she gave birth to her firstborn, a son.* She wrapped him in cloths and placed him in a manger, because there was no guest room available for them. —Luke 2:1-7 (*emphasis added*)

Second, contextual theology encompasses the larger societal events that are part of personal and group experiences. For example, in our most recent history, events of September 11, 2001, Barack Obama's presidential election, the bank and Wall Street failures of 2008, and the wars in Iraq and Afghanistan had a global impact and served to frame our human understanding of reality.

Third, as we've alluded to elsewhere, the broader social context of a people (what we might call "public culture" or "society's culture") contributes to understanding about theological issues (for example, American, European, African, Asian, and so on).

A fourth aspect of contextual theology is the recognition that social location frames theological understanding. Within the broader social context, the places in which different peoples and groups reside provide a lens for engaging in theological reflection. So, for example, being young or old, male or female, poor or wealthy, powerful or powerless, gives shape to one's theology.

Finally, a fifth aspect of contextual theology is the sea of social change and flux within cultures. The global spread of technology, particularly in the area of personal communication; global media; and rapid and wide-ranging political and economic changes all serve as significant frameworks for the theological perspectives of people.

These five components of contextual theology provide the framework for developing an appropriate theology of youth cultures. Contextual theologians contend that the historical traditions of our Christian faith provide the impetus for doing contextual theology. Specifically, Bevans cites Christian teaching in five areas—incarnation, human experience, revelation, the Trinity, and the catholicity of the Church—that support contextual theology.

DYNAMICS OF CHRISTIAN FAITH THAT DEMAND A THEOLOGY THAT IS CONTEXTUAL

The Incarnation

God, in divine wisdom, in order to reveal his character and nature to humanity and, as Bevans highlights, in order to "encourage human beings to enter into relationship with God," chose to reveal himself in and through the person of Jesus Christ. God chose a *particular* person, a *particular* time, and a *particular* place to reveal himself. "Incarnation is a process of becoming *particular*" (*emphasis added*) (2006, 12).

We know God and enter into relationship with God by a personal encounter with the particular person of Jesus Christ. "The incarnation unmistakably demonstrates God's intention to make himself known from within the human situation" (Bevans 2006, 12). Without

The Nicene Creed

I believe in one God, the Father Almighty, Maker of heaven and earth, and of all things visible and invisible.

And in one Lord Jesus Christ, the only-begotten Son of God, begotten of the Father before all worlds; God of God, Light of Light, very God of very God; begotten, not made, being of one substance with the Father, by whom all things were made.

Who, for us men and for our salvation, came down from heaven, and was incarnate by the Holy Spirit of the virgin Mary, and was made man; and was crucified also for us under Pontius Pilate; He suffered and was buried; and the third day He rose again, according to the Scriptures; and ascended into heaven, and sits on the right hand of the Father; and He shall come again, with glory, to judge the quick and the dead; whose kingdom shall have no end.

And I believe in the Holy Ghost, the Lord and Giver of Life; who proceeds from the Father and the Son; who with the Father and the Son together is worshipped and glorified; who spoke by the prophets.

And I believe one holy catholic *and apostolic Church. I acknowledge one baptism for the remission of sins; and I look for the resurrection of the dead, and the life of the world to come. Amen. (emphasis added)*

question, God's revelation is contextualized! A first-century Jew was born in Bethlehem, with a particular genealogy, during a time when Palestine was under Roman rule, at a particular time in Israel's history—in that context God is revealed.

It's imperative, then, that Christians in the twenty-first century recognize the importance of communicating the truths of God in context—to serve as incarnational witnesses—by recognizing the need to communicate the message of the gospel contextually. As followers of Christ, Christians are called to, in a sense, "re-enact that incarnation as we encounter the world" (Bevans 2006).

Sacramental Nature of Reality

Recognizing the significance of human experience and context shifts the work of theology from solely, or even primarily, being about ideas to concrete reality. When we acknowledge that "encounters with God in Jesus continue to take place in our world through concrete things," we raise the nature of that reality from simply the profane or mundane to the sacramental (Bevans 2006, 12).

Any activity of youth or youth ministry has the potential of raising the awareness of the reality of God. Winter snow camps, summer mission trips, youth worship Sundays, worship leader teams, as well as events outside the church—"at any time and in any place and through any person... things can become transparent and reveal their creator as acting and lovingly present to creation" (Bevans 2006, 13).

> "The whole of the movement of the Bible is one of interpreting the ordinary, the secular, in terms of religious symbolism." This is the continuing task of theology: to reveal God's presence in a truly sacramental world. —*Stephen Bevans,* Models of Contextual Theology, *13*

A Shift in the Understanding of the Nature of Divine Revelation

Writing from a Catholic perspective, Bevans (2006) highlights here the traditional Catholic teaching that said that revelation had ended with the "death of the last apostle" (13). He argues for a shift in understanding, acknowledging that revelation is complete in Jesus Christ from the sense that God's revelation was full in Jesus Christ. That is, God has expressed himself completely and fully in the person of Jesus Christ. God's redemptive act is full and complete in Jesus Christ's life, death, and resurrection.

The shift he calls for, though, is one that recognizes that God's revelation isn't complete in the sense that all revelation has ended. Bevans argues for an understanding of God's revelation that acknowledges that God continues to reveal himself in and through the lives of his people and their daily lives. This notion of revelation "points to the necessity of a theology that takes seriously the actual context in which men and women experience God" (2006, 14).

> *After this I looked, and there before me was a great multitude that no one could count,* from every nation, tribe, people and language, *standing before the throne and in front of the Lamb. They were wearing white robes and were holding palm branches in their hands. And they cried out in a loud voice: "Salvation belongs to our God, who sits on the throne, and to the Lamb." All the angels were standing around the throne and around the elders and the four living creatures. They fell down on their faces before the throne and worshiped God, saying: "Amen! Praise and glory and wisdom and thanks and honor and power and strength be to our God for ever and ever. Amen!" —Revelation 7:9-12 (emphasis added)*

The Catholicity of the Church

Bevans contends for an understanding of the catholicity of the Church that sees the Church as a place that is embracing and inclusive of all peoples and all cultures, across the full span of human history and experience (Bevans 2006). Doing theology outside a contextual understanding tends to limit our abilities to recognize the full breadth and depth of the nature of the Church. A full appreciation of God and of humanity necessitates that all peoples and cultures participate in the dialogue of theology.

As Bevans states:

> Andrew Walls writes: "The full-grown humanity of Christ requires all the Christian generations, just as it embodies all the cultural variety that six continents can bring." For such a dialogue to take place, all persons and cultural groups have to dig deep into their own social situation, personal experience, and cultural existence to see how these interact with God's offer of friendship and relationship in Jesus Christ. (2006, 15)

The Trinity

Finally, Bevans contends that God, by his very nature, compels us to do theology contextually because the Godhead is a dynamic, relational community. The triune nature of God calls us, as Christians, to be active in culture and human experience to foster greater understanding of the communal nature of God and to communicate the communal, personal reality of our Creator God.

Bevans concludes his discussion of the compelling need for contextual theology by stating that context is at the very center of the work of theology. If one of the goals of doing theology is to reach the world with the gospel message, then, he argues, "the person [is] one's starting-point and [we are] always coming back to the relationships of people among themselves and with God" (Bevans quoting Pope Paul VI, 2006, 15). This brings us back to the heart of youth ministry: Encouraging young people to embrace a relationship with God. The work of contextual theology starts with the world of youth and helps us and young people make sense of God and human life within that context.

REFLECTION ACTIVITY (5 TO 10 MINUTES)

Stephen Bevans states: "at any time and in any place and through any person...things can become transparent and reveal their creator as acting and lovingly present to creation" (2006, 13). Choose one particular youth ministry activity—one that wouldn't ordinarily be considered as revealing the presence of the Creator—and identify ways in which that activity reveals the loving and personal nature of God. Take a moment to write down your thoughts.

DIGGING DEEPER (10 TO 15 MINUTES)

Read the three narrative accounts at the beginning of the chapter. Identify at least three cultural themes that are present in all three accounts. Write a brief essay relating how each of these three themes is different for each student and how their cultural experiences may have shaped their values and beliefs, particularly beliefs regarding their sense of self.

- Contextual Theology begins and ends in cultural context, recognizing that Scripture, God's revelation, and the theological traditions of the Church come to us from particular contexts and that as we proclaim the gospel message of Jesus, we do so in particular contexts.

- Historically, Christian traditions and teachings regarding the incarnation, the human experience, divine revelation, the Trinitarian nature of God, and the catholicity of the Church call for Christians to engage in the task of contextual theology.

WORKS CITED

Barth, Karl. 1933. *The epistle to the Romans.* 6th ed. Trans. Edwyn C. Hoskyns. London: Oxford University Press.

Benedict, Ruth. 1934. *Patterns of culture.* Boston: Houghton-Mifflin.

Bevans, Stephen B. 2006. *Models of Contextual Theology.* 6th ed. Ed. Robert J. Schreiter. Maryknoll, New York: Orbis Books.

BookRags.com. 2005-2006. *Encyclopedia of world biography on Karl Barth.* Thomson Gale. http://www.bookrags.com/biography/karl-barth.

Bulman, Raymond F. 1981. *A blueprint for humanity: Paul Tillich's theology of culture.* East Brunswick, NJ: Associated University Presses.

Cyzewski, Ed. 2008. *Coffeehouse theology: Reflecting on God in everyday life.* Colorado Springs: NavPress.

Elwell, Walter A., ed. 1988. *Baker encyclopedia of the Bible.* Vol. 1: A-I. Grand Rapids, MI: Baker Book House.

Hartford Institute for Religion Research. 1998. *Encyclopedia of Religion and Society.* William H. Swatos Jr., ed. Hartford, CT: AltaMira Press.

King, William McGuire. 1983. "History as revelation" in the theology of the social gospel. *Harvard Theological Review* 76 (1): 109–129.

Lynch, Gordon. 2005. *Understanding theology and popular culture.* Malden, MA: Blackwell Publishing.

Marshall, I. Howard, Stephen Travis, and Ian Paul. 2002. *Exploring the New Testament: A guide to the letters and Revelation.* Vol. 2. Downers Grove, IL: InterVarsity Press.

Metzger, Paul Louis. 2003. *The word of Christ and the world of culture: Sacred and secular through the theology of Karl Barth.* Grand Rapids, MI: Eerdmans.

Niebuhr, H. Richard. 1951. *Christ and culture.* New York: Harper & Brothers Publishers.

Palma, Robert J. 1983. *Karl Barth's theology of culture: The freedom of culture for the praise of God.* Ed. Dikran Y. Hadidian. Allison Park, PA: Pickwick Publications.

Rachels, James. 1993. *The elements of moral philosophy.* 2nd ed. New York: McGraw-Hill.

Tanner, Kathryn. 1997. *Theories of culture: A new agenda for theology.* Guides to Theological Inquiry Series. Minneapolis: Fortress Press.

Tillich, Paul. 1951. *Systematic theology.* Vol. 1. Chicago: University of Chicago Press.

———. 2000. *The courage to be.* 2nd ed. New Haven, CT: Yale University Press.

———. 1959. *Theology of culture.* New York: Oxford University Press.

Time Magazine. 1962. Religion: Witness to an ancient truth. Time.com. April 20, 1962. http://www.time.com/time/magazine/article/0,9171,873557,00.html.

Wildman, Wesley J. 1994–2009. Boston collaborative encyclopedia of Western theology. http://people.bu.edu/wwildman/bce/tillich.htm.

CONCLUSION
A Practical Approach to
Understanding Youth Culture

LEARNING OBJECTIVE

When you've finished this section, you should be able to:

1. Summarize the ways to integrate ethnography, human development, and theological thinking to youth cultural experiences

In the previous chapters, this text explored different skills and ways of critically thinking about youth culture. Specifically, chapters 5 through 8 offered ideas about developing an ethnographic ability with which to view youth culture. Chapters 9 through 12 considered the interactions between adolescent development and culture. And chapters 13 through 17 discussed a number of theological perspectives for thinking about an appropriate response to culture.

Bringing together each of these three considerations, this final chapter seeks to construct a framework for engaging in the study of youth culture. This framework isn't a rigid methodology, but a holistic approach to contemplate all aspects of cultural influences.

Most of us have experienced throwing a rock into a lake or a pond and seeing the expanding circles of water appear. My limited skills in physics prevent me from being able to adequately explain what happens, but the image is a good one for describing the integrated theological task for youth workers examining the influence of youth culture. Starting with very specific cultural experiences, the task of thinking about culture gradually widens as we continue to draw upon the different skills and ideas shared in this text.

In setting forth this integrated framework, we'll look to some of the recent works of practical theologians, particularly the works of Richard Osmer and Kevin Vanhoozer, Charles Anderson, and Michael Sleasman. The chart on the next page illustrates this approach.

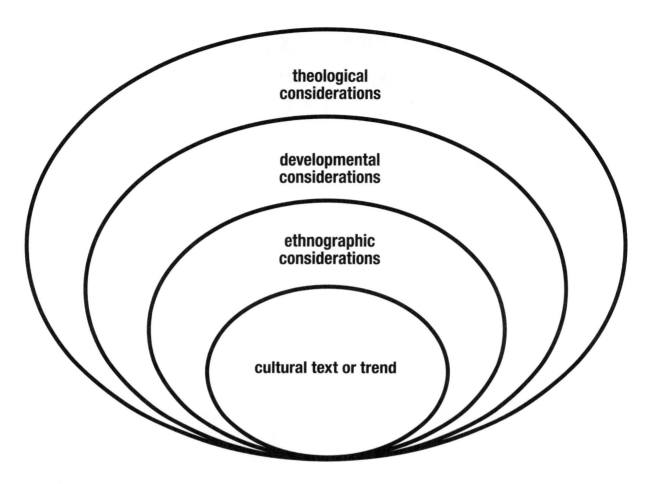

theological
considerations

developmental
considerations

ethnographic
considerations

cultural text or trend

THE STARTING POINT: WHAT IS HAPPENING HERE?

An integrated theological approach to youth culture begins with a specific point within a cultural setting. In his book *Practical Theology: An Introduction*, Richard Osmer describes this specific point as an episode, a situation, or a context. And in *Everyday Theology*, authors Kevin Vanhoozer, Charles Anderson, and Michael Sleasman separate specific points into cultural texts or trends. That is, cultural *texts* are specific, well-defined situations or events. Cultural *trends* are cultural movements or themes and more broadly influence cultural phenomena.

So, for example, the individual songs on the Billboard Weekly Top Ten Singles list are each cultural texts; rap music, though, is a cultural trend. As Vanhoozer, Anderson, and Sleasman aptly note, cultural texts are typically less complicated than cultural trends. Cultural texts are restricted to a particular "happening," whereas cultural trends most likely encompass a broad swath of cultural texts and are, thus, more complicated to critique (2007).

In youth culture, there are myriad examples of cultural texts and cultural trends. As highlighted in Part Two of this text, the skills of ethnography, through focused observation and intense listening, help youth workers identify texts and trends that are relevant for a particular group. Once a text or trend has been identified for study, Vanhoozer, Anderson, and Sleasman pose a set of questions that can open up a conversation about a specific aspect of culture:

- What is good and meaningful in this situation? (For example, what about this text or trend is conducive to human flourishing?)

- How and where is God being revealed in this?

- How can we pay attention to what is really there? (For example, how can we judge this event or experience on its own merits?) (2007)

These questions serve to get the conversation started and, generally speaking, will be the impetus for developing a different set of questions to guide further discussion.

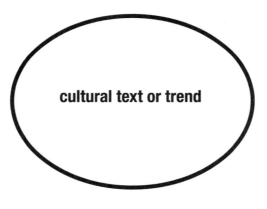

cultural text or trend

Integrating an Ethnographic Perspective

As one moves from identifying a particular cultural experience, the objective is to construct the best picture possible, using critical skills of reflection and interpretation from the disciplines of theology, human development, and ethnography to shed light on a particular

Food for Thought

Can you identify a cultural text and a cultural trend in your present-day experience of youth culture?

situation. It should be stated at the outset that in the practical experience of youth ministry, it's probably impossible to separate each of these different approaches from the others. This discussion, though, is designed to portray each in a linear fashion, recognizing that in practice the work will be done in a more seamless way.

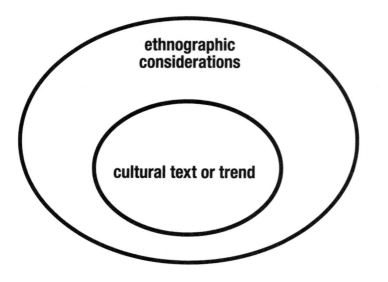

Ethnographic Considerations:

• Develop an insider's view. (What do I know and How do I know it?)

• Be watchful, observing and listening carefully.

• Be curious, asking questions that bring insight.

• Be a caring observer.

To that end, after identifying a cultural experience, the conversation moves to applying ethnographic skills of personal observation and listening, gathering details and data from those people intimately connected with the cultural dynamic.

Leonardo Boff calls this aspect of practical theology the "seeing analytically" stage (Bevans 2006). At this point, it's important to hear as many voices as possible to get the broadest picture possible. Think of it as a sort of Town Hall informational meeting where the goal is to listen—to get people talking. Before you talk to "experts"—including social scientists, as well as biblical and theological people and texts—gather information from those who have a firsthand perspective and those who have a vested interest. While this kind of information gathering is most often informal, it shouldn't be limited to a small segment of the community. A good eye requires listening to multiple levels of experience and calls for careful listening (Osmer 2008).

Still Talking, but Broadening the Conversation

This stage of "seeing analytically" involves extending the conversation in an investigative manner to gather information regarding the developmental influences and how they might shape the cultural experiences of young people. This phase moves beyond the firsthand-experience experts to consult and bring into the conversation those who can provide social science expertise. The emphasis is still on gathering information and facilitating conversation, but the conversation moves out to include other voices.

For example, in Part Three of this text, the practices of dating and online communication are discussed. In each of these aspects of youth culture, insights from developmental psychologists, social workers, and others involved in the social science professions relating to adolescents provide insightful guidance into understanding youth culture. Social science experts can give further insights into cultural events by helping a community evaluate cultural symbols and understand

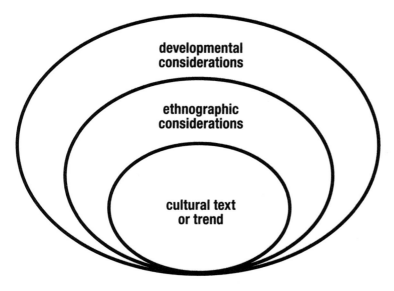

Developmental Considerations:

- What are the micro-level relation-ship influences?

- How do the different immedi-ate contexts shape this specific experience?

- What are the social role expecta-tions involved?

- Are there broader cul-tural influences (exo- and macro- contexts)?

social systems (such as family and peer networks) and psychosocial dynamics (for example, "Why are adolescents so passionate about their music?")

As Osmer and others note, this phase of cultural study is a communal effort. Osmer calls for a thoughtful, ongoing interpretive response, one that recognizes the flawed limitations of human effort but nonetheless moves forward, digging deeper for greater breadth and depth of under-standing. What's called for here is "a spirituality of sagely wisdom [that] puts aside the quest for certainty and the one true perspective. Loving God with the mind is a way of moving more deeply into the mystery of God and God's creation" (Osmer 2008, 84).

Judging Theologically

Leonardo Boff calls this stage "judging theologically," which aptly describes the tasks involved. As a community judges theologically (and this aspect continues to be a communal effort), three principles need to be a part of the discussion: (1) Thoughtful interpretation, (2) wise judgment, and (3) acting pastorally (Bevans 2006). These three principles can be implemented through a process of theological reflection.

An example for engaging in judging theologically is presented below:

Theological Reflection Process

1. Describe the event, dilemma, situation
2. Response (What are the initial reactions of the community?)
   a. Feelings (How do I feel about this?)
   b. Convictions (What do I think is appropriate or inappropriate?)

c. Beliefs (What do I believe to be true?)
3. Suspend action to gather more information
    a. Don't act on feelings, convictions, or beliefs
    b. What do others think? (colleagues, teachers, family, church)
    c. What is the cultural perspective? (What does society think?)
4. Scriptural Consideration
    a. What Scripture passages (or believed Scripture passages) immediately come to mind that speak to the event, dilemma, or situation?
    b. What does a study of Scripture reveal?
5. Church tradition and heritage
    a. How does your church tradition and heritage address the issue?
    b. How has the church's understanding changed over time?
6. Now what?
    a. Feelings
    b. Convictions
    c. Beliefs
    d. Ongoing questions?

Biblical study and theological reflection place the contemporary cultural experience in the context of church history and tradition and help a community consider such experiences in the light of theological concepts. In this stage, a community is called upon to develop a spirituality of prophetic discernment to enable them to sift through the issues presented and to weigh out the evidence. As Osmer notes, theological interpretation focuses on the present in light of theological concepts. Though theology carries out this task "in dialogue with other forms of human knowledge" (Osmer 2008), there is the recognition that the "lens of biblical faith...offers a high-definition worldview" (Vanhoozer, Anderson, and Sleasman 2007, 41).

Response

The task of constructing an integrated response to youth culture ends as it began—in culture, encouraging a community to construct culture, to become culture makers and culture bearers, bringing to bear the influences of God's community on the culture around it. In turn, new responses bring new experiences, which bring new questions regarding youth culture. So the process continues. The critical task of evaluating the influences of youth culture is an integral and unceasing one for youth workers. There are always new trends and texts to explore and more questions to encounter.

WORKS CITED

Bevans, Stephen B. 2006. *Models of contextual theology.* 6th ed. Maryknoll, NY: Orbis Books.

Osmer, Richard R. 2008. *Practical theology: An introduction.* Grand Rapids: Eerdmans.

Vanhoozer, Kevin J., Charles A. Anderson, and Michael J. Sleasman, eds. 2007. *Everyday theology: How to read cultural texts and interpret trends.* Grand Rapids, MI: Baker Academic.

TERMS AND DEFINITIONS

Accommodationist: Niebuhr's typology, also called "Christ of Culture" response, in which cultural leaders and institutions develop more divine ways of thinking and acting in moving toward God's kingdom.

Antinomianism: The belief that because salvation comes by faith—we aren't bound by moral laws.

Biological Inheritance: A person's characteristics that are passed down genetically at birth.

Calling: A particular practice of courtship in which a young woman and her family extended an invitation to a young man to visit *(call on)* her at her family's home.

Clergy Privilege: The responsibility to maintain confidentiality regarding private information told to clergy in the professional execution of their duties.

Clique: A small, often exclusive, group of friends; typically numbering six to eight.

Code-switching: The process of changing modes of behavior from one context to another.

Connotation: The intended meaning(s) of a cultural sign.

Context: The experiences, events, or circumstances within which an individual exists.

Contextual Theology: Theology that seeks to understand Christian faith in terms of a particular context.

Conversionist: Niebuhr's typology, also called "Christ the Transformer of Culture" response, in which the premier concern is with the renewal of God's creation *now*, rather than in a future eschatological moment.

Courtship: A romantic relationship between young people prior to marriage.

Crowd: Large reputation-based groups of adolescent peers who share similar characteristics and stereotypes (for example, jocks, brains, loners, and so on) but aren't necessarily friends and don't necessarily spend time together.

Cultural Inheritance: A person's characteristics that are passed down through one's environment and experience.

Cultural Patterns: Formalized forms of behavior established on societal values and beliefs.

Cultural Relativism: The concept that people shouldn't judge another person's culture based on their own cultural values. Instead, they should evaluate each culture and its practices on its own merits.

Culture: The total way of life of a people, including ways in which people think and act in community.

Culture Bearer: Reflecting the values, beliefs, and behaviors of a society.

Culture Maker: Participating in creating the values, beliefs, and behaviors of a society.

Custom Complex: Based on a customary or usual practice, along with a set of beliefs, values, sanctions, rules, motives, and satisfactions associated with the practice.

Dating: A form of romantic courtship in which two people go out together independent from family.

Denotation: The literal meaning of a cultural sign.

Derived Etic: The fourth step in the S. E. E. Spiral, in which the youth pastor-ethnographer, after closely observing a group of people, reaches a deeper understanding of the culture of that group from the perspective of an outsider.

Development: The evolving nature and scope of perceived reality as it emerges and expands in the child's awareness and in his active involvement with the physical and social environment.

Developmental Psychology: A branch of psychology that studies how a human being changes over his or her life span in all aspects of what it means to be human (cognitive, physical, emotional, spiritual, as well as one's personality).

Dualist: Niebuhr's typology, also called "Christ and Culture in Paradox," which is characterized by a conflict between the righteousness of God and the unrighteousness of humanity and the unavoidable influence of sinful culture.

Ecological Development: An approach to understanding human behavior that focuses on the interactions between cultural environments and human development.

Emic: To describe actions, beliefs, or behaviors of a culture or group based on an insider's perspective.

Enhanced Self-disclosure Hypothesis: A theory proposing that Internet usage enhances intimate self-disclosure, which fosters greater feelings of closeness and increases the quality of social relationships.

Environment: The natural and created world of a human being, consisting of all of his or her contexts of relating and the self.

Ethnography: A field of study in the broader scientific field of anthropology that studies groups of people in their natural settings through methods of inquiry and discovery.

Ethnocentrism: When a person assumes that one's cultural practice is superior to another's cultural practice.

Etic: To describe actions, beliefs, or behaviors of a culture or group based on an outsider's perspective.

Exosystem: *Exo*, meaning "outside," describes those settings in which an adolescent doesn't regularly participate. But what happens in those settings has great potential to shape what happens in the micro and meso settings of the adolescent.

Faith: The level of personal trust and devotion that a person places in God.

Familiar-Strange Phenomenon: Observed occurrences that seem abnormal to an observer in the context of a familiar environment.

Feminine: Those qualities, activities, or behaviors that are socially thought to be associated with women or girls.

Fiduciary Duty: Any relationship in which one party accepts the responsibility to act for the care and benefit of another party.

Free Culture: Human activity that's grounded in God's own freedom and humanity and serves as a sign of God's kingdom.

Friend Influence (Peer Pressure): The influence asserted in direct and indirect ways, in subtle and not-so-subtle ways, primarily by peer friends.

Ideology: A system of ideas about life and culture.

Imaging Signs: Cultural signs in which the signifier images or reflects the signified, such as photos, cartoon drawings, or imitated sounds.

Indicative Signs: Cultural signs in which the signifier and signified have a logical or causal connection.

Intimate Self-disclosure: Sharing worries, fears, secrets, and embarrassing experiences with another person.

Gender: The psychological and sociocultural dimensions of being male or female.

Gnosticism: The belief that the spiritual world was good and the physical world was evil and that a heavenly redeemer came into the world to save people from bondage to the physical world by giving them divine knowledge.

Human Ecology: A branch of sociology that studies the relationships between individuals and their natural and created environments.

Independent Self: A personal identity that seeks to act autonomously from others.

Interdependent Self: A personal identity that, in some degree, seeks to function through mutually connected and supportive relationships.

Isolates: Youth who aren't members of a clique and have few or no links to other peer networks.

Language: A symbolic system of communication, consisting of verbal and written sets of words and meanings.

Langue: (French word for "language" or "tongue") An aspect of language consisting of a system of rules and conventions that's independent of individual users.

Liaisons: Youth who interact with two or more adolescents who belong to cliques, but aren't members of a clique themselves.

Local Emic: The third step in the S. E. E. Spiral, in which a youth pastor-ethnographer engages in intense personal observation of a group or group's activities.

Macrosystem: The way the institutional elements of the other systems (micro, meso, and exo) function consistently because of broader cultural beliefs, values, and patterns of behavior.

Masculine: Those qualities, activities, or behaviors that are socially thought to be associated with men or boys.

Mesosystem: Comprises the interrelations among two or more settings in the microsystem in which the adolescent actively participates.

Microsystem: Consisting of one's immediate environment, involving those regular and daily interactions in which an adolescent is an active agent.

Parole: (French word for "speech") The aspect of language that refers to the use of language—the system—in particular instances, oral or written.

Peer: Someone who has a similar status—age, social class, and location.

Peer Friendship: A dynamic, interrelating relationship with a peer that includes intimacy, trust, and mutuality.

Perception: An attitude or understanding derived from personal experiences.

Pro-social Behaviors: Behaviors that promote the well-being of self and others.

Public Culture: Those specific forms of thoughts and actions expected in the communal and social arenas of society.

Radicalist: Niebuhr's typology, also called "Christ against Culture," in which Christ embodies absolute truth, and culture is evil and must be resisted.

Reciprocity: A characteristic of a relationship in which there is mutual exchange and recognition.

Reduction Hypothesis: A theory that proposed that Internet usage was associated with subsequent reduction in family communication, declines in the size of social relationship networks, and increases in loneliness.

Religion: The deepest expression in all aspects of a person's spirit, encompassing the totality of the human spirit.

Religiosity: The measure of a person's religious commitment.

Ritual: "A symbolic-expressive aspect of behavior that communicates something about social relations, often in a relatively dramatic or formal manner."

Self-regulation: The capacity for exercising self-control and curbing impulses to act in accordance with social norms.

Sex: Refers to the biological dimension of being male or female.

Sign: A cultural element that represents or expresses something else.

Signified: The concept or meaning of a cultural sign expressed by a signifier.

Signifier: The aspect of a cultural sign that is the physical or material means by which a concept is expressed.

Social Competency: The ability to negotiate social relationships, particularly with individuals within the immediate (micro) context of one's environment.

Socialization: The process of becoming skilled in the beliefs, behaviors, and customs of a particular society's culture.

Spirituality: Concerns the aspect of a person's identity that addresses issues of the transcendent and questions about ultimate meaning in one's life.

Starting Emic: The first step in the S. E. E. Spiral, in which the youth pastor-ethnographer engages in a personal reflection of what he or she knows and how he or she knows it regarding a particular cultural phenomenon.

Stimulation Hypothesis: Theory that proposed that use of the Internet may actually stimulate relationship formation with strangers *and* improve the quality of pre-existing social relationships.

Strange-Familiar Phenomenon: Observed occurrences that are familiar to an observer but appear in a particular context that is strange to the observer.

Strengthened, Imposed Etic: The second step in the S. E. E. Spiral, in which a youth pastor-ethnographer seeks to gain increased knowledge and gather data from a study of a particular cultural phenomenon.

Subject-Object Phenomenon: The dynamic in an ethnographic observation in which observed groups are the objects of study, but also serve as the experts of a cultural phenomenon (subject).

Symbol: A cultural sign that is removed from its actual representation and used to impose meaning upon experience.

Synthetic: Niebuhr's typology, also called "Christ above Culture," in which culture is perceived to be both holy and sinful and can be a means for mediating God's truth and grace.

BIBLIOGRAPHY
(NOT INCLUDING WORKS CITED)

Ajrouch, Kristine J. "Gender, Race, and Symbolic Boundaries: Contested Spaces of Identity among Arab American Adolescents." *Sociological Perspectives* 47, no. 4 (Winter 2004): 371–391.

Allen, Joseph P., et al. 1994. Autonomy and relatedness in family interactions as predictors of expressions of negative adolescent affect. *Journal of Research on Adolescence* 4 (4): 535–552.

Angrosino, Michael V., ed. *Doing Cultural Anthropology: Projects for Ethnographic Data Collection.* Prospect Heights, IL: Waveland Press, Inc., 2002.

Arnett, Jeffrey Jensen. "Adolescents' Use of Media for Self-Socialization." *Journal of Youth and Adolescence* 24, no. 5 (1995): 519–533.

Baer, Roberta D., and Susan C. Weller. "Designing a Questionnaire for Cross-cultural Research." In *Doing Cultural Anthropology: Projects for Ethnographic Data Collection*, by Michael V. Angrosino, 115–122. Prospect Heights, IL: Waveland Press, Inc., 2002.

Bartko, W. Todd, and Jacquelynne S. Eccles. 2003. Adolescent participation in structured and unstructured activities: A person-oriented analysis. *Journal of Youth and Adolescence* 32 (4): 233–241.

Basow, Susan A. "Gender Role and Gender Identity Development." Chapter 26 in *Handbook of Girls' and Women's Psychological Health*, edited by Judith Worell and Carol D. Goodheart, 242–251. Oxford: Oxford Unversity Press, 2006.

Baugh, John, and Joel Sherzer. *Language in Use: Readings in Sociolinguistics.* Englewood Cliffs, NJ: Prentice Hall Publishers, 1984.

Bieschke, Kathleen J. "Charting the Waters." *The Counseling Psychologist* 30, no. 4 (July 2002): 575–581.

Boingeanu, Corneliu. "Personhood in its Protological and Eschatological Patterns: An Eastern Orthodox View of the Ontology of Personality." *Evangelical Quarterly* 78, no. 1 (2006): 3–19.

Branje, Susan J., Tom Frijns, Catrin Finkenauer, Rutger Engels, and Wim Meeus. "You Are My Best Friend: Commitment and Stability in Adolescents' Same-Sex Friendships." *Personal Relationships* 14, no. 4 (2007): 587–603.

Brown, B. Bradford, and Nina S. Mounts. 2007. The cultural context of family-peer linkages in adolescence. *New Directions for Child and Adolescent Development* 2007 (116): 1–15, in *Linking parents and family to adolescent peer relations: Ethnic and cultural considerations.* San Francisco: Jossey-Bass Publishers.

Browning, Don S. 1996. *A fundamental practical theology: Descriptive and strategic proposals.* Minneapolis: Fortress Press.

Bukowski, William M., Ana Maria Velasquez, and Mara Brendgen. 2008. Variations in patterns of peer influence: Considerations of self and other. In *Understanding peer influence in children and adolescents,* ed. Mitchell J. Prinstein and Kenneth A. Dodge, 125–140. New York: The Guilford Press.

Carlo, Gustavo, Richard A. Fabes, Deborah Laible, and Kristina Kupanoff. "Early Adolescence and Prosocial/Moral Behavior II: The Role of Social and Contextual Influences." *The Journal of Early Adolescence* 19, no. 2 (May 1999): 133–147.

Cass, V. C. "Homosexual Identity Formation: A Theoretical Model." *Journal of Homosexuality* 4, no. 3 (1979): 219–235.

Chen, Chuansheng, Ellen Greenberger, Susan Farruggia, Kevin Bush, and Qi Dong. "Beyond Parents and Peers: The Role of Important Non-Parental Adults (VIPS) in Adolescent Development in China and the United States." *Psychology in the Schools* 40, no. 1 (2003): 35–50.

Clark, Chap. "Youth Ministry as Practical Theology." Edited by Mark W. Cannister. *The Journal of Youth Ministry* (Evangel Publishing, Inc.) 7, no. 1 (Fall 2008): 9–38.

Collins, W. Andrew, Deborah P. Welsh, and Wyndol Furman. "Adolescent romantic relationships." *Annual Review of Psychology* 60 (January 2009): 631–652.

Connolly, Jennifer, Wendy Craig, Adele Goldberg, and Debra Pepler. 2004. Mixed-gender groups, dating, and romantic relationships in early adolescence. *Journal of Research on Adolescence* 14 (2): 185–207.

Cox, Harvey. *Religion in the Secular City: Toward a Postmodern Theology.* New York: Simon & Schuster, 1984.

Coyne-Beasley, Tamera, and Victor J. Schoenbach. 2000. The African-American church: A potential forum for adolescent comprehensive sexuality education. *Journal of Adolescent Health* 26 (4): 289–294.

Crosnoe, Robert, and Clea McNeely. "Peer Relations, Adolescent Behavior, and Public Health Research and Practice." *Family Community Health* 31, no. 1S (2008): S71–S80.

Dean, Kenda Creasy. "We Will Find the Answers as We Go: A Response to Chap Clark's *Youth Ministry as Practical Theology*." Edited by Mark W. Cannister. *The Journal of Youth Ministry* (Evangel Publishing, Inc.) 7, no. 1 (Fall 2008): 39–48.

de Bruyn, Eddy H., and Dymphna C. van den Boom. "Interpersonal Behavior, Peer Popularity, and Self-esteem in Early Adolescence." *Social Development* 14, no. 4 (2005): 555–573.

Dekovic, Maja, Rutger C. M. E. Engels, Toshiaki Shirai, Gerard de Kort, and Arjen L. Anker. "The Role of Peer Relations in Adolescent Development in Two Cultures." *Journal of Cross-Cultural Psychology* 33, no. 6 (November 2002): 57–595.

Diamond, Milton J. "Sex and Gender Are Different: Sexual Identity and Gender Identity Are Different." *Clinical Child Psychology and Psychiatry* 7, no. 3 (2002): 320–334.

Dimitriadis, Greg. "'In the Clique': Popular Culture, Constructions of Place, and the Everyday Lives of Urban Youth." *Anthropology and Education Quarterly* 32, no. 1 (March 2001): 29–51.

Dishion, Thomas J., Timothy F. Piehler, and Michael W. Myers. 2008. Dynamics and ecology of adolescent peer influence. Chap. 4 in *Understanding peer influence in children and adolescents*. Ed. Mitchell J. Prinstein and Kenneth A. Dodge, 72–93. New York: The Guilford Press.

Dunn, Richard R., and James W. Mohler. "The 'Fourth Wave': A Theological Perspective." *Christian Education Journal* 3 NS, no. 2 (Fall 1999): 47–61.

Eliason, Michele J. "Accounts of Sexual Identity Formation in Heterosexual Students." *Sex Roles* 32, nos. 11-12 (June 1995): 821–834.

Ewing, Katherine P. "The Illusion of Wholeness: 'Culture,' 'Self,' and the Experience of Inconsistency." *Ethos* 18, no. 3 (September 1990): 251–278.

Fassinger, R. E., and B. A. Miller. "Validation of an Inclusive Model of Sexual Minority Identity Formation on a Sample of Gay Men." *Journal of Homosexuality* 32, no. 2 (1996): 53–78.

Fife, Wayne. *Doing Fieldwork: Ethnographic Methods for Research in Developing Countries and Beyond*. New York: Palgrave Macmillan Publishers, 2005.

Friedman, Herbert L. "Culture and Adolescent Development." *Journal of Adolescent Health* 25, no. 1 (1999): 1–6.

Gardner, Kelli A., and Carolyn E. Cutrona. "Social Support Communication in Families." Chapter 22 in *Handbook of Family Communication*, edited by Anita L. Vangelisti, 495–512. Mahwah, NJ: Lawrence Erlbaum Associates, 2004.

Gilmore, David D. *Manhood in the Making: Cultural Concepts of Masculinity.* New Haven, CT: Yale University Press, 1990.

Good, Marie, and Teena Willoughby. "The Identity Formation Experiences of Church-Attending Rural Adolescents." *Journal of Adolescent Research* 22, no. 4 (July 2007): 387–412.

Grotevant, Harold D. "Toward a Process Model of Identity Formation." *Journal of Adolescent Research* 2, no. 3 (1987): 203–222.

Grusec, Joan E., and Paul D Hastings. *Handbook of Socialization: Theory and Research.* New York: The Guilford Press, 2007.

Güroglu, Berna, Cornelis F. M. van Lieshout, Gerbert J. T. Haselager, and Ron H. J. Scholte. "Similarity and Complementarity of Behavioral Profiles of Friendship Types and Types of Friends: Friendships and Psychosocial Adjustment." *Journal of Research on Adolescence* 17, no. 2 (2007): 357–386.

Hall, Douglas John. *The Cross in our Context: Jesus and the Suffering World.* Minneapolis: Fortress Press, 2003.

———. "Finding Our Way Into the Future." *The Princeton Lectures on Youth, Church, and Culture,* 2006: 14–29.

———. "Where in the World Are We?" *The Princeton Lectures on Youth, Church, and Culture,* 2006: 1–13.

Hardway, Christina, and Andrew J. Fuligni. "Dimensions of Family Connectedness Among Adolescents with Mexican, Chinese, and European Backgrounds." *Developmental Psychology* 42, no. 6 (2006): 1246–1258.

Hartup, Willard W., and Nan Stevens. 1997. Friendships and adaptation in the life course. *Psychological Bulletin* 121 (3): 355–370.

Hartup, Willard W. "The Company They Keep: Friendships and Their Developmental Significance." *Child Development* 67, no. 1 (February 1996): 1–13.

Joinson, Adam N. 2001. Self-disclosure in computer-mediated communication: The role of self-awareness and visual anonymity. *European Journal of Social Psychology* 31 (2): 177–192.

Jones, Diane Carlson, and Joy K. Crawford. "The Peer Appearance Culture During Adolescence: Gender and Body Mass Variations." *Journal of Youth and Adolescence* 35, no. 2 (April 2006): 257–269.

Jorgenson, Danny L. *Participant Observation: A Methodology for Human Studies.* Newbury Park, CA: Sage Publications, 1989.

Killen, Melanie. "Culture, Self, and Development: Are Cultural Templates Useful or Stereotypic?" *Developmental Review* 17, no. 3 (1997): 239–249.

Killen, Melanie, and Cecilia Wainryb. "Independence and Interdependence in Diverse Cultural Contexts." *New Directions for Child & Adolescent Development*, no. 87 (Spring 2000): 5–21.

Klaczynski, Paul A. "Cultural-Developmental Tasks and Adolescent Development: Theoretical and Methodological Considerations." *Adolescence* 25, no. 100 (Winter 1990): 811–823.

Kraft, Charles H. 2008. *Worldview for Christian witness.* Pasadena, CA: William Carey Library.

Kutsche, Paul. *Field Ethnography: A Manual for Doing Cultural Anthropology.* Upper Saddle River, NJ: Prentice Hall, 1998.

Ladd, G. W., and K. D. Lesieur. 1995. Parents and children's peer relationships. Vol. 4 of *Handbook of parenting: Applied and practical parenting.* Ed. M. H. Bornstein. Mahwal, NJ: Erlbaum.

Lam, Ching Man. "A Cultural Perspective on the Study of Chinese Adolescent Development." *Child and Adolescent Social Work Journal* 14, no. 2 (April 1997): 95–113.

Lerner, Richard M., and Laurence Steinberg. 2009. *Handbook of adolescent psychology: Contextual influences on adolescent development.* Vol. 2. 3rd ed. Hoboken, NJ: John Wiley & Sons, Inc.

Livermore, David A. *Cultural Intelligence: Improving Your CQ to Engage Our Multicultural World.* Edited by Chap Clark. Grand Rapids, MI: Baker Academic, 2009.

Marcia, James E. "Development and Validation of Ego Identity Status." In *Ego Identity: A Handbook for Psychosocial Research.* Edited by J. R. Marcia, A. S. Waterman, D. R. Matteson, S. L. Archer, and J. L. Orlofsky, 1-21. New York: Springer-Verlag, 1966.

Marsh, Penny, Joseph P. Allen, Martin Ho, Maryfrances Porter, and F. Christy McFarland. "The Changing Nature of Adolescent Friendships: Longitudinal Links with Early Adolescent Ego Development." *The Journal of Early Adolescence* 26, no. 4 (November 2006): 414–431.

Mascolo, Michael F. "The Coactive Construction of Selves in Cultures." Edited by Michael F. Mascolo and Jinn Li. *New Directions for Child and Adolescent Development* 2004, no. 104 (Summer 2004): 79–90.

McDonald, Suzanne. "Barth's 'Other' Doctrine of Election in the *Church Dogmatics.*" *International Journal of Systematic Theology* 9, no. 2 (2007): 134–147.

McKenna, Katelyn Y. A., and John A. Bargh. 2000. Plan 9 from cyberspace: The implications of the Internet for personality and social psychology. *Personality and Social Psychology Review* 4 (1): 57–75.

McFarlane, Graham. "Living on the Edge—Moving Towards the Centre: The Place of Jesus Christ in Our Quest for Personhood." *Evangelical Quarterly* 78, no. 1 (2006): 37–50.

Miller, Joan G. "Essential Role of Culture in Developmental Psychology." *New Directions for Child and Adolescent Development* 2005, no. 109 (Fall 2005): 33–41.

Miller, Peggy J., and Sarah C. Mangelsdorf. "Developing Selves Are Meaning-Making Selves: Recouping the Social in Self-Development." *New Directions for Child and Adolescent Development* 2005, no. 109 (Fall 2005): 51–59.

Morris, Michael W., Kwok Leung, Daniel Ames, and Brian Lickel. "Views from Inside and Outside: Integrating Emic and Etic Insights about Culture and Justice Judgment." *Academy of Management Review* 24, no. 4 (October 1999): 781–796.

Mounts, Nina S., and Hyun-Soo Kim. "Parental Goals Regarding Peer Relationships and Management of Peers in a Multiethnic Sample." *New Directions for Child and Adolescent Development* 2007, no. 116 (Summer 2007): 17–33.

Mueller, Walt. *Engaging the Soul of Youth Culture: Bridging Teen Worldviews and Christian Truth.* Downers Grove, IL: IVP Books, 2006.

Nelson, R. Michael, and Teresa K. DeBacker. "Achievement Motivation in Adolescents: The Role of Peer Climate and Best Friends." *The Journal of Experimental Education* 76, no. 2 (2008): 170–189.

O'Sullivan, Lucia F., M. C. McCrudden, and Deborah L. Tolman. "To Your Sexual Health! Incorporating Sexuality Into the Health Perspective." Chapter 21 in *Handbook of Girls' and Women's Psychological Health: Gender and Well-Being Across the Life Span,* by Judith Worell and Carol D. Goodheart, 192–199. Oxford: Oxford University Press, 2006.

Paddison, Angus. "Karl Barth's Theological Exegesis of Romans 9-11 in the Light of Jewish-Christian Understanding." *Journal for the Study of the New Testament* 28, no. 4 (2006): 469–488.

Padilla, Amado M. "Bicultural Social Development." *Hispanic Journal of Behavioral Sciences* 28, no. 4 (November 2006): 467–497.

Padilla, C. René. 1985. *Mission between the times: Essays on the kingdom.* Grand Rapids, MI: Eerdmans.

Parrett, Gary A. "Toward What End? A Response to Chap Clark's *Youth Ministry as Practical Theology.*" Edited by Mark W. Cannister. *The Journal of Youth Ministry* (Evangel Publishing, Inc.) 7, no. 1 (Fall 2008): 49–66.

Penner, Myron B., ed. *Christianity and the Postmodern Turn: Six Views.* Grand Rapids, MI: Brazos Press, 2005.

Perry, Pamela. "White Means Never Having to Say You're Ethnic: White Youth and the Construction of 'Cultureless' Identities." *Journal of Contemporary Ethnography* 30, no. 1 (February 2001): 56–91.

Poulin, Francois, and Sara Pedersen. "Developmental Changes in Gender Composition of Friendship Networks in Adolescent Girls and Boys." *Developmental Psychology* 43, no. 6 (2007): 1484–1496.

Quigley, Richard. "Positive Peer Groups: 'Helping Others' Meets Primary Developmental Needs." *Reclaiming Children and Youth* 13, no. 3 (Fall 2004): 134–137.

Raeff, Catherine. "Individuals in Relationships: Cultural Values, Children's Social Interactions, and the Development of an American Individualistic Self." *Developmental Review* 17, no. 3 (1997): 205–238.

———. "Within-Culture Complexities: Multifaceted and Interrelated Autonomy and Connectedness Characteristics in Late Adolescent Selves." Edited by Michael F. Mascolo and Jin Li. *New Directions for Child and Adolescent Development* 2004, no. 104 (Summer 2004): 61–78.

Regnerus, Mark D., and Glen H. Elder. 2003. Religion and vulnerability among low-risk adolescents. *Social Science Research* 32 (4): 633–658.

Riggs, John W. *Postmodern Christianity: Doing Theology in the Contemporary World.* Harrisburg, PA: Trinity Press International, 2003.

Root, Andrew. "Practical Theology: What Is it and How Does It Work?" Edited by Mark W. Cannister. *The Journal of Youth Ministry* (Evangel Publishing, Inc.) 7, no. 2 (Spring 2009): 55–72.

Ryan, Linda G., Karen Miller-Loessi, and Tanya Nieri. "Relationships with Adults as Predictors of Substance Use, Gang Involvement, and Threats to Safety Among Disadvantaged Urban High-School Adolescents." *Journal of Community Psychology* 35, no. 8 (2007): 1053–1071.

Sauter, Gerhard. *Protestant Theology at the Crossroads: How to Face the Crucial Tasks for Theology in The Twenty-First Century.* Grand Rapids, MI: Eerdmans, 2007.

Schwartz, Seth J. "A New Identity for Identity Research: Recommendations for Expanding and Refocusing the Identity Literature." *Journal of Adolescent Research* 20, no. 3 (May 2005): 293–308.

———. "Self and Identity in Early Adolescence: Some Reflections and an Introduction to the Special Issue." *Journal of Early Adolescence* 28, no. 1 (February 2008): 5–15.

Seginer, Rachel, Shirli Shoyer, Rabiaa Hossessi, and Hyam Tannous. "Adolescent Family and Peer Relationships: Does Culture Matter?" Edited by B. Bradford Brown and Nina S. Mounts. *New Directions for Child and Adolescent Development* 2007, no. 116 (Summer 2007): 83–100.

Sheriffs, Deryck. "Personhood in the Old Testament: Who's Asking?" *Evangelical Quarterly* 77, no. 1 (2005): 13–34.

Smith, Christian, Melinda Lundquist Denton, Robert Faris, and Mark Regnerus. "Mapping American Adolescent Religious Participation." *Journal for the Scientific Study of Religion* 41, no. 4 (2002): 597–612.

Spinrad, Tracy L., Nancy Eisenberg, and Frank Bernt. "Introduction to the Special Issues on Moral Development: Part II." *The Journal of Genetic Psychology* 168, no. 3 (2007): 229–230.

Stanton-Salazar, Ricardo D., and Stephanie Urso Spina. "Adolescent Peer Networks as a Context for Social and Emotional Support." *Youth & Society* 36, no. 4 (June 2005): 379–417.

Steinberg, Laurence, and Kathryn Monahan. "Age Differences in Resistance to Peer Influence." *Developmental Psychology* 43, no. 6 (2007): 1531–1543.

Subrahmanyam, Kaveri, David Smahel, and Patricia M. Greenfield. 2006. Connecting developmental constructions to the Internet: Identity presentation and sexual exploration in online teen chat rooms. *Developmental Psychology* 42 (3): 395–406.

Sussman, Steve, Pallav Pokhrel, Richard D. Ashmore, and B. Bradford Brown. "Adolescent Peer Group Identification and Characteristics: A Review of the Literature." *Addictive Behaviors* 32, no. 8 (August 2007): 1602–1627.

Swain, Jon. "An Ethnographic Approach to Researching Children in Junior School." *International Journal of Social Research Methodology* 9, no. 3 (July 2006): 199–213.

Tilton-Weaver, Lauree C., Erin T. Vitunski, and Nancy L. Galambos. "Five Images of Maturity in Adolescence: What Does 'Grown Up' Mean?" *Journal of Adolescence* 24, no. 2 (2001): 143–158.

Triandis, Harry C. "The Self and Social Behavior in Differing Cultural Contexts." *Psychological Review* 96, no. 3 (1989): 506–520.

Turiel, Elliot. "Commentary: Beyond Individualism and Collectivism—A Problem, or Progress?" Edited by Michael F. Mascolo and Jin Li. *New Directions for Child and Adolescent Development* 2004, no. 104 (Summer 2004): 91–100.

Turner, Max. "Approaching 'Personhood' in the New Testament, with Special Reference to Ephesians." *Evangelical Quarterly* 77, no. 3 (2005): 211–233.

Underwood, Marion K., and Lisa H. Rosen. "Gender, Peer Relations, and Challenges for Girlfriends and Boyfriends Coming Together in Adolescence." *Psychology of Women Quarterly* 33, no. 1 (January 2009): 16–20.

Ward, Pete. *God at the Mall: Youth Ministry That Meets Kids Where They're At.* Peabody, MA: Hendrickson Publishers, 1999.

Wells, David F. *Above All Earthly Pow'rs: Christ in a Postmodern World.* Grand Rapids, MI: Eerdmans, 2005.

———. "A More Excellent Way: A Response to Chap Clark's *Youth Ministry as Practical Theology.*" Edited by Mark W. Cannister. *The Journal of Youth Ministry* (Evangel Publishing, Inc.) 7, no. 1 (Fall 2008): 49–58.

Worthington, Roger L., Holly Bielstein Savoy, Frank R. Dillon, and Elizabeth R. Vernaglia. "Heterosexual Identity Development: A Multidimensional Model of Individual and Social Identity." *The Counseling Psychologist* 30, no. 4 (July 2002): 496–531.

Zeldin, Shepherd, Reed Larson, Linda Camino, and Cailin O'Connor. "Intergenerational Relationships and Partnerships in Community Programs: Purpose, Practice, and Directions for Research." *Journal of Community Psychology* 33, no. 1 (2005): 1–10.

INDEX

A

Abelard, Peter, 173
Acting for another's benefit, 93
Adolescence. *See* Development, adolescent; Youth
Adult leader training, 68–69
Advice, expert, 96
Affection and intimacy in peer relationships, 128
Aggarwal, Neelam, 7 (box)
American culture, 8 (box), 15, 18–19
    bald eagle in, 40, 41 (box)
    Thanksgiving in, 44–46 (box)
Anderson, Charles, 211
Anderson, Elijah, 21 (box)
Anthropological discussion of culture, 27
Aquinas, St. Thomas, 175
Arnett, Jeffrey Jensen, 110, 130
Assessing harm, 97
Assigned character traits, 18–19
Augustine, 178

B

Bailey, Beth L., 141, 143 (box)
Bald eagle, 40, 41 (box)
Ball, Joanna, 91
Barth, Fritz, 189 (box)
Barth, Karl, 161, 181–182, 189 (box)
    definition of culture, 184–185
    on free culture, 185–186
    on God's revelation, 183
    on relationships between God and humanity,
        182–184
    on rightness of free culture, 187–188
    on role of the church, 189–190
    on task of theology, 188
Barth, Markus, 184
Bearers, culture, 8
Beatnik generation, 31–32 (box)
Behavior
    rituals and extraordinary, 43–44
    socially consistent patterns of, 28–29
    symbols as blueprints for, 41–42
Beliefs, consensus on, 194–195
Benedict, Ruth, 28–29, 193
Bennett, John W., 28
Bevans, Stephen, 201–202, 204–205

Biological inheritance, 7–8, 17 (box)
Blais, Julie J., 134, 135, 136
Boff, Leonardo, 213
Bonhoeffer, Dietrich, 71, 72
Boundaries, cultural, 196, 197
Broderick, Carlfred B., 141 (box)
Bronfenbrenner, Urie, 105–109, 127, 131
    ecological model of, 110–114
    on religious affiliation of youth, 147
Brown, B. Bradford, 121
Bucholtz, Mary, 56
Buhrmester, Duane, 119, 123
Bulman, Raymond, 164, 166, 167

C

Calling practices, 141–144
Catholicity of the church, 205
Chandler, Daniel, 49
Character traits, assigned, 18–19
Christ and Culture, 169
Church, the
    Barth on role of, 189–190
    Catholicity of, 205
    Tillich on function of, 166–167
Church Dogmatics, 181
Cliques, 129–130
Closeness between parents and adolescents, 120–121
Cobb, Nancy, 119
Code of the Street, 21 (box)
Code-switching, 21 (box)
Collins, W. Andrew, 121
Communication technologies, online, 133–138
Community matters and ethnography, 69
Companionship in peer relationships, 127
Competency, social, 123
Confidentiality
    keeping, 94–96
    mandated reporting and, 97–100
    when to break, 96–97
Connolly, Jennifer, 138, 139
Consensus on beliefs, 194–195
Contextual theology
    Catholicity of the church and, 205
    components of, 202–203
    defined, 201–202

dynamics of Christian faith that demand, 203–206
incarnation and, 204
sacramental nature of reality and, 204
shift in understanding of nature of divine
revelation and, 204–205
the trinity and, 205–206
Conversionists, 177–178
Coptic cross, 37 (box)
Courtship, 141 (box)
Creativity, culture as, 30
Critical response, proper, 187
Critical thinking about youth culture, 210–215
Cross, image of the, 36, 37 (box)
Crowds, 130–131
Cultural distinctions, 17 (box), 196, 197
Cultural inheritance, 7–8, 23
Cultural patterns, 30 (box)
Cultural relativism, 22 (box)
Culture. See also Youth culture
    American, 8 (box), 15, 18–19
    as an internally consistent whole, 194
    anthropological discussion of, 27
    assigned character traits in, 18–19
    bearers, 8
    boundaries, 196, 197
    chief characteristics of, 171
    Christ above, 173–175
    Christ against, 172
    Christ as transformer of, 177–178
    and Christ in paradox, 175–176
    as creativity, 30
    critique of modern understanding of, 193–196
    defined, 15, 17, 165, 170–171, 184–185
    dominant, 54
    free, 185–188
    as a guidance system, 32–33
    as a historical phenomenon, 29
    historical understandings of, 16–17
    human potential for ideas and, 27–28
    ideology fit in defining, 33 (box)
    makers, 8
    of niceness, 15
    operating, 19–20
    of peer relationships, 117–118, 122–127, 127–131
    people assigning meaning and, 28
    pool, 25
    popular, 8 (box), 9, 15
    primacy of stability in, 196
    problem solving and, 30–32
    public, 20–23

    of relationships, 10–11
    rightness of free, 185–188
    set of public, 23–24
    seven senses of, 17–25
    shaping the identity of adolescents, 9
    socially consistent patterns of behavior and,
    28–29
    social order and, 195
    society's, 25
    sub-, 53–56
    systems of standards in, 18
    theology of, 181–182
    visualizing, 17
Culture: A Critical Review of Concepts and Definitions, 27
Curiosity, 75
Custom complex, 109
Cyzewski, Ed, 201 (box)

D
Definition of culture, 15, 17
    Barth's, 184–185
    ideology fit in, 33 (box)
Depression, 91
Derived etic, 85
Development, adolescent, 105–106
    ecological model of, 110–114
    environment in, 108
    exosystem of, 111 (figure), 113–114
    importance of cultural beliefs to, 110
    macrosystem of, 111 (box), 114
    mesosystem of, 111 (figure), 112, 121–122
    micro-level of, 111 (figure), 112
    preliminary concepts and terms in, 107–109
    the self in, 108–109
    socialization in, 109
    web of relationships in, 114–115
Developmental psychology, 106
Discernment, 63–65
Distinctions, cultural, 17 (box)
Dodge, Kenneth, 129
Dominant culture, 54
Drug abuse, 91
    religiosity and, 149
Dualism, 175–176
Dworkin, Jodi B., 151

E
Eagle, bald, 40, 41 (box)
Eastman Kodak, 10
Ecological model of human development, 110–114

Ecology, human, 106
Ego support in peer relationships, 127
Elias, Maurice J., 147
Emic perspective on ethnography, 79
    local, 84–85, 85–87
    S. E. E. Spiral of, 80–85
    starting, 81–82
Engels, Friedrich, 33 (box)
Enhanced self-disclosure hypothesis, 134
Ethics, 75
Ethnocentrism, 19 (box)
Ethnography
    adult leader training and, 68–69
    basis for, 67
    community matters and, 69
    cultivating all the senses, 73–74
    curiosity and, 75
    emic perspective on, 79–85
    ethics and, 75
    etic perspective on, 79–85
    facilitating new practices, 70–71, 73
    facilitating theological thinking, 70
    humility and, 74
    humor and, 75
    identifying the familiar in the strange, 87
    identifying the strange in the familiar, 87
    increased understanding of youth through, 68
    listening and, 72–73
    ministry as, 65, 71
    pastoral-, 68–71
    subject-object phenomenon, 86
    vision and, 78–80
    watchfulness and, 71–72
    youth culture, 212–213
Etic perspective on ethnography, 79–80
    derived, 85
    S. E. E. Spiral of, 80–85
    strengthened, imposed, 84
Everyday Theology, 211
Exosystem of adolescent development, 111 (figure), 113–114
Expert advice, 96

F
Facebook, 131
Faith, 148
Feedback, 123
Fiduciary duty, 93–94
Fourchée, cross, 37 (box)
Fowler, H. W., 50 (box)

Free culture, 185–186
    rightness of, 187–188
Freilich, Morris, 16
Furman, Wyndol, 119
Furrow, James L., 150

G
Gannon, Michael, 45 (box)
Geertz, Clifford, 27, 28
Gender differences in peer friendships, 124–126
Getahun, Linde, 80
Global youth culture, 55 (box), 56
Gnosticism, 173, 174 (box)
Goals and ordering, right, 187–188
God
    incarnation of, 204
    relationship with humanity, 182–184
    revelation of, 183, 204–205
    triune nature of, 205–206
    "yes/no" of, 183–184
Goodenough, Ward, 17, 18, 19, 23, 25
Greek cross, 37 (box)
Guidance system, culture as a, 32–33

H
Hannerz, Ulf, 28, 30
Harm, assessing, 97
Harnack, Adolf, 189 (box)
Harris, Marvin, 27, 80
Hiebert, Paul, 19 (box)
Hip-hop culture, 55 (box)
Historical understandings of culture, 16–17
Hitler, Adolf, 189 (box)
Hoffman, Nelly, 189 (box)
Homogeneity of dominant cultures, 54
Hopelessness, 91
Human ecology, 106
Humanity
    free culture and, 185–186
    relationship between God and, 182–184
    religiosity and, 164–165
Human potential for ideas, 27–28
Humility, 74
Humor, sense of, 75

I
Iconic signs, 39
Icons, 39
Ideas, human potential for, 27–28
Identity, rituals and social, 44

Ideology
    fit in defining culture, 33 (box)
    religiosity and, 150–151
Imaging signs, 39
Incarnation, 204
Indexical signs, 39
Indicative signs, 39, 40 (box)
Inheritance, biological versus cultural, 7–8, 17 (box), 23
Instant messaging, 135
Internet, the
    communication technology use and, 133–138
    culture of adolescence, 132–133
    ethics of youth workers and, 136–137 (box)
    as a negative influence on social relationships, 136, 138
Interviewing, 67
Intimacy and affection in peer relationships, 128
Isolates, 130

J

Jean, Jesse, 8 (box)
Jesus Christ, 42 (box)
    ability to See Things, 64
    above culture, 173–175
    birth of, 203
    and culture in paradox, 175–176
    against culture typology, 172
    of culture typology, 173
    definition of, 170
    incarnation of God in, 204
    revelation in, 183, 204–205
    as the transformer of culture, 177–178
Judging theologically, 213–215

K

King, Pamela E., 150
Kluckhohn, Clyde, 27
Kraft, Charles, 202
Kroeber, Alfred L, 27, 29

L

Language, 46–50
Larson, James, 121
Latin cross, 37 (box)
Laursen, Brett, 121
Leader training, adult, 68–69
Lévi-Strauss, Claude, 27, 49 (box)
Liaisons, 130
Liberman, Anatoly, 49–50 (box)

Lincoln, Abraham, 45 (box)
Listening, 72–73
Local emic, 84–85, 85–87
Lord's Supper, 42 (box)
Luther, Martin, 176
Lynch, Gordon, 172

M

Macrosystem of adolescent development, 111 (box), 114
Mah, Ann, 8 (box)
Ma Jingxuan, 8 (box)
Makers, culture, 8
Malinowski, Bronislaw, 170
Mandated reporting, 97–100
Markstrom, Carol, 148
Marshall, Gordon, 54 (box)
Marx, Karl, 33 (box)
McDonald's, 115 (box)
McIsaac, Caroline, 138, 139
Mead, Margaret, 28
Meaning
    culture and, 28
    language and, 49–50 (box)
    management, symbols as system of, 43
    signs as vehicles of, 35–36
    universal aspects of being human and, 88
Media, 131–132
Mesosystem of adolescent development, 111 (figure), 112, 121–122
Metzger, Paul, 183, 188
Micro-level of adolescent development, 111 (figure), 112
Mission trips, 77–78
Models of Contextual Theology, 201
Morality, 163
Moschella, Mary Clark, 70, 73–74
Moses, 74
Motivation, human, 187
Mulkeen, Patricia, 120
Muñoz, Caroline Lego, 137 (box)
Mutuality, 123
MySpace, 131

N

Namenwirth, J. Zvi, 28
Newman, Barbara M., 123
Newman, Philip R., 123
Nicene Creed, 203 (box)
Niebuhr, Richard, 161, 169–170

on Christ, 170
on culture, 170–171
paradoxes highlighted by, 176–178
typologies, 171–176
Nonnemaker, James M., 91
Nouwen, Henri, 74

O

Obama, Barack, 203
Objectivity, 187
Online communication technologies, 133–138
Online culture of adolescence, 132–133
Operating culture, 19–20
Order, social, 195
Ordering and goals, right, 187–188
Osmer, Richard, 211, 213, 215

P

Palma, Robert, 184, 186
Paradox, Christ and culture in, 175–178
Parental leave, 30 (box)
Passover, 42 (box)
Pastoral-ethnography, 68–71
Patterns of behavior, socially consistent, 28–29
Paul, apostle, 72, 99, 176–177
Peer pressure, 128
Peer relationships. *See also* Relationships
    change from preadolescence to adolescence,
        126–127
    cliques in, 129–130
    crowds and, 130–131
    culture of, 117–118, 122–127, 127–131
    family influences on, 118–122
    feedback and mutuality from, 123
    gender differences in, 124–126
    negative influences on, 136, 138
    online communication technologies and, 133–138
    self-disclosure in, 123–124, 128, 134
Peirce, C. S., 38, 40
Perry, Katy, 9
Peter, Jochen, 133, 134
Pew Internet Research, 135
Physical support in peer relationships, 127
Pike, Kenneth, 80
Pledge of Allegiance, 42
Pool, culture, 25
Popular culture, 8 (box), 9, 15
Positive development and behaviors promoted by
        religiosity, 150
Potential for ideas, human, 27–28
Power dynamic, unequal, 93–94

Practical Theology: An Introduction, 211
Prager, Karen, 123
Pressure, peer, 128
Prinstein, Mitchell, 129
Privilege, clergy, 97–100
Problem solving and culture, 30–32
Proper critical response, 187
Psychology, developmental, 106
Public culture, 20–23
    set of, 23–24

R

Rachels, James, 163
Rap music, 55 (box)
Rappaport, Roy A., 27
Reality, sacramental nature of, 204
Reduction hypothesis, 133–134
Referrals, 96–97
Reflection, theological, 214–215
Regional public cultures, 23–24
Reich, Alice, 78, 79, 85–86, 87
Relationships. *See also* Peer relationships
    culture of, 10–11
    family support and, 119
    mesosystem dynamics in, 121–122
    romantic, 138–144
    standards, norms, and values in, 118–119
    web of, 114–115
Relativism, cultural, 22 (box)
Reliance, 93
Religion
    defined, 162
    defining time and space through, 164–165
    expressed in form of culture, 165
    function of church in, 166–167
    humanity and, 164
    morality and, 163
Religiosity
    defined, 147–148
    faith and, 148
    ideological context of, 150–151
    promoting positive development and behaviors,
        150
    protection from risk behaviors with, 149–150
    salience during adolescence, 148–152
    social context of, 151
    spirituality and, 148, 151–152
Reporting, mandated, 97–100
Return of the Prodigal Son, The, 74
Revelation, God's, 183, 204–205
Rice, Kenneth, 120

Rightness of free culture, 187–188
Right ordering and right goals, 187–188
Risk behaviors and religiosity, 149–150
Rituals, 43–46
Roeser, Robert W., 150
Romantic relationships. *See also* Relationships
    calling practices and, 141–144
        function of, 140–141
        quality of, 139
        quantity of, 138, 139 (box)
Roosevelt, Franklin D., 45 (box)
Ross, Diana, 9

S
S. E. E. Spiral, 80–85
Sacramental nature of reality, 204
Same-gender romantic relationships, 139
Santrock, John, 127
Saussure, Ferdinand de, 36, 46
Scott, John, 54 (box)
Self, the, 108–109
    independence versus interdependence of, 119 (box)
Self-concept, 148
Self-disclosure, 123–124, 128
    hypothesis, enhanced, 134
Self-esteem, 119
Self-regulation, 109
Set of public cultures, 23–24
Seven senses of culture, 17–25
Sexual activity and religiosity, 149–150
Shady, Sara, 163
Signification, true, 187
Signified concepts, 36, 38–40
Signifiers, 36, 38–40
    language as, 47
Signs, 35–38
    aspects of cultural, 38–39
    imaging, 39
    indicative, 39, 40 (box)
Simon, Paul, 10
Slang, 47–48 (box)
Sleasman, Michael, 211
Smith, Christian, 23 (box), 147 (box)
Social comparison in peer relationships, 128
Social competency, 123
Social context of religiosity, 151
Social identity and rituals, 44
Socialization, 109, 124–126
Socially consistent patterns of behavior, 28–29
Social networking sites, 136–137 (box)
Social order, principle of, 195

Society's culture, 25
Soda, 24 (box)
Sombat, Windy, 141 (box), 143
Spiral, S. E. E., 80–85
Spirituality, 148, 151–152
Stability, cultural, 196
Standards, cultural systems of, 18
Starting emic, 81–82, 82–84 (box)
Steinberg, Laurence, 130
Stimulation hypothesis, 134
Stimulation in peer relationships, 127
Strengthened, imposed etic, 84
Subcultural theory, 53–56
Subject-object phenomenon, 86
Substance abuse, 91
    religiosity and, 149
Suicide, 91
Support
    family, 119
    for youth workers, 97
Symbols, 40–43
    language as, 47
    rituals and, 43
Synthetic view, 173
Systematic Theology, 164
Systems of standards, cultural, 18

T
Tanner, Kathryn, 161, 193, 201
    on consensus in beliefs, 194–195
    critique of modern understanding of culture,
        193–196
    on cultural boundaries, 196
    on exploring cultural norms and products, 196–197
    on primacy of cultural stability, 196
    on principle of social order, 195
Task of theology, 188
Tattooing, 81–82, 82–84 (box)
Tau cross, 37 (box)
Terrorism, 203
Thanksgiving, 44–46 (box)
Theological judging, 213–215
Theological reflection, 214–215
Theological thinking, 70
Theology, contextual. *See* Contextual theology
Theology of Culture, 161, 166
Theories of Culture: A New Agenda for Theology, 193
Tierney, Gerry, 72
Tillage, 16
Tillich, Paul, 161–162, 164–167
Tolstoy, Leo, 172

Towner, Terri L., 137 (box)
Tradition, culture as, 29
Training, adult leader, 68–69
Trends, youth culture, 211–212
Trinity, the, 205–206
True signification, 187
Trust, 93
Tylor, E. B., 17, 28
Typologies, 171–172
    Christ above culture, 173–175
    Christ against culture, 172
    Christ and culture in paradox, 175–176
    Christ as transformer of culture, 177–178
    Christ of culture, 173

U

Understanding Theology and Popular Culture, 172
Unequal power dynamic, 93–94

V

Valkenburg, Patti M., 133, 134
Values
    religiosity and, 150
    society, 28
Van Dyke, Cydney J., 147
Vanhoozer, Kevin, 211
Vision, 78–80
Visualizing culture, 17

W

Walls, Andrew, 205
Watchfulness, cultivating, 71–72
Weber, Robert Philip, 28
Web of relationships, 114–115
Wuthnow, Robert, 43

Y

Youth. *See also* Development, adolescent
    closeness between parents and, 120–121
    code-switching by, 21 (box)
    culture shaping the identity of, 9
    drug abuse by, 91
    family support of, 119
    media in culture of, 131–132
    mission trips by, 77–78
    online communication technologies used by, 133–138
    online culture of, 132–133

pastoral-ethnography for increased
        understanding of, 68
    religion and positive behaviors among, 23 (box)
    typical aspects of life for American, 199–200
    well-being and peer groups, 127–129
    worldwide number of, 7
Youth culture, 9–10, 15. *See also* Culture
    Beatnik generation and, 31–32 (box)
    critical thinking about, 210–215
    dominant culture and, 54
    emic perspective on, 79
    ethnographic perspective on, 212–213
    etic perspective on, 79–80
    global, 55 (box), 56
    language in, 47–48 (box)
    tattooing in, 81–82, 82–84 (box)
    trends, 211–212
Youth workers. *See also* Ethnography
    acting for another's benefit, 93
    assessing harm, 97
    care and compassion of, 91–92
    discernment and, 64
    ethnographic skills for, 67, 68–71
    expert advice for, 96
    fiduciary duty of, 93–94
    keeping things confidential, 94–96
    mandated reporting by, 97–100
    mission trips by, 77–78
    personal support for, 97
    public culture and, 20
    referrals made by, 96–97
    role and responsibility of, 92
    social networking sites and, 136–137 (box)
    trust and reliance of, 93
    unequal power dynamic and, 93–94
    vision of, 78–80
    and when to break confidentiality, 96–97

Z

Zimmer-Gembeck, Melanie J., 139

LINCOLN CHRISTIAN UNIVERSITY